Dessert Cook Book

By the Editors of

Better Homes and Gardens

Cream Puff topped
with Chocolate Sauce

Coconut Ribbon Loaf

Cranberry Sherbet

Fluffy Strawberry Parfait
along with a Coconut Kiss

Crunch-crust Pie

Cherry Divinity,   Ginger Creams

Feathery Fudge Cake, Chocolate Satin Frosting

Peach Sundae Melba

*Ambrosia with a
crown of coconut*

*Lemon-
Orange
Sherbet*

Delicious desserts for a grand finale!

When you serve a simply terrific dessert, chances are good that your meal—or party—is a big success! That's why Better Homes & Gardens is bringing you a Dessert Cook Book with over 400 wonderful recipes, each polished to perfection in our Test Kitchen.

The book includes long-time favorites, everything from velvety chocolate cake to marvelous Bavarians! Desserts easy as 1-2-3, spectaculars for special occasions, treats for weight-watchers, desserts to make ahead—you'll find all these plus many more!

Contents

On our cover: Down front is Americana Key Lime Pie—a beauty! Next comes Rich Strawberry Shortcake. On tiered tray: Brownies, decorated Sugar Cookies, Cherry Winks, Jam Shortbread Cookies; above: Divinity and coconut-coated marshmallows. In back is Lemon-drop Ice Cream, with fluffs of marshmallow creme.

Luscious desserts—more to come!

Tops on everybody's list—oven-warm Pineapple Upside-down Cake (page 15). Check the cake chapter for lots of old favorites, along with new recipes you'll be anxious to try.

Magic with cake mix! Ribbons of chocolate shot in delicate angel cake—a super dessert and a breeze to make with packaged helpers! You'll find many other easy desserts.

When it's your turn to serve, choose Chocolate Charlotte Russe —just right when you want to roll out the red carpet! See how to make this beauty on page 149.

Page through our chapter of spectaculars—each one is a "best!"

This seal tells you that every recipe in this book is endorsed by the Better Homes & Gardens Test Kitchen. Each one is tested over and over till it rates excellent in practicality, family appeal, and in deliciousness!

Better Homes and Gardens TEST KITCHEN

A "big" on the popularity poll of fine eating! Our Red Cherry Pie (page 78) tastes just like Mother used to make, but it's easier.

Pastry pointers, fruit pies, meringue pies, airy chiffon pies—this book has them all!

Come to a fruit festival! Here it's peaches and blueberries, color- and flavor-schemed to taste wonderful. Take your choice from page after page of absolutely marvelous fruit desserts. Use fresh, frozen, canned, and dried fruit; turn out fritters or dumplings, sauce or shortcake, an old-time cobbler or compote.

Time a-flying? Our 1-2-3 chapter includes delectable fruit treats that are a snap to make.

All peaches 'n cream! It's refreshing Peach-tree Ice Cream—super-smooth! Recipe is easy—just four ingredients (page 152).

You'll find many more desserts to make ahead and keep in the refrigerator or freezer till serving time. No last-minute hubbub—you'll be a carefree hostess!

Look for weight-watcher specials, too—desserts low in calories, high in goodness.

One glance through our treasury of

fruit desserts, and you'll

want to try each one! Some are

company fare, others for

family night—all are delicious!

Fruit desserts

Pick a berry-patch beauty

Come to our apple spree!

Start with canned or dried fruit

Sunny citrus desserts

Yes, we have bananas, too!

Pears on parade

Summer fruit spectaculars

Old-fashioned strawberry shortcake

←Sugared strawberries, biscuit-shortcake layers, whipped cream—it all adds up to wonderful eating! Take your choice of butter shortcake or one that's not so rich. In a rush? Make shortcake from packaged biscuit mix.

These are the berries!

Strawberry Tree

Drama for a simple dessert! Guests pluck big, juicy berries from the tree, then dunk them in one or all of the accompaniments—

Set out a Strawberry Tree and a bowl each of sour cream (trimmed with shredded orange peel or brown sugar), toasted flaked coconut, and powdered sugar. To "grow" a Strawberry Tree: Start with a ball of plastic foam about the size of a large orange (from florist shop or variety store). Insert a small wood dowel or long pencil for tree trunk. Cover the ball with strawberry or other green leaves, tacking them with pins. To support trunk, fill a small flowerpot with sand or anything else that will do the job; cover top surface with green-tinted flaked coconut or with chocolate shot. Poke one end of a toothpick into the green cap of each strawberry; anchor other end in the ball.

Lime-Pineapple Fluff

Sugared raspberries atop add just the right flavor bouquet for this tangy gelatin whip—

1 No. 2 can (2½ cups) crushed pineapple
1 envelope (1 tablespoon) unflavored
  gelatin
⅓ cup sugar
Dash salt
¼ cup lime juice
. . .
1 cup heavy cream, whipped
Few drops green food coloring

Drain pineapple and add enough water to syrup to make 1½ cups. Combine gelatin, sugar, and salt; add syrup. Heat and stir till gelatin dissolves. Remove from heat; add lime juice. Chill till partially set; beat with rotary or electric beater till light and fluffy. Fold in drained pineapple and whipped cream. Tint pale green with few drops food coloring. Pour into 1-quart mold. Chill till firm. Unmold. Top with additional whipped cream and sweetened red raspberries; or pass a bowl of thawed frozen raspberries (a few crystals remaining) for a sauce. Makes 6 to 8 servings.

French Strawberry Tart

A bridge-club dazzler!—

2 8-ounce packages cream cheese,
  softened
¼ cup sugar
1 to 2 teaspoons grated lemon peel
2 tablespoons lemon juice
1 baked 9-inch Rich Tart Shell
1 quart fresh strawberries, sliced
2 tablespoons cornstarch
¼ cup cold water
1 12-ounce jar (1 cup) strawberry
  preserves
2 tablespoons lemon juice

Combine cheese, sugar, lemon peel, and 2 tablespoons lemon juice; mix well. Spread in bottom of baked shell. Top with strawberries. Combine cornstarch and water; add preserves. Bring to boiling, stirring constantly; cook and stir until thick and clear. Remove from heat; add 2 tablespoons lemon juice. Cool to room temperature. Pour over berries. Chill. If you like, garnish with whipped cream. Makes 12 servings.

Rich Tart Shell

½ cup butter or margarine
¼ cup sugar
¼ teaspoon salt
1 unbeaten egg
1½ cups sifted enriched flour

Stir butter to soften; blend in sugar and salt. Add egg and mix well. Stir in flour. Chill slightly. On floured surface, roll out in 12-inch circle, ⅛ to ¼ inch thick. Using rolling pin to transfer dough, carefully place over *outside* of 9x1½-inch round cake pan. (Shape dough to sides of pan *almost* to rim. Be sure there are *no thin places* in crust, especially where sides and bottom of pan join.) Trim off excess crust. Place pan, with crust up, on cooky sheet. Bake in very hot oven (450°) 8 to 10 minutes or till crust is lightly browned. Cool a few minutes; while slightly warm, transfer crust to serving plate.

Note: If you prefer, bake a regular 10-inch pie shell (Plain Pastry recipe, page 70).

Start with a basket of berries . . . turn out delicious desserts

1 French Strawberry Tart. Glazed berries, cream cheese in tart shell. **2** Strawberry Tree, dunks. **3** Peach Sundae Melba (recipe, page 67). **4** Lime-Pineapple Fluff. **5** Raspberry Chiffon Pie (recipe, page 86).

Rich Strawberry Shortcake

2 cups sifted enriched flour
2 tablespoons sugar
3 teaspoons baking powder
½ teaspoon salt
½ cup butter or margarine
1 beaten egg
⅔ cup light cream
Soft butter or margarine
3 to 4 cups sugared sliced strawberries
1 cup heavy cream, whipped

Sift together dry ingredients; cut in butter till mixture is like coarse crumbs. Combine egg and cream; add all at once to dry ingredients, stirring only to moisten.

Big Biscuit Style: Spread dough in greased 8x1½-inch round pan, slightly building up dough around edges. Bake in very hot oven (450°) 15 to 18 minutes or till golden brown. Remove from pan to cooling rack; cool about 3 minutes. With serrated knife, split in 2 layers, lifting top off carefully. Butter bottom layer. Spoon berries and whipped cream between layers and over top. Cut in 6 wedges; serve warm.

Individual Shortcakes: Turn dough out on floured surface; knead gently ½ minute. Pat or roll dough to ½ inch. Cut 6 biscuits with floured 2½-inch round or fluted cutter. Bake on ungreased baking sheet in very hot oven (450°) about 10 minutes. Split shortcakes; butter bottom layers. Fill and top with berries, whipped cream. Serve warm.

Plain Strawberry Shortcake

"Plain" describes the shortcake part—it's not so rich, more like a true biscuit—

2 cups sifted enriched flour
1 tablespoon sugar
3 teaspoons baking powder
½ teaspoon salt
⅓ cup shortening
1 beaten egg
⅔ cup milk
Soft butter or margarine
3 to 4 cups sugared sliced strawberries
1 cup heavy cream, whipped

Sift together dry ingredients; cut in shortening till mixture is like coarse crumbs. Combine egg and milk; add all at once to dry ingredients, stirring only to moisten.

Big Biscuit Style: Follow method above, except bake shortcake 18 to 20 minutes.

Individual Shortcakes: Follow method above.

Blueberry Buckle

Serve this homey dessert warm with cream—

½ cup shortening
½ cup sugar
1 beaten egg
2 cups sifted enriched flour
2½ teaspoons baking powder
¼ teaspoon salt
½ cup milk
2 cups fresh blueberries
½ cup sugar
½ cup sifted enriched flour
½ teaspoon cinnamon
¼ cup butter or margarine

Thoroughly cream shortening and ½ cup sugar; add egg, mix well. Sift 2 cups flour, baking powder, and salt; add to creamed mixture alternately with milk. Pour into well-greased 11½x7½x1½-inch pan; sprinkle blueberries over batter. Combine ½ cup sugar, ½ cup flour, cinnamon, butter till crumbly; sprinkle over blueberries. Bake in moderate oven (350°) 45 to 50 minutes. Cut in 8 to 10 squares. Serve warm.

Peach-Blueberry Torte

6 egg whites
1 teaspoon white vinegar
½ teaspoon vanilla
Dash salt
1¾ cups sugar
¼ cup chopped drained maraschino cherries
8 cooked or canned peach halves, chilled and drained
1 pint peach ice cream
Fresh blueberries

Cover cooky sheet with piece of heavy paper; draw an 11x8-inch rectangle in center.

To make meringue shell, beat egg whites, vinegar, vanilla, and salt until very soft peaks form. Add sugar gradually, beating till very stiff peaks form and all sugar has dissolved. Fold in maraschino cherries. Spread meringue within rectangle, hollowing out center and building up sides. Bake in very slow oven (250°) 1 hour; turn off heat and leave in oven (door closed) till cool.

Peel off paper. Fill shell with 2 rows of peach halves (hollow side up); spoon blueberries between rows and top with ice cream. Sprinkle peaches with blueberries. Pass bowl of extra blueberries to spoon over, if desired. Makes 10 servings.

Lush desserts with apples

It's apple-cooking time! Pop one of these desserts in the oven . . . let the wonderful aroma of apple goodness flood your kitchen.

Revel in old-fashioned favorites—baked apples, plump dumplings, crusty fritters. Take time to try new apple treats—mincemeat crisp, spicy apple pizza. Easy dessert needed? Team rosy ripe apples with favorite cheeses, crackers, other fruits.

Whiff the spicy fragrance of Apple Dumplings . . . each apple wears a crisp pastry jacket; near by is fruit and cheese on an apple platter; lower left, Big Apple Pizza; above are golden Apple Fritters.

Homespun apple favorites

Applesauce

Whole pieces: Quarter and core tart apples. (Pare, if desired.) Add small amount of water; cover and cook slowly till tender. Add sugar to taste—about ¼ cup sugar to 4 medium apples—and continue cooking till sugar dissolves. Add ½-inch stick cinnamon or 1 to 2 whole cloves, if desired.

Puree type: Cook apples as above. Before adding sugar, press through sieve or colander; beat smooth if apples are soft. Add sugar; cook till sugar dissolves.

Baked Apples

Select 6 large baking apples. Core apples and pare strip from top of each. Place in baking dish. In center of each apple, place 1 to 2 tablespoons brown or granulated sugar and ½ teaspoon butter. Pour 1 cup water around apples; bake uncovered in moderate oven (375°) 45 to 60 minutes. Baste apples several times during baking.

Apple centers may be filled with chopped dates, raisins, or mincemeat. Or mix ¼ teaspoon anise seed and 1 tablespoon chopped nuts with the sugar for each apple.

Brown Betty

    2 cups bread crumbs or graham-cracker
        crumbs
    3 tablespoons melted butter
    3 or 4 medium apples, pared and sliced
    ½ cup brown or granulated sugar
    1 tablespoon lemon juice
    ½ teaspoon grated lemon peel
    ⅓ cup hot water

Combine crumbs and butter; stir over low heat until lightly browned. Place ⅓ in buttered 8x8x2-inch pan. Arrange half of apples over crumbs. Sprinkle with half the sugar, lemon juice and peel.

Add second layer of crumbs and remaining apples, sugar, lemon juice and peel. Cover with remaining crumbs. Pour water over. Bake in moderate oven (375°) 30 to 40 minutes. Serve warm with Lemon Sauce (page 65). Makes 6 servings.

Harvest Torte

Easy! Just stir ingredients together—

    4 cups diced unpared tart apples
    1 cup sugar
    ½ cup sifted enriched flour
    2 teaspoons baking powder
    1 egg
    1 tablespoon melted butter or margarine
    1 teaspoon vanilla
    ½ cup broken California walnuts
    ½ cup pitted dates, cut up

Combine all ingredients. Mix thoroughly—do not beat. Turn into greased 8x8x2-inch pan. Bake in hot oven (400°) 40 minutes, or till apples are tender (test with fork). Cut in 6 to 8 squares. Serve with whipped cream.

Apple Crisp

    5 cups sliced pared tart apples
    1 cup brown sugar
    ¾ cup enriched flour
    ¾ cup quick-cooking rolled oats
    1 teaspoon cinnamon
    ½ cup butter or margarine

Arrange apples in buttered 9-inch pie plate. Combine brown sugar, flour, oats, and cinnamon; cut in butter till crumbly. Press mixture over apples. Bake in moderate oven (350°) 45 to 50 minutes or till top is browned. Serve warm with ice cream.

Mincemeat Apple Crisp

    1¾ cups prepared mincemeat *or* 1 9-
        ounce package
    4 medium apples, pared and sliced
    ½ cup brown sugar
    ⅓ cup enriched flour
    1 teaspoon cinnamon
    ¼ cup butter or margarine

If using packaged mincemeat, prepare according to package directions. Place half of apples in buttered 8x1½-inch round baking dish. Top with half the mincemeat; repeat layers. Mix remaining ingredients till crumbly; sprinkle over top. Bake in moderate oven (350°) about 45 minutes. Serve warm.

13

Big Apple Pizza

Aluminum foil
Plain Pastry
7 tart medium apples
½ cup sugar
1 teaspoon cinnamon
¼ teaspoon nutmeg
¾ cup enriched flour
½ cup sugar
½ cup butter or margarine

Cut a 15-inch circle from 18-inch-wide aluminum foil. Use a pastry recipe calling for 2 cups flour (page 70); roll pastry on foil to fit circle. Trim edge with pastry wheel. Place foil and pastry on a large cooky sheet. Core apples, but do not pare; slice a little less than ½ inch thick (7 cups sliced). Beginning ¾ inch from edge of pastry, overlap apple slices, making 2 circles (see picture, page 11).

Combine ½ cup sugar and the spices; sprinkle over apples. Combine flour and ½ cup sugar; cut in butter till crumbly; sprinkle over top. Turn up the ¾-inch rim of pastry and foil; flute. Bake in very hot oven (450°) 20 to 25 minutes or till crust is brown and apples are done. Center with a small whole apple and a few green leaves for garnish. Cut pie in 10 wedges and serve warm.

Apple Fritters

1⅓ cups sifted enriched flour
1 tablespoon sugar
2 teaspoons baking powder
½ teaspoon salt
2 beaten eggs
⅔ cup milk
1 tablespoon salad oil or melted
    shortening
3 cups *small* strips of apple*

Sift dry ingredients together. Blend eggs, milk, and salad oil; add dry ingredients all at once and mix just till moistened. Stir in apple strips. Drop from tablespoon into deep, hot fat (375°). Fry till puffy and golden, 3 to 4 minutes; turn once. Drain on paper towels. While warm, sprinkle with confectioners' sugar and serve at once. Makes about 3 dozen.

Note: To keep first fritters hot while you fry remaining batter, place them in a very slow oven (250°) for short time.

*Pare and core 3 or 4 tart, medium apples; cut crosswise in ⅛-inch slices. Stack several slices and cut in ⅛-inch strips.

Apple Dumplings

1½ cups sugar
1½ cups water
¼ teaspoon cinnamon
¼ teaspoon nutmeg
6 to 10 drops red food coloring
3 tablespoons butter or margarine
2 cups sifted enriched flour
2 teaspoons baking powder
1 teaspoon salt
⅔ cup shortening
½ cup milk
6 medium, whole apples,
    pared and cored

Combine sugar, water, spices, and food coloring; bring to boiling. Remove from heat; add butter. Sift dry ingredients together; cut in shortening till mixture resembles coarse crumbs. Add milk all at once and stir just until flour is moistened. On lightly floured surface, roll to between ⅛ and ¼ inch thick into 18x12-inch rectangle. Cut into 6-inch squares. Place whole apple in each square. Sprinkle each apple generously with sugar, cinnamon, and nutmeg; dot with butter. Moisten edges of squares. Fold corners to center and pinch edges together. Place 1 inch apart in ungreased 11½x7½x 1½-inch baking pan. Pour the syrup over dumplings; sprinkle with sugar. Bake at 375° 35 minutes, or till apples are done. Serve warm with cream. Makes 6 servings.

Note: If you wish, you may use ½ apple, sliced, in each square of pastry.

*Wonderful desserts—
that apple flavor is
always a hit!*

Delicious desserts with canned fruit

Polynesian Parfait

Stir 1 cup mint jelly. Add one No. 2 can (2½ cups) crushed pineapple, chilled and drained; mix well. Add few drops green food coloring, if desired. In parfait glasses, alternate layers of the pineapple with 1 quart pineapple sherbet. Makes 6 servings.

Fruit-cocktail Cobbler

1 No. 2½ can (3½ cups) fruit cocktail
¼ cup brown sugar
2 tablespoons cornstarch
1 teaspoon grated orange peel
¾ cup diced orange sections
2 tablespoons butter or margarine
1 cup packaged biscuit mix
⅓ cup light cream
1 tablespoon butter or margarine, melted

Drain fruit cocktail, reserving syrup. Mix brown sugar and cornstarch; add reserved syrup. Cook and stir till thick. Add fruit cocktail, peel, and orange; heat just to boiling. Pour into 8x8x2-inch baking dish; dot with 2 tablespoons butter. Combine biscuit mix, cream, and 1 tablespoon butter; mix just to moisten. Quickly drop by spoonfuls onto hot fruit. Bake in hot oven (400°) 20 minutes or till biscuits are done. Serve warm with cream. Makes 9 servings.

Cooky Fruit Freeze

Line bottom and sides of 8x8x2-inch pan with about 2 dozen chocolate wafers.

Combine 1 cup heavy cream, whipped, with 1 tablespoon sugar and 1 teaspoon rum flavoring or vanilla. Fold in one No. 2½ can (3½ cups) fruit cocktail, drained, 1 ripe banana, sliced, ½ cup tiny marshmallows, and ¼ cup chopped California walnuts. Pile into cooky-lined pan. Freeze firm.

Remove from freezer ½ hour before serving. Cut in squares. Makes 9 servings.

A breeze to make, a joy to eat—that's Cooky Fruit Freeze. The crust is speedy with chocolate cooky wafers. Garnish dessert with a few extra wafers cut in half.

Fruit-cocktail Cobbler—homespun and wonderful! Orange sections add tangy goodness. Topping is quick with biscuit mix. Serve cobbler warm, pass cream.

Pineapple Upside-down Cake—delightful!

Bottoms up and there's the topping—built-in! You don't stop to mix frosting—cake's ready to serve when timer bell rings. If you like, make the cake batter from a loaf-size cake mix. You'll have this dessert in the oven in no time!

Pineapple Upside-down Cake

3 tablespoons butter or margarine
1 No. 2 can (2½ cups) pineapple
   tidbits or crushed pineapple
Maraschino cherries
California walnut halves
⅔ cup brown sugar

. . .

⅓ cup shortening
½ cup granulated sugar
1 egg
1 teaspoon vanilla

. . .

1¼ cups sifted cake flour
1½ teaspoons baking powder
½ teaspoon salt

Topping: Melt butter in 9x1½-inch round pan. Drain pineapple, reserving ½ cup syrup. Arrange maraschino cherries and nuts in bottom of pan. Cover with brown sugar, then the pineapple.

Cake*: Cream together shortening and granulated sugar. Add egg and vanilla; beat till fluffy. Sift together dry ingredients; add alternately with reserved pineapple syrup, beating after each addition. Spread over pineapple. Bake in moderate oven (350°) 45 to 50 minutes. Let stand 5 minutes; invert on plate. Serve warm. Top each piece with a dollop of whipped cream, if desired.

*Or call on loaf-size yellow-cake mix. Follow package directions, using reserved pineapple syrup for the liquid.

Golden Pineapple Fritters

Pineapple spears take on a crisp batter coating. A real treat!—

1 No. 2 can (16) pineapple spears
1½ cups sifted enriched flour
⅓ cup sugar
3 teaspoons baking powder
1½ teaspoons salt
2 beaten eggs
1 tablespoon salad oil
Enriched flour

. . .

Sweetened whipped cream
Nutmeg

Drain pineapple, reserving ⅓ cup syrup. Place spears on paper towels to dry. Sift together 1½ cups flour, the sugar, baking powder, and salt. Combine eggs, reserved ⅓ cup pineapple syrup and the salad oil; add to dry ingredients, stirring just till smooth. Roll pineapple spears in flour; spread with batter. Fry a few at a time, in deep hot fat or oil (375°), about 1 minute on each side, or till golden brown. Drain on paper towels. (Fritters stay crisp 15 to 20 minutes—keep hot in slow oven.) Serve warm, topped with sweetened whipped cream sprinkled with nutmeg. Makes 6 to 8 servings.

Note: For easier handling, insert a skewer lengthwise in pineapple spear before spreading it with the batter. Push pineapple spear off skewer into hot fat.

Rosy Pear Sundaes

1 cup currant jelly
1 tablespoon grated orange peel
⅓ cup orange juice
Few drops red food coloring
1 No. 2½ can (3½ cups) pear
  halves, drained
1 quart vanilla ice cream

Melt jelly in saucepan; remove from heat and stir in orange peel and juice. Tint with red food coloring. Cut pear halves in two lengthwise and add to jelly sauce; chill several hours. For each serving, arrange 2 or 3 pieces of pear over scoop of ice cream. Pour sauce over all. Makes 6 to 8 servings.

Topsy-turvy Peach Cups

Cake Cups: Thoroughly drain 1 No. 2½ can (3½ cups) peach halves, reserving ½ cup syrup for sauce. Butter six or seven 6-ounce custard cups; place a peach half in each. Prepare 1 package white-cake mix according to package directions. Spoon about half the batter over peaches, filling cups ⅔ full. (Bake the remaining batter in a layer.) Bake in moderate oven (350°) 25 minutes or till done. Prepare sauce.

Melba Sauce: In saucepan, mix one 10-ounce package frozen raspberries, thawed, the reserved peach syrup, and 2 teaspoons cornstarch. Cook and stir till clear and slightly thick; strain. Add 1 tablespoon lemon juice. Invert cakes in dishes. Serve warm topped with sauce.

Cinnamon Cherry Cobbler

1 No. 2 can (2½ cups) pitted tart red
  cherries
⅓ cup sugar
⅓ cup red cinnamon candies
1 tablespoon quick-cooking tapioca
2 tablespoons butter or margarine
1 package refrigerated quick cinnamon
  rolls or refrigerated biscuits

Drain cherries, reserving juice. Combine sugar, candies, tapioca, and reserved juice. Cook, stirring constantly, over low heat until candies melt and mixture is thick and clear. Stir in butter and cherries. Pour into 10x6x1½-inch baking dish. Top *hot* cherries with rolls. Bake in moderate oven (375°) about 20 minutes; drizzle with icing that comes in cinnamon-roll package. Serve warm with cream. Makes 8 servings.

Red-and-White Cherry Freeze

1 3-ounce package cream cheese
1 9-ounce can (1 cup) crushed pineapple
2 cups tiny marshmallows
1 9-ounce can (1 cup) pitted Royal
  Anne cherries, drained
⅓ cup quartered maraschino cherries
1 cup heavy cream, whipped

Soften cream cheese; blend in pineapple. Add marshmallows and cherries. Fold in cream. Pile into 10x6x1½-inch dish or refrigerator tray. Freeze firm. Cut in squares; top with whipped cream. Makes 6 servings.

Peach Ambrosia Dessert

1 No. 2 can (2½ cups) pineapple
  tidbits, drained
1 cup Tokay grape halves or seedless
  white grapes
1 cup orange sections (undrained)
1 cup tiny marshmallows
1 3½-ounce can (1¼ cups) flaked
  coconut
1 cup dairy sour cream
1 No. 2½ can (3½ cups) peach halves

Combine first 5 ingredients, stir in sour cream. Chill several hours or overnight. Serve in chilled, drained peach halves on endive. Makes 6 or 7 servings.

Pineapple Bridge Dessert

1½ cups crushed vanilla wafers
⅓ cup butter or margarine, melted
1 No. 2 can (2½ cups) crushed pineapple
1 package lemon-flavored gelatin
⅓ cup butter or margarine
½ cup sugar
3 egg yolks
½ cup broken California walnuts

· · ·

3 egg whites
¼ cup sugar

Combine crumbs and melted butter. Line bottom of a buttered 9x9x2-inch pan with *1 cup* of the crumb mixture. Thoroughly drain pineapple, reserving syrup. Heat syrup to boiling; remove from heat. Add gelatin; stir to dissolve. Cool to room temperature. Cream ⅓ cup butter and ½ cup sugar. Add yolks; beat well. Stir in gelatin, pineapple, and nuts. Beat whites till soft peaks form; gradually add ¼ cup sugar, beating till stiff peaks form; fold into gelatin. Pour into pan; top with remaining crumbs. Chill firm. Cut in 9 squares.

Heavenly Hawaiian Cream—you'll agree, it's just that!

Pineapple tidbits, marshmallows, maraschino cherries go together in whipped cream—toasted almonds and coconut atop. We're serving ours in scooped-out coconut shells for drama.

Heavenly Hawaiian Cream

You'll like this dessert for its luscious flavor, for saving you time—

1 No. 2 can (2½ cups) pineapple tidbits
¼ pound (16) marshmallows, cut in eighths *or* 2 cups tiny marshmallows
¼ cup well-drained maraschino cherries, cut in fourths
. . .
1 cup heavy cream, whipped
. . .
¼ cup slivered blanched almonds, toasted
Shredded coconut

Drain pineapple, reserving ¼ cup of the syrup. Combine pineapple, marshmallows, cherries, and reserved ¼ cup syrup. Let stand for 1 hour. Fold in whipped cream. Spoon into dessert dishes and chill. To serve, sprinkle with nuts and top with coconut. Makes 6 to 8 servings.

Pineapple-Cherry Squares

1½ cups fine vanilla-wafer crumbs
1 3½-ounce can (1¼ cups) flaked coconut
½ cup butter or margarine
1½ cups sifted confectioners' sugar
2 eggs
1 9-ounce can (1 cup) crushed pineapple, drained
1 cup broken California walnuts
¾ cup chopped maraschino cherries, well drained
1 cup heavy cream, whipped

Place half of crumbs in bottom of 9x9x2-inch pan; sprinkle with half the coconut. Cream butter; gradually add confectioners' sugar, creaming till light. Add eggs, one at a time, beating well after each. Spread mixture over coconut. Fold pineapple, nuts, and cherries into whipped cream; spread over mixture in pan. Sprinkle with remaining coconut and crumbs. Chill about 4 hours. Cut in squares. Makes 9 servings.

Citrus specials

Sherbet Ambrosia Cups

Orange shells are sherbet-lined for extra goodness, then heaped with fruit—

3 large oranges
1 pint orange sherbet

. . .

1 9-ounce can (1 cup) pineapple
tidbits, drained
1 3½-ounce can (1¼ cups) flaked
coconut
6 strawberries or maraschino
cherries, halved
Aromatic bitters (optional)

Slice oranges in half lengthwise. Scoop out the fruit with a spoon and break in sections. If "cups" tip, cut off sliver of peel to level. Line bottom and sides of the cups with sherbet; freeze firm. Combine the orange sections with remaining ingredients; chill. Just before serving, fill orange cups with fruit; dash with aromatic bitters, if desired. Trim with mint sprigs. Makes 6 servings.

Orange Fluff

Easiest dessert ever! And so good—

24 marshmallows
½ cup frozen orange-juice
concentrate

. . .

1 cup heavy cream, whipped
1 recipe Vanilla-wafer Crust

Heat marshmallows and juice concentrate in top of double boiler over simmering water, stirring occasionally till marshmallows melt. Cool thoroughly. Fold in whipped cream. Pile into Vanilla-wafer Crust; top with reserved crumbs. Chill until firm.

To serve, cut in wedges and top with additional whipped cream and walnut halves. Makes 7 or 8 servings.

Vanilla-wafer Crust: Mix together ¾ cup fine vanilla-wafer crumbs, ¼ cup finely chopped California walnuts, and ¼ cup melted butter or margarine. Line bottom of 1-quart refrigerator tray with half of crumb mixture; reserve remainder for top.

Ambrosia

2 13½-ounce cans (3 cups) frozen
pineapple chunks
5 medium oranges
2 fully ripe, flecked-with-brown bananas
2 cups white seedless grapes
or halved grapes, seeded
1 3½-ounce can (about 1¼ cups)
flaked coconut

. . .

1 7-ounce bottle ginger ale (optional)
Whole maraschino cherries

Drain pineapple, reserving syrup. Pare oranges with sharp knife; remove sections by cutting close to membrane, reserving juice. (You'll need about 2 cups orange sections.)

Peel bananas, slice on bias, and place in the orange juice. For beautiful arrangement, use a crystal bowl and keep the pineapple, oranges, bananas, and grapes separate, allotting one-fourth of the bowl to each. Following this plan, place *half* of each fruit in bowl, sprinkle with *half* of coconut; top with remaining fruit.

Pour reserved pineapple syrup over all; chill thoroughly. At serving time, pour ginger ale over. Sprinkle with remaining coconut and dot with whole maraschino cherries. Makes 8 to 12 servings.

Lemonade 'n Cake Loaf

1 10x4x2-inch loaf angel cake
1 quart vanilla ice cream
1 6-ounce can frozen pink-lemonade
concentrate
1 cup heavy cream, whipped

. . .

1 quart fresh strawberries, sliced
and sweetened

Slice cake lengthwise in three even layers. Stir ice cream to soften. With spoon zigzag lemonade concentrate through ice cream till marbled; spread between cake layers. Freeze. About 1 hour before serving time, spread top and sides of loaf with whipped cream. Return to freezer. To serve, slice and top with sweetened strawberries.

Makes 8 to 10 servings.

Ambrosia—party-pretty! Here's the perfect light dessert after a hearty feast. The fruit combination is wonderful—pineapple chunks, orange sections, banana slices, grapes, maraschino cherries.

Lemonade Ladyfinger Torte

1½ cups sifted confectioners' sugar
½ cup soft butter
2 eggs
2 teaspoons grated lemon peel
2½ to 3 tablespoons lemon juice
4 dozen 4-inch-long single ladyfingers
  or 2 dozen double
1 cup heavy cream, whipped

Gradually add sugar to butter, creaming at medium speed on mixer till light and fluffy. Add eggs, one at a time, beating well after each. Gradually add peel and juice. (Mixture may look curdled.) Beat at high-speed till fluffy and smooth, about 10 minutes. On cake plate, place 12 single ladyfingers, curved side down, in 2 rows; top with a third of the lemon mixture. Add another layer of ladyfingers in opposite direction; repeat layers ending with ladyfingers. Frost with sweetened whipped cream. Chill overnight. Makes 12 to 16 servings.

Citrus Creme Dessert

1½ teaspoons unflavored gelatin
½ cup cold water
2 egg yolks
⅓ cup sugar
⅓ cup orange juice
2½ tablespoons lemon juice
Dash salt
2 egg whites
¼ cup sugar

Soften gelatin in cold water; heat and stir over medium heat till dissolved. Cool to room temperature. Beat egg yolks; gradually add ⅓ cup sugar, beating till thick and lemon colored. Stir in fruit juices, salt, and gelatin. Chill till partially set; stir occasionally. Beat egg whites to soft peaks; gradually add ¼ cup sugar, beating to stiff peaks. Fold whites into yolk mixture. Pour into serving bowl. Chill thoroughly, several hours or overnight. Spoon over fresh fruit. Pass crisp cookies. Makes 4 to 6 servings.

Yes, we have banana desserts!

Banana Fritters

Bananas get orange-juice dip, then crispy coat. Delicious dessert or meat go-with—

3 firm bananas
2 tablespoons orange juice
1 tablespoon sugar
1 cup sifted enriched flour
½ teaspoon baking powder
¼ teaspoon salt
1 slightly beaten egg
½ cup milk
2 tablespoons butter, melted
¼ teaspoon vanilla
1 teaspoon grated orange peel

Peel bananas; cut in half crosswise, then lengthwise; let stand in mixture of orange juice and sugar. Sift together flour, baking powder, and salt. Mix remaining ingredients; add to dry ingredients, stirring only till moistened. Drain bananas; dip into batter, spreading batter evenly over bananas. Fry in deep hot fat (375°) 2 to 3 minutes or till fritters are golden brown. Drain. Makes 4 servings. Serve with dessert topping or whipped cream. Pass Orange-Lemon Sauce.

Orange-Lemon Sauce: Mix ½ cup sugar, 1½ tablespoons cornstarch, and dash salt; stir in ¾ cup water. Bring to boiling, stirring constantly. Cook and stir till thick and clear. Remove from heat; add 2 tablespoons butter, ¼ cup orange juice, and 1 tablespoon lemon juice. Serve warm.

Chilled Banana Cheesecake

Combine 2 cups graham-cracker crumbs, ⅓ cup sugar, and 1 teaspoon cinnamon. Blend in ½ cup melted butter. Press ¾ of mixture into bottom and sides of 8-inch spring-form pan; reserve rest for topping.

Make filling as for Lemon Refrigerator Cheesecake (page 136). Thinly slice 3 large, fully ripe bananas. Pour ⅓ of filling into crumb-lined pan. Cover with half the banana slices. Add another ⅓ of gelatin mixture and remaining banana slices. Top with remaining gelatin mixture. Sprinkle with reserved crumbs. Chill till firm (4 to 6 hours or overnight). Makes 8 to 10 servings.

Beauties with banana goodness

← Clockwise: Banana Cream Pie in Coconut Crust; Banana-Coconut Rolls on fruit platter; Banana-Nut Cake with Cocoa Whipped Cream; Chilled Banana Cheesecake; Banana Ice Cream topped with Fudge Sauce.

Choose bananas of best flavor

These bananas are *all yellow;* the peel is buttercup color—good ripeness for a fruit tray, for baking, or for eating as fresh fruit.

For Banana Fritters, select light yellow bananas that are *tipped with green.* Tops for broiling, too.

Fully ripe bananas, *flecked with brown,* are just right to eat "as is," or in desserts, pies, or cakes.

Banana Ice Cream

1½ teaspoons (½ envelope) unflavored gelatin
2 tablespoons cold water
¾ cup light cream, scalded
½ cup sugar
¼ teaspoon salt
1 cup mashed fully ripe bananas
2 well-beaten egg yolks
2 teaspoons lemon juice
1 teaspoon vanilla
2 cups heavy cream, whipped
2 egg whites
¼ cup sugar

Soften gelatin in cold water. Add hot scalded cream; stir to dissolve gelatin. Stir in ½ cup sugar and the salt. Chill till partially set. Whip till smooth. Blend in bananas, egg yolks, lemon juice, and vanilla. Fold in whipped cream. Beat egg whites to soft peaks; gradually add ¼ cup sugar, beating till stiff. Fold into banana mixture. Pour into refrigerator trays. Freeze till firm. Serve plain or with warm Fudge Sauce. Makes about 2 quarts.

Banana-Coconut Rolls

Peel all-yellow or fully ripe bananas. Cut in half crosswise. Dip in honey, then roll in shredded coconut, coating well.

Pass *Citrus Fluff:* In saucepan, beat 1 egg; add ½ cup sugar, 1 tablespoon grated orange peel, 2 teaspoons grated lemon peel, and 2 tablespoons lemon juice. Cook and stir over *low* heat till thick (about 5 minutes). Cool thoroughly. Fold in 1 cup heavy cream, whipped. Chill. Makes 2⅓ cups.

Desserts from dried fruits

Baked Prune Whip

2 cups cooked prunes, drained
1 teaspoon grated lemon peel
2 teaspoons lemon juice
4 tablespoons confectioners' sugar
Dash salt
4 stiff-beaten egg whites

Pit prunes; mash to a pulp. Blend in lemon peel, juice, *2 tablespoons* confectioners' sugar, and salt. To beaten egg whites, add remaining confectioners' sugar; beat till stiff. Fold prune mixture into whites. Pile lightly in ungreased 1½-quart baking dish. Bake in moderate oven (350°) 20 to 30 minutes or till knife inserted in center comes out clean. Serve warm with Custard Sauce (page 64). Makes 6 to 8 servings.

Swedish Fruit Soup

1 11-ounce package (1¾ cups) mixed dried fruits
½ cup golden seedless raisins
3 to 4 inches stick cinnamon
4 cups water
1 medium orange, unpared, cut in ¼-inch slices
1 No. 2 can (2¼ cups) unsweetened pineapple juice
½ cup currant jelly
¼ cup sugar
2 tablespoons quick-cooking tapioca
¼ teaspoon salt

Combine mixed dried fruits, raisins, cinnamon, and water. Bring to boiling, then simmer uncovered till fruits are tender, about 30 minutes. Add remaining ingredients. Bring to a boil; cover, cook over low heat 15 minutes longer, stirring occasionally. Serve warm or chilled. Makes 8 to 10 servings.

Date Bridge Dessert

Crush 12 chocolate sandwich cookies (about 1⅓ cups crumbs); reserve ¼ cup crumbs. Spread remaining crumbs in bottom of 10x6x1½-inch baking dish.

In saucepan, combine 1 cup pitted dates, cut up, ¾ cup water and ¼ teaspoon salt. Bring to a boil, then simmer about 3 minutes. Remove from heat; add ¼ pound (16) marshmallows or 2 cups tiny marshmallows; stir till marshmallows melt. Cool to room temperature, about 20 minutes. Stir in ½ cup chopped California walnuts. Spread over crumbs in dish. Whip 1 cup heavy cream with ½ teaspoon vanilla; swirl whipped cream over date mixture. Sprinkle with reserved cooky crumbs. Chill overnight. Cut in squares to serve. Makes 8 servings.

Easy way to plump dried fruit

Place 1 pound prunes in jar or other container with snug lid. Add 1 quart boiling water. Cover tightly and cool. Chill in refrigerator at least 24 hours.

Want dried fruit of just-right plumpness for baking or cooking? Cover 1 pound prunes or apricots with 1 quart cold water; cover, let stand 24 hours.

How to cook dried fruit

You need not soak dried fruit. Just rinse, then cover generously with water. Simmer fruit gently for time specified below. If desired, add sugar (amount given below) during the last five minutes of cooking.

One pound dried fruit	Cooking time in minutes*	Added sugar
Prunes—2¾ cups	20 to 30	2 tablespoons per cup uncooked fruit
Apricots—3 to 3¾ cups	20 to 25	¼ to ½ cup per cup uncooked fruit
Peaches—3 cups	30 to 35	¼ cup per cup uncooked fruit
Figs—3 cups	30 to 40	1 tablespoon per cup uncooked fruit
Pears—3½ cups	15 to 30	¼ cup per cup uncooked fruit
Apples—6 cups	20 to 30	¼ cup per cup uncooked fruit
Raisins—3 to 3¼ cups	10	½ tablespoon per cup uncooked fruit

*Some dried fruits are processed to cut cooking time. See cooking directions on package.

Pears on parade!

Baked Pears

In 2-quart casserole put 2 tablespoons lemon juice and enough water to cover bottom. Add 6 medium fresh pears, pared; cover and bake in moderate oven (375°) 20 to 25 minutes or until tender.

Remove from oven. Sprinkle each pear with 1 to 2 teaspoons sugar; bake uncovered 10 minutes longer to glaze. Serve warm or chilled. Top with whipped cream and chocolate decorettes, if desired.

Pears a la Compote

Combine 1 cup sugar, 3 cups water, ⅓ cup lime or lemon juice, and dash salt. Heat to boiling. Meanwhile halve 4 fresh pears lengthwise, leaving stem intact; core but do not pare. Add pears to syrup; cover and cook 20 minutes or till tender.

Arrange 2 cups seeded Tokay or Emperor grapes and the pears in serving dish. Dash aromatic bitters into syrup to taste. Pour syrup over fruits. Chill. Makes 8 servings.

Ginger Pear Crumble

Just sniff the spices! Is it Grandmother's kitchen? No, yours—

1½ cups fine gingersnap crumbs
½ cup brown sugar
¼ teaspoon salt
¼ cup butter or margarine, melted

• • •

3 fresh pears, halved, pared, and cored,
   or 1 1-pound can pear halves, drained
1 tablespoon lemon juice

• • •

Maraschino cherries

Combine crumbs, brown sugar, salt, and butter. Place half of mixture in bottom of buttered 8¼x1¾-inch round baking dish. Top with pear halves, cut side up. Sprinkle with lemon juice and remaining crumbs.

Bake in moderate oven (350°) 25 to 30 minutes or till pears are tender and top is crisp. Center each pear half with a maraschino cherry. Serve warm topped with ice cream or whipped cream. Makes 6 servings.

Cheese-and-Fruit Tray— nothing tastier, nothing less complicated!

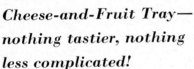

Here's the prettiest treat ever to turn on a Lazy Susan! Keep the makings on hand for an impromptu dessert that looks planned!

Here, pears and lush green grapes get together with cheese and crackers. Choose mellow Camembert or a mild cream cheese. If you like, line tray with grape leaves.

The possibilities are unlimited for fruit-cheese combinations. Try aged Cheddar, lacy Swiss, robust blue and Roquefort, a red-jacketed Gouda or Edam. For best flavor, serve cheeses at room temperature.

Summertime favorites

Wonderful Plum Crunch

3 pounds fresh prune-plums, quartered
   and pitted (5 cups)
¼ cup brown sugar

. . .

1 cup sifted enriched flour
1 cup granulated sugar
½ teaspoon salt
½ teaspoon cinnamon
1 beaten egg

. . .

½ cup butter or margarine, melted

Combine prunes and brown sugar. Spoon into 11½x7½x1½-inch baking dish. Sift together dry ingredients; add egg, tossing with fork till mixture is crumbly; sprinkle evenly over plums. Drizzle with butter.

Bake in moderate oven (375°) about 45 minutes or till lightly browned. Serve warm topped with ice cream or whipped cream. Makes 8 servings.

*Turn summer's
bounty into lush
desserts*

Peach-a-berry Cobbler

1 tablespoon cornstarch
¼ cup brown sugar
½ cup cold water
2 cups sugared sliced fresh peaches
1 cup fresh blueberries
1 tablespoon butter or margarine
1 tablespoon lemon juice
Cobbler Crust:
  1 cup sifted enriched flour
  ½ cup granulated sugar
  1½ teaspoons baking powder
  ½ teaspoon salt

. . .

  ½ cup milk
  ¼ cup soft butter or margarine

. . .

  2 tablespoons sugar
  ¼ teaspoon nutmeg

Mix first 3 ingredients; add fruits. Cook and stir till mixture thickens. Add butter and lemon juice. Pour into 8¼x1¾-inch round ovenware cake dish.

Cobbler Crust: Sift together flour, ½ cup sugar, baking powder, and salt. Add milk and butter all at once; beat smooth. Pour over fruit. Mix 2 tablespoons sugar and nutmeg. Sprinkle over batter. Bake in moderate oven (350°) 30 minutes or till done. Serve warm with cream. Makes 6 servings.

Note: Or use canned or frozen fruits. Drain; use ½ cup syrup instead of water.

Persian Peaches

Combine 4 cups sliced peaches, ½ cup orange juice, 3 tablespoons honey, 2 tablespoons finely chopped candied ginger, and dash salt. Mix gently. Cover; chill thoroughly. Spoon into 5 chilled sherbets. Or spoon over vanilla ice cream.

Color bright: When you are slicing peaches for dessert or for trim, you can keep that pretty golden tone with a color keeper (the same ascorbic-acid mixture you add when freezing light-colored fruits). Follow label directions for mixing color keeper with sugar or dissolving in water.

Another way is to brush the cut fruit with a little lemon juice.

Dunk a melon ball!

Cantaloupe or honeydew—take your pick! Skewer a melon ball and swirl in Blue-cheese Melon Dip—flavor combination is terrific! Makes a refreshing dessert; next time, serve as appetizer.

Rich Peach Shortcakes

Mix dough as for Rich Strawberry Shortcake (page 10). Roll out, cut in 2½-inch rounds, and bake following the directions given for Individual Shortcakes.

Split shortcakes; butter bottom layers. Fill and top with 4 cups sugared, sliced peaches and 1 cup heavy cream, whipped. Serve warm. Makes 6 servings.

Cherry-Berry Compote

1 1-pound can pitted Bing cherries
1 10-ounce package frozen raspberries
2 tablespoons cooking sherry

Pour undrained cherries over frozen raspberries; add sherry. Let stand about 1 hour (berries should have some ice crystals remaining). Spoon into 4 to 6 sherbets.

Blue-cheese Melon Dip

Combine one 4-ounce package blue cheese, one 3-ounce package cream cheese, 2 tablespoons milk, and 2 tablespoons salad dressing. Beat at low speed of electric mixer till light and fluffy. Makes about 1 cup.

Melon Memo

From the melon vine come quick and easy desserts! More good ideas along this line, page 120. (An aside to waistline watchers: Melons are vitamin high, calorie low.)

Blueberry-Peach Compote

Chill blueberries and peaches. Just before serving, peel peaches and slice. Line sides of serving bowl with peaches. Mound blueberries in center. Pass sugar and cream.

Cakes

Pointers for cake-making perfection

Layer and loaf cakes

Cakes that frost themselves

Luscious chocolate cakes

Easy quick-mix cakes

Chiffon, angel, and sponge cakes

Fruitcakes to bring compliments

Jelly rolls—filled with flavor

Small-size cakes to meet big occasions

Desserts from ready-baked cakes

Two from our collection of wonderful cakes

High on a pink pedestal is our Devil's-food Cake—red-brown and velvety, blanketed with fluffy Peppermint-stick Frosting. On the blue platter is Grandma's Chocolate Cake. We frosted it with smooth Chocolate Satin Frosting, added circle of walnuts.

Cake-making pointers

You can turn out a cake that's even-grained, tender, light, and delicately flavored—if you carefully follow a few proved rules.

Cake-making success is not due to good luck or to a knack. It's due to accurate measurements . . . a complete understanding of the method of mixing . . . using a technique that's best for the kinds and amounts of ingredients . . . correct baking.

All cakes fall into three classifications: those with shortening (conventional and quick-mix cakes), those without shortening (angel and sponge cakes), and a combination angel and shortening-type cake (chiffon cake). They differ in ingredients, the way they're mixed, and the appearance and characteristics of the final product; however, many rules for cake making apply to all three kinds.

The cake you bake is only as good as the ingredients you put into it. The cake needs fine granulated sugar for delicate texture. You may use vegetable fats, butter, or margarine as shortening; all should be at room temperature when you use them.

Cake flour is best for cakes made with shortening and for angel and sponge cakes. In our recipes, enriched flour is used where cake flour is not specified.

Use fresh eggs—eggs that have thick whites and yolks that don't spread when eggs are broken. Eggs beat easier if they are at room temperature. However, keep eggs refrigerated until ready to use for baking.

Recipes in this chapter all call for double-acting baking powder. If you want to use single-acting baking powder, use 1½ times the amount called for in the recipe.

Baking your cake

Before you start mixing, turn on the oven and preheat to the right temperature.

You may bake cakes as layers, loaves, sheets, tubes, or cupcakes—but many recipes can't be used interchangeably. To be safe, use type and size pan specified in recipe.

Place pans as near the center of the oven as possible. Don't let pans touch each other or the sides of the oven. Do not place pans directly under each other. If necessary, stagger the pans on two shelves.

When is your cake done? There are several tests you can use. The cake will shrink slightly from the sides of the pan; it will spring back when pressed lightly with finger; a cake tester or a toothpick inserted in the center will come out clean. Regardless of the baking time given in a recipe, always test the cake for doneness.

Slick trick! Slice a layer cake this way—get more servings

To cut your layer cake like this, choose a sharp knife with thin blade. First, cut a circle about 2 inches in from the edge of the cake. If the frosting is soft, dip the knife in hot water before you start cutting cake.

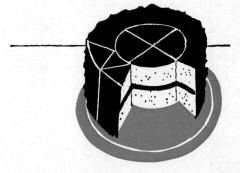

Now cut the cake as shown. From each slice you'll get two servings. Do not press down — hold handle of knife up and slice by pulling it toward you. You may get into family arguments over who gets the outside pieces!

High-altitude changes

If you happen to live in a high-altitude region (3,000 feet above sea level and up), you may find that many cakes will tend to fall and give unpredictable results.

Here is a general guide to help you make adjustments in the baking powder, liquid, and sugar proportions.

	3,000 ft.	5,000	7,000
Liquid: add for each cup	1-2 table-spoons	2-3 table-spoons	3-4 table-spoons
Baking powder: decrease for each teaspoon	⅛ tea-spoon	⅛-¼ tea-spoon	¼-½ tea-spoon
Sugar: decrease for each cup	no change	usually no change	1-2 table-spoons

These aren't hard and fast rules. Since each recipe is different in its proportion of ingredients and richness, you may have to experiment a few times with each recipe to discover the best proportions.

Cakes with shortening

Before you start to mix the cake, read the recipe carefully to make sure you understand the method. Then assemble all the ingredients and utensils. Measure accurately, using standard measuring cups and spoons. Use the type and size pan called for. Preheat oven to specified temperature.

Prepare the pans. You'll find that cakes will be easier to remove if *plain* paper is used, cut to fit the bottom of the pans. It is unnecessary to grease pans.

Pour batter into pans, spreading it to the sides and filling all corners so that the baked cake will be even. Tap the batter-filled pans lightly on the table to break up air bubbles that form.

Cakes with shortening are done when the top is delicately browned and cake shrinks a little from sides of pan. Cake will spring back when you press it lightly in center.

Warm cake is fragile so let it stand in the pan 5 minutes before removing. This way it becomes rigid enough to take the necessary handling. Loosen the edge with a knife and turn cake out on wire rack to cool. Remove paper immediately.

Cool cake before frosting. Brush off loose crumbs and place bottom sides together with frosting or filling between. Frost top and sides.

Causes for failure with a shortening-type cake

Coarse texture
Too much leavening
Not enough liquid
Insufficient creaming of shortening and sugar
Insufficient mixing with increased amount of shortening and sugar
Too slow an oven

Heavy, compact texture
Too much shortening
Too much sugar
Too slow an oven
Extreme overbeating

A dry cake
Too much flour
Not enough shortening or sugar
Too much leavening
Overbeaten egg whites
Overbaking

Thick, heavy crust
Too much flour
Too-long baking
Too hot an oven
Not enough sugar or shortening

Hump or cracks on top
Too much flour
Too hot an oven

Soggy layer or streak at bottom
Undermixing of ingredients
Too much sugar
Too much baking powder

Moist, sticky crust
Too much sugar

Cake falling
Too much leavening
Too much shortening
Too much sugar
Too slow an oven
Insufficient baking
Moving cake during baking

Undersized cake
Too large a pan
Too hot an oven
Not enough leavening

Batter running over pan
Too small a pan
Too slow an oven
Too much sugar or shortening
Too much leavening

Layer and loaf cakes

White Cake Supreme

¾ cup shortening
1½ cups sugar
1½ teaspoons vanilla
2¼ cups sifted cake flour
3 teaspoons baking powder
1 teaspoon salt
1 cup skim milk
5 stiff-beaten egg whites

Stir shortening to soften. Gradually add sugar, and cream together until light and fluffy (beat about 10 minutes at medium-high speed on mixer, scraping bowl occasionally to guide batter into beaters). Add vanilla. Sift flour with baking powder and salt; add to creamed mixture alternately with milk, beginning and ending with flour mixture; beat after each addition. Fold in egg whites. Bake in 2 paper-lined 9x1½-inch round pans in moderate oven (375°) 18 to 20 minutes. Cool. Frost as desired.

Lady Baltimore Cake

¾ cup shortening
2 cups sugar
1 teaspoon vanilla
¼ teaspoon lemon extract
2½ cups sifted cake flour
3 teaspoons baking powder
¾ teaspoon salt
½ cup milk
½ cup water
6 stiff-beaten egg whites

Stir shortening to soften. Gradually add sugar, and cream together until light and fluffy. Add extracts. Sift together flour, baking powder, and salt; add to creamed mixture alternately with milk and water, beginning and ending with flour. Beat after each addition. Fold in egg whites.

Bake in 2 paper-lined 9x9x2-inch pans in moderate oven (350°) about 25 minutes.

Put layers together with Lady Baltimore Filling; frost with ⅔ recipe for Seven-minute Frosting (page 56).

Lady Baltimore Filling: To ⅓ of Seven-minute Frosting, add ¼ cup each chopped figs, seedless raisins, candied cherries, and chopped pecans.

Golden Layer Cake

½ cup shortening
1 cup sugar
1 teaspoon vanilla
½ teaspoon lemon extract *or*
    1 teaspoon grated lemon peel
2 eggs
2 cups sifted cake flour
1 teaspoon baking powder
¾ teaspoon soda
¼ teaspoon salt
1 cup buttermilk

Stir shortening to soften. Gradually add sugar, and cream until light and fluffy. Add extracts. Add eggs, 1 at a time, beating well after each. Sift together dry ingredients; add to creamed mixture alternately with buttermilk, beginning and ending with flour. Beat after each addition. Bake in 2 paper-lined 8x1½-inch round pans in moderate oven (350°) about 30 minutes.

Put cooled layers together with Lemonade Filling (page 61); frost with Seven-minute Frosting. Cover with Lemon Coconut.

Lemon Coconut: In jar mix together 1 tablespoon frozen lemonade concentrate (or a bit of grated lemon peel) and a few drops yellow food coloring. Add one 3½-ounce can flaked coconut. Cover and shake till coconut is colored. Dry on paper towels.

Best Two-egg Cake

½ cup shortening
1½ cups sugar
1 teaspoon vanilla
2 eggs
2¼ cups sifted cake flour
2½ teaspoons baking powder
1 teaspoon salt
1 cup plus 2 tablespoons milk

Stir shortening to soften. Gradually add sugar, creaming thoroughly (12 to 15 minutes at medium-high speed on mixer). Add vanilla. Add eggs, 1 at a time, beating well after each. Sift flour with baking powder and salt; add to creamed mixture alternately with milk, beating after each addition. Bake in 2 paper-lined 9x1½-inch round pans at 375° about 23 minutes.

Golden Layer Cake—it's lemon all the way! Here's triple lemon flavor—cake, filling, and trim! To match picture, double the recipe for Golden Layer Cake and bake in three 9-inch layers. Double the recipe for Lemonade Filling.

Hot-milk Sponge Cake

A feathery, company-style cake—

1 cup sifted enriched flour
1 teaspoon baking powder
¼ teaspoon salt
2 tablespoons butter or margarine
½ cup hot milk
2 eggs
1 cup sugar
1 teaspoon vanilla

Sift together flour, baking powder, and salt. Add butter to milk; keep hot. Beat eggs till thick and lemon-colored, about 3 minutes at high speed on mixer. Gradually add sugar, beating constantly at medium speed 4 to 5 minutes.

Quickly add sifted dry ingredients to egg mixture; stir just till blended. Stir in hot milk mixture and vanilla. Pour into paper-lined 9x1½-inch round pan. Bake in moderate oven (350°) about 25 minutes. Cool cake in pan 15 minutes before removing.

Applesauce Loaf

½ cup shortening
1 cup sugar
2 eggs
1¾ cups sifted enriched flour
1 teaspoon salt
1 teaspoon baking powder
½ teaspoon soda
½ teaspoon cinnamon
½ teaspoon nutmeg
1 cup sweetened applesauce
½ cup chopped California walnuts

Stir shortening to soften; gradually add sugar, creaming till light. Add eggs; beat till light and fluffy. Sift together dry ingredients; add to creamed mixture alternately with applesauce, beating after each addition; stir in nuts. Pour into paper-lined 9½x5x3-inch loaf pan. Bake at 350° about 1 hour. Cool in pan 10 minutes; remove. While still warm, spread top with *Sugar Glaze:* Combine ½ cup sifted confectioners' sugar and 1 tablespoon water.

Banana-Nut Cake

⅔ cup shortening
2½ cups sifted cake flour
1⅔ cups sugar
1¼ teaspoons baking powder
1 teaspoon soda
1 teaspoon salt
1¼ cups mashed fully ripe bananas
⅔ cup buttermilk
2 eggs
⅔ cup chopped California walnuts

Stir shortening to soften. Sift in dry ingredients. Add bananas and half the buttermilk; mix until all flour is dampened. Beat vigorously 2 minutes. Add remaining buttermilk and the eggs; beat 2 minutes longer. Fold in nuts. Bake in 2 paper-lined 9x1½-inch round pans in moderate oven (350°) 35 minutes, or till done. Cool 10 minutes in pans. Remove and cool thoroughly. Spread one layer with about ⅓ of Cocoa Whipped Cream and top with 2 bananas, sliced. Add second layer; frost top, sides with remainder.

Cocoa Whipped Cream: Combine ½ cup sugar, ⅓ cup cocoa, and 1½ cups heavy cream. Chill at least 1 hour. Beat until stiff.

Burnt-sugar Cake

1½ cups sugar
½ cup shortening
1 teaspoon vanilla
2 eggs
2½ cups sifted cake flour
3 teaspoons baking powder
½ teaspoon salt
¾ cup cold water
3 tablespoons Burnt-sugar Syrup

Gradually add sugar to shortening, creaming thoroughly. Add vanilla, then eggs, one at a time, beating 1 minute after each. Add sifted dry ingredients to creamed mixture alternately with water, a small amount at a time, beating smooth after each addition. Add *3 tablespoons* Burnt-sugar Syrup.

Now beat batter *very well*, 4 minutes. Bake in 2 paper-lined 9x1½-inch round pans in moderate oven (375°) about 20 minutes. Cool 10 minutes in pans; turn out. Cool. Frost with Burnt-sugar Frosting.

Burnt-sugar Syrup: In heavy skillet, melt ⅔ cup sugar over low heat, stirring constantly. When a dark brown syrup, remove from heat; slowly add ⅔ cup boiling water. Heat and stir till all dissolves. Boil to reduce syrup to ½ cup. Cool.

Date Cake

1 cup chopped dates
1 cup boiling water
½ cup shortening
1 cup sugar
1 teaspoon vanilla
1 egg
1⅔ cups sifted cake flour
1 teaspoon soda
¼ teaspoon salt
½ cup chopped California walnuts

Combine dates with water; cool to room temperature. Stir shortening to soften. Gradually add sugar; cream thoroughly. Add vanilla and egg; beat well. Sift flour, soda, and salt together 2 times; add to creamed mixture alternately with date mixture, beating after each addition. Add nuts. Bake in paper-lined 9x9x2-inch pan in moderate oven (350°) about 35 to 40 minutes.

Choco-Date Cake: In Date Cake recipe above, sift 2 tablespoons cocoa with dry ingredients and omit nuts from batter. Pour into greased 13x9½x2-inch pan; sprinkle with the nuts and ½ to 1 cup semisweet chocolate pieces. Bake as above.

Spice Layer Cake

¾ cup shortening
2¼ cups sifted cake flour
1 cup granulated sugar
1 teaspoon baking powder
1 teaspoon salt
¾ teaspoon soda
¾ to 1 teaspoon cinnamon
¾ to 1 teaspoon cloves

• • •

¾ cup brown sugar
1 cup buttermilk
3 eggs

Stir shortening to soften. Sift in flour, granulated sugar, baking powder, salt, soda, and spices. Add brown sugar and buttermilk. Mix till all flour is dampened; beat vigorously 2 minutes. Add eggs; beat 2 minutes more. Bake in 2 paper-lined 9x1½-inch round pans at 350° for 30 to 35 minutes.

Spice Layer Cake—delicious!

Set for a party! Spice Layer Cake is blanketed with luscious Brown-sugar Frosting (page 56), circled with walnuts and candy corn. Between layers is a wide ribbon of Date-Nut Filling (recipe, page 61). Go-with: hot cider.

Wonderful Pound Cake

⅔ cup shortening
1¼ cups sugar

• • •

1 teaspoon grated
    lemon peel
1 tablespoon lemon juice
⅔ cup milk

• • •

2¼ cups sifted cake flour
1¼ teaspoons salt
1 teaspoon baking powder
3 eggs

• • •

Confectioners' sugar

Stir the shortening to soften. Gradually add sugar, and cream together until light and fluffy. (Beat about 3 minutes on medium speed of mixer.) Add lemon peel and juice. Add milk, and mix enough to break up creamed mixture. Sift together flour, salt, and baking powder; add to creamed mixture, and mix until smooth (about 2 minutes on low speed of mixer). Scrape sides of bowl often. Add eggs, 1 at a time, beating for 1 minute after each (low speed of mixer). Beat additional 1 minute at end. Scrape sides and bottom of bowl often. Pour into greased 9½x5x3-inch loaf pan. Bake in slow oven (300°) about 1 hour and 20 minutes. When thoroughly cool, sift confectioners' sugar over top of loaf.

Note: If desired, butter may be substituted for shortening. When substituting, cut down the amount of milk to ½ cup.

Mocha Pound Cake

Stir ⅔ cup shortening to soften. Sift in 2 cups sifted cake flour, 1¼ cups sugar, 1 tablespoon instant coffee, 1 teaspoon salt, ½ teaspoon cream of tartar, and ¼ teaspoon soda. Add ½ cup water and 1 teaspoon vanilla; mix until flour is dampened, then beat vigorously 2 minutes. Add 3 eggs and two 1-ounce squares unsweetened chocolate, melted; beat 1 minute. Pour into paper-lined 9½x5x3-inch loaf pan. Bake in slow oven (325°) 65 to 70 minutes, or till done. Cool in pan 10 minutes; remove.

Gingerbread

½ cup shortening
½ cup sugar
1 egg
½ cup light molasses
1½ cups sifted enriched flour
¾ teaspoon salt
¾ teaspoon soda
½ teaspoon ginger
½ teaspoon cinnamon
½ cup boiling water

Stir shortening to soften. Gradually add sugar, creaming till light and fluffy. Add egg and molasses; beat thoroughly. Sift together dry ingredients; add to molasses mixture alternately with boiling water, beating after each addition. Bake in greased 8x8x2-inch pan in moderate oven (350°) about 35 to 40 minutes. Serve warm.

Wonderful Pound Cake

A recipe to treasure! Wonderful Pound Cake is easy to make, turns out perfect every time. It has a silky grain, fairly melts in your mouth. For pretty top, dust with confectioners' sugar. Cut thin slices and serve with tea or hot chocolate. This cake is moist, and keeps well—if your family will let it!

Another time, try the Mocha Pound Cake (above). You'll like the coffee-chocolate blend of flavors.

These cakes frost themselves

Coconut-top Spice Cake

¼ cup butter or margarine
¼ cup shortening
1½ cups sugar
½ teaspoon vanilla
3 beaten eggs
2 cups sifted enriched flour
1 teaspoon baking powder
1 teaspoon soda
2 teaspoons nutmeg
¼ teaspoon salt
1 cup buttermilk

. . .

1 recipe Broiled Coconut Frosting

Cream butter and shortening together; gradually add sugar, creaming till light. Add vanilla. Add eggs; beat till light and fluffy. Sift together dry ingredients; add to creamed mixture alternately with buttermilk, beating after each addition. Pour into greased 13x9x2-inch pan. Bake in moderate oven (350°) 40 minutes or till done. Top with **Broiled Coconut Frosting:** Cream ¼ cup butter or margarine and 1 cup brown sugar. Add 2 tablespoons light cream; mix well. Stir in 1 cup flaked or shredded coconut. Spread mixture over warm cake. Broil 4 to 5 inches from heat, about 4 minutes or till golden brown. Serve cake warm.

Party Meringue Cake (*Blitz Torte*)

¼ cup shortening
½ cup sugar
½ teaspoon vanilla
2 egg yolks
1 cup sifted cake flour
1½ teaspoons baking powder
¼ teaspoon salt
½ cup milk
2 egg whites
½ cup sugar
¼ cup slivered blanched almonds
Fresh sweetened halved strawberries or drained thawed frozen berries

Cream shortening; gradually add ½ cup sugar and vanilla, creaming till fluffy. Beat in egg yolks. Sift together flour, baking powder, and salt; add alternately with milk to creamed mixture, beating after each addition. Pour into 2 paper-lined 8x1½-inch round pans. Beat egg whites till frothy; gradually add ½ cup sugar and beat till stiff peaks form. Spread evenly over cake batter; sprinkle with almonds. Bake at 350° for 30 to 35 minutes. Cool in pans 10 minutes; remove, cool thoroughly. Spread strawberries between layers (meringue side up). Serve with whipped cream and extra sweetened strawberries.

Lazy Mary Frosting— *easiest of all!*

Bake a white, spice, or chocolate cake. (Use one of our recipes or a mix.) While cake's hot, sprinkle with package of semisweet chocolate pieces; let stand till chocolate softens; spread smooth with spatula. Your cake's frosted and ready to serve in about the same time it takes to bake it!

Try this trick with chocolate-covered peppermints for a marbled, mint-flavored frosting.

Chocolate cakes

Red Devil's Food Cake

½ cup shortening
1 cup sugar
1 teaspoon salt
1 teaspoon vanilla
⅓ cup cold water
½ cup cocoa
2½ cups sifted cake flour
1 cup cold water
3 egg whites
¾ cup sugar
1½ teaspoons soda
⅓ cup cold water

Stir shortening to soften. Gradually add 1 cup sugar, creaming together till light and fluffy. Add salt and vanilla. Combine ⅓ cup cold water and the cocoa; beat into creamed mixture. Add flour alternately with 1 cup cold water, beginning and ending with flour; beat after each addition. Beat egg whites till soft peaks form; gradually add ¾ cup sugar, beating till stiff peaks form. Fold into batter. Dissolve soda in ⅓ cup cold water; stir into batter, mixing thoroughly. Bake in 2 paper-lined 9x1½-inch round pans at 350° about 30 minutes.

Prize Chocolate Cake

1 cup shortening
2 cups sugar
2 teaspoons vanilla
4 1-ounce squares unsweetened
  chocolate, melted
5 eggs
2¼ cups sifted cake flour
1 teaspoon soda
1 teaspoon salt
1 cup sour milk or
  buttermilk

Stir shortening to soften. Gradually add sugar, creaming till light and fluffy. Blend in vanilla and cooled chocolate. Add eggs, 1 at a time, beating well after each.

Sift together flour, soda, and salt; add to creamed mixture alternately with milk, beating after each addition. Bake in 3 paper-lined 9x1½-inch round pans in moderate oven (350°) 20 to 25 minutes.

Grandma's Chocolate Cake

2 cups brown sugar
1 cup milk
3 1-ounce squares unsweetened
  chocolate
½ cup shortening
1 teaspoon vanilla
½ teaspoon red food coloring
3 eggs
2 cups sifted enriched flour
1 teaspoon soda
½ teaspoon salt

Heat and stir *1 cup* brown sugar, ½ *cup* milk, and chocolate over very low heat till chocolate melts. Cool. Stir shortening; gradually add remaining brown sugar; cream till fluffy. Add vanilla and red food coloring. Beat in eggs, one at a time. Blend in chocolate mixture. Sift together flour, soda, salt; add to creamed mixture alternately with ½ *cup* milk, beginning and ending with flour; beat after each addition. Bake in 2 paper-lined 9x1½-inch round pans at 350° about 25 minutes.

Chocolate Fudge Cake

A favorite at California's Nut Tree—

¾ cup softened butter
½ cup cocoa
1½ cups sugar
1 teaspoon vanilla
3 egg yolks
2¼ cups sifted cake flour
3 teaspoons baking powder
1 cup ice water
3 stiff-beaten egg whites

Beat butter with cocoa. Gradually add sugar, beating till fluffy and light. Add vanilla. Beat in egg yolks, one at a time. Sift flour with baking powder; add to creamed mixture alternately with water, beginning and ending with flour; beat after each addition. Fold in egg whites. Bake in 2 paper-lined 9x1½-inch round pans in slow oven (300°) 30 to 35 minutes or until done. Cool in pans 10 minutes; turn out and cool on racks. Frost with Rich Chocolate Icing (page 58).

Rich and luscious—
Feathery Fudge Cake

Here's the kind of cake men like—chocolate through and through! It's full of that old-fashioned goodness. Swirl with Chocolate Satin Frosting, ring with walnut halves for the finishing touch. Better whisk this out of sight till dessert time!

Feathery Fudge Cake

⅔ cup soft butter or margarine
1¾ cups sugar
2 eggs
1 teaspoon vanilla
2½ 1-ounce squares unsweetened
   chocolate, melted
2½ cups sifted cake flour
1¼ teaspoons soda
½ teaspoon salt
1¼ cups ice water

Cream together butter, sugar, eggs, and vanilla till fluffy (beat 5 minutes at high speed on mixer, scraping bowl occasionally to guide batter into beaters; or beat 5 minutes by hand). Blend in cooled chocolate. Sift together flour, soda, and salt; add to creamed mixture alternately with ice water, beginning and ending with flour; beat after each addition. Bake in 2 paper-lined 9x1½-inch round pans in moderate oven (350°) 30 to 35 minutes or till done. Frost cooled cake with Chocolate Satin Frosting (page 59).

Sweet Chocolate Layer Cake

1 4-ounce package sweet cooking
   chocolate
1 cup sugar
⅔ cup softened butter or margarine
3 egg yolks
1 teaspoon vanilla
1¾ cups sifted cake flour
1 teaspoon soda
½ teaspoon salt
⅔ cup buttermilk
3 stiff-beaten egg whites

Combine chocolate with ⅓ cup water; stir over low heat till chocolate melts; cool. Gradually add sugar to butter, creaming till light and fluffy. Beat in egg yolks, one at a time. Blend in vanilla and chocolate mixture. Sift together flour, soda, and salt; add to creamed mixture alternately with buttermilk, beating after each addition. Fold in egg whites. Bake in 2 paper-lined 9x1½-inch round pans at 350° about 25 minutes. Fill and frost with Coconut Frosting (page 60.)

Choco-Cherry Cake This feather-light cake is full of scrumptious bits of mara-schino cherries and walnuts. Swirl with No-cook Fudge Frosting. Top each piece with a perfect walnut half.

Choco-Cherry Cake

Luscious and rich! For a casual supper dessert, serve right from the pan at your kitchen snack bar. Better cut big pieces!—

½ cup shortening, butter, or margarine
1 cup sugar
1 egg
2 1-ounce squares unsweetened
  chocolate, melted

• • •

1½ cups sifted cake flour
1 teaspoon soda
¾ teaspoon salt
1 cup milk
¼ cup chopped maraschino cherries
2 tablespoons maraschino-cherry syrup
½ cup chopped California walnuts

Stir shortening to soften. Gradually add sugar, creaming till light and fluffy. Add egg, beat well; stir in chocolate.

Sift together dry ingredients; then add to creamed mixture alternately with milk, beginning and ending with flour mixture; beat after each addition. Add cherries, syrup, and nuts.

Grease bottom of 8x8x2-inch baking dish*; pour in batter. Bake in slow oven (325°) 50 to 55 minutes, or till cake tests done. Cool. Frost in pan, if desired, with No-cook Fudge Frosting (recipe, page 59).

*Or use square metal pan and bake in moderate oven (350°) about 40 minutes.

Chocolate Marble Loaf Cake

Two favorite cakes combined, yet you stir up only one batter. If you like, frost cooled loaf with chocolate icing—

⅓ cup shortening
1 cup sugar
1 teaspoon vanilla
2 cups sifted cake flour
2½ teaspoons baking powder
¼ teaspoon salt
⅔ cup milk
3 stiff-beaten egg whites

• • •

1 1-ounce square unsweetened
  chocolate, melted
2 tablespoons hot water
¼ teaspoon soda
⅛ teaspoon red food coloring

Stir shortening to soften. Gradually add sugar, creaming till light and fluffy. Add vanilla. Sift together flour, baking powder, and salt; add to creamed mixture alternately with milk, beginning and ending with flour mixture. Beat after each addition. Fold in egg whites.

Combine chocolate, water, soda, and food coloring; add to ½ the batter, stirring just to blend. (Leave other part plain.) Spoon light and dark batters alternately into paper-lined 9½x5x3-inch loaf pan. Zigzag spatula through batter. Bake in moderate oven (350°) about 45 minutes.

Easy quick-mix cakes

Use special recipes for quick-mix cakes—don't try to adapt conventional cake recipes to the quick-mix method, or you face the possibility of sad results.

You'll find that there is less chance for failure with this method of making cakes because minutes may be timed exactly if you use an electric mixer or strokes may be counted. (If you count, 150 strokes are equal to 1 minute of beating by mixer.)

Streamlined

cake-making—

one bowl,

no creaming

Gold Layer Cake

½ cup shortening
2¼ cups sifted cake flour
1½ cups sugar
3 teaspoons baking powder
1 teaspoon salt

• • •

1 cup milk
2 eggs
1½ teaspoons vanilla

Stir shortening just to soften. Sift in dry ingredients. Add ⅔ cup of the milk; mix until all flour is dampened. Beat vigorously 2 minutes. Add remaining milk, eggs, and vanilla; beat vigorously 2 minutes more. Bake in 2 paper-lined 9x1½-inch round pans in moderate oven (350°) about 30 minutes.

Busy-day Cake

⅓ cup shortening
1¾ cups sifted cake flour
¾ cup sugar
2½ teaspoons baking powder
½ teaspoon salt
1 egg
¾ cup milk
1½ teaspoons vanilla

Stir shortening just to soften. Sift in dry ingredients. Add egg, ½ the milk; mix till all flour is dampened. Beat 2 minutes at medium speed on electric mixer. Add remaining milk, vanilla; beat 2 minutes longer. Bake in paper-lined 9x9x2-inch pan in moderate oven (375°) about 25 minutes.

Note: If you like, substitute ⅓ cup salad oil for shortening in Busy-day Cake. When substituting oil, follow method below.

Sift together flour, ½ *cup sugar*, baking powder, and salt. Add salad oil, milk, and vanilla; stir till all flour is dampened. Then beat till satin smooth (2 minutes at medium speed on mixer). Beat egg till thick and light (3 minutes at high speed on mixer). Gradually add remaining ¼ cup sugar, beating constantly. Fold egg mixture thoroughly into batter. Bake as above.

Devil's-food Cake

⅔ cup shortening
2¼ cups sifted cake flour
2 cups sugar
1 teaspoon salt
1 teaspoon soda
1 teaspoon baking powder
1¼ cups milk
3 eggs
3 1-ounce squares unsweetened chocolate, melted

Stir shortening just to soften. Sift in dry ingredients. Add ½ cup of the milk; mix until all flour is dampened. Beat vigorously 2 minutes. Add remaining milk, eggs, melted chocolate, and 1 teaspoon red food coloring; beat vigorously 2 minutes longer. Bake in 2 paper-lined 9x1½-inch round pans at 350° for 30 to 35 minutes or till done.

Chiffon cakes

Chiffon cakes give the lightness of an angel cake along with the melting richness of a shortening-type cake. The method for making this cake is different—it combines some of the steps used in making an angel cake with some for a shortening-type cake; study the method before you start mixing.

Assemble all the ingredients, preheat the oven, and measure ingredients accurately. Use the type and size pans specified in the recipe. *Do not grease pans.*

To make chiffon cake, follow step-by-step photographs on next page. Pour batter into ungreased tube pan and bake. The cake is done when it springs back when you touch the surface lightly. Cool as shown.

Pineapple Chiffon Cake

2¼ cups sifted cake flour
1½ cups sugar
3 teaspoons baking powder
1 teaspoon salt
½ cup salad oil
5 egg yolks
¾ cup unsweetened pineapple juice
1 cup (8) egg whites
½ teaspoon cream of tartar

Sift dry ingredients into mixing bowl; make a well in dry ingredients. In this order, add: salad oil, egg yolks, and pineapple juice. Beat until satin smooth.

In large mixing bowl, combine egg whites and cream of tartar. Beat until they form *very stiff peaks* (stiffer than for meringue or angel cake). Pour egg-yolk batter in thin stream over entire surface of egg whites, gently cutting and folding just until blended. Bake in ungreased 10-inch tube pan in slow oven (325°) 55 minutes; increase heat to 350° and bake 10 minutes longer. Invert and cool thoroughly.

Split cooled cake in 2 layers. Fill with part of the Pineapple-whip Topping; frost with remainder. Trim with pineapple daisies.
Pineapple-whip Topping: Thoroughly drain 1 No. 2 can (2½ cups) crushed pineapple, chilled. Gently fold drained pineapple into 2 cups heavy cream, whipped.

Maple-nut Chiffon Cake

2¼ cups sifted cake flour
¾ cup granulated sugar
3 teaspoons baking powder
1 teaspoon salt
¾ cup brown sugar

. . .

½ cup salad oil
5 egg yolks
¾ cup cold water
2 teaspoons maple flavoring
1 cup (8) egg whites
½ teaspoon cream of tartar
1 cup finely chopped California walnuts

Sift flour, granulated sugar, baking powder, and salt into mixing bowl; stir in brown sugar. Make a well in dry ingredients. In this order, add: salad oil, egg yolks, water, and flavoring. Beat till satin smooth.

Combine egg whites and cream of tartar in large mixing bowl. Beat until they form *very stiff peaks* (stiffer than for meringue or angel cake). Pour egg-yolk batter in thin stream over entire surface of egg whites, gently cutting and folding—down, across bottom, up the side, and over—just till blended. Fold in nuts.

Bake in ungreased 10-inch tube pan in slow oven (325°) 55 minutes; increase heat to 350° and bake 10 to 15 minutes more. Invert pan; let cool thoroughly. Frost cooled cake with Golden Butter Frosting.

Golden Butter Frosting

½ cup butter or margarine
4 cups sifted confectioners' sugar
½ cup light cream
1 to 1½ teaspoons maple flavoring or vanilla

Melt butter in saucepan; keep over low heat until golden brown, watching carefully so it doesn't scorch. Remove from heat and stir in confectioners' sugar. Blend in cream and flavoring. Place pan in ice water and beat till of spreading consistency (add more cream if needed). Makes enough to frost 10-inch round chiffon or angel cake.

Maple-nut Chiffon Cake— *you'll treasure the recipe*

So light and airy—this cake fairly takes wing! And the flavor's a delicious blend of maple and brown sugar and walnuts. Gild this beauty with easy-to-work-with Golden Butter Frosting. For a party-going trim, adorn with coppery mums and a cluster of green grapes.

Follow these picture steps for a chiffon cake you'll be proud of

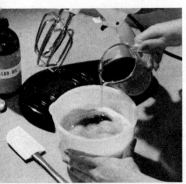

Sift flour, sugar, baking powder, and salt into bowl. Make well in center; add in this order: salad oil, unbeaten egg yolks, water, flavoring. Beat till batter is satin smooth.

Beat egg whites and cream of tartar till *very stiff* peaks form—when you pull dry rubber spatula through, a clear path should remain. Add egg-yolk batter in thin stream, gently folding into the whites to blend.

Soon as cake comes from oven, invert pan and all, on funnel or bottle until it cools to room temperature. With metal spatula or knife, loosen cake around sides and tube. Turn upside down; remove the pan. Now for the frosting!

Burnt-sugar Chiffon Cake

¾ cup sugar
1 cup boiling water
2¼ cups sifted cake flour
1¼ cups sugar
3 teaspoons baking powder
1 teaspoon salt
½ cup salad oil
5 egg yolks
6 tablespoons water
1 teaspoon vanilla
1 cup (8) egg whites
½ teaspoon cream of tartar

In heavy skillet, melt ¾ cup sugar over low heat, stirring constantly till medium brown and smooth. Remove from heat. Slowly add boiling water, stirring and heating to blend; cool. Sift dry ingredients into mixing bowl; make well in center. In this order, add: salad oil, egg yolks, 6 tablespoons water, vanilla, and 6 tablespoons of the burnt-sugar syrup. Beat till satin smooth.

Combine egg whites and cream of tartar. Beat till *very stiff peaks* form. Fold egg-yolk batter gradually into egg whites. Bake in 10-inch tube pan in slow oven (325°) 55 minutes, then in moderate oven (350°) 10 to 15 minutes. Invert pan; cool thoroughly. Frost with Burnt-sugar Frosting (page 56).

Mocha Chiffon Cake

4 teaspoons instant coffee
¾ cup hot water
2¼ cups sifted cake flour
1½ cups sugar
3 teaspoons baking powder
1 teaspoon salt
½ cup salad oil
5 egg yolks
1 teaspoon vanilla
3 1-ounce squares semisweet chocolate, thinly shaved
1 cup (8) egg whites
½ teaspoon cream of tartar

Dissolve instant coffee in hot water; cool. Sift flour, sugar, baking powder, and salt into mixing bowl; make a well in dry ingredients. In this order, add: salad oil, egg yolks, coffee, and vanilla. Beat until satin smooth. Stir in chocolate. Combine egg whites and cream of tartar in large mixing bowl. Beat till *very stiff peaks* form (stiffer than for meringue or angel cake). Pour egg-yolk batter in thin stream over entire surface of egg whites, gently cutting and folding just till blended. Bake in ungreased 10-inch tube pan in slow oven (325°) 55 minutes, then in moderate oven (350°) 10 to 15 minutes. Invert pan; cool.

Burnt-sugar Chiffon—

glamorous with

trim of broken pecans

Boston Cream Pie

This pie's a fooler. It's really a fluffy, 2-egg chiffon cake! Or, when minutes matter, try the Boston cream-pie mix—

2 egg whites
½ cup sugar

• • •

2¼ cups sifted cake flour
1 cup sugar
3 teaspoons baking powder
1 teaspoon salt
⅓ cup salad oil
1 cup milk
1½ teaspoons vanilla
2 egg yolks

Beat egg whites till foamy. Gradually beat in ½ cup sugar. Continue beating till very stiff and glossy. Sift remaining dry ingredients into another bowl. Add salad oil, *half* of the milk, and the vanilla. Beat 1 minute at medium speed on mixer or 150 strokes by hand, scraping sides and bottom of bowl constantly. Add remaining milk and egg yolks. Beat 1 minute longer, scraping bowl constantly. Gently fold in egg-white mixture with down-up-and-over motion, turning the bowl. Bake batter in 2 paper-lined 9x1½-inch round pans in moderate oven (350°) 25 to 30 minutes. When the cake is thoroughly cool, fill between layers with Vanilla Cream Filling. Top with Confectioners' Glaze and Chocolate Spiral.

Note: For easy assembly, frost and decorate top layer, then fill between layers. For make-ahead dessert, put together 1 to 3 hours before serving time and keep chilled.

Vanilla Cream Filling: Prepare 1 package vanilla pudding according to package directions, *using only* 1¾ cups milk. Cover and chill. Beat till fluffy and smooth.

Confectioners' Glaze: Combine 1 cup sifted confectioners' sugar, 1 tablespoon *warm* water, 1½ teaspoons light corn syrup, and ¼ teaspoon vanilla; stir until blended. Leaving a ½- to ¾-inch border of cake, quickly spread frosting over top layer. Immediately add *Chocolate Spiral:* Start at center of cake. Using a teaspoon, pour chilled canned chocolate syrup from the tip in a thin stream to form spiral. Quickly run tip of spatula from the center of cake to edge, "pulling" each band of chocolate slightly. Repeat, making 16 or 24 spokes, evenly spaced. (Wipe the spatula with a damp cloth after making each stroke.)

Washington Pie: Mix and bake chiffon cake as in Boston Cream Pie recipe. Fill between layers with strawberry or raspberry jam. Sift confectioners' sugar over top. Or, split one of the layers, fill with jam. (Frost second layer for another meal.)

Golden Lemon Chiffon Cake

1 cup plus 2 tablespoons sifted cake flour
¾ cup sugar
1½ teaspoons baking powder
½ teaspoon salt
¼ cup salad oil
2 egg yolks
¼ cup plus 2 tablespoons cold water
1 teaspoon vanilla
1 teaspoon grated lemon peel
½ cup (4) egg whites
¼ teaspoon cream of tartar

Sift flour, sugar, baking powder, and salt into mixing bowl; make well in dry ingredients. In this order, add: salad oil, egg yolks, water, vanilla, and grated lemon peel. Beat till satin smooth. Combine egg whites and cream of tartar. Beat till *very stiff peaks* form. Pour egg-yolk batter in thin stream over entire surface of egg whites, gently cutting and folding just till blended. Bake in ungreased 8x8x2- or 9x9x2-inch pan in moderate oven (350°) 30 to 35 minutes.

Cherry Chiffon Loaf Cake: In Golden Lemon Chiffon Cake recipe, decrease water to 3 tablespoons; omit lemon peel. Add 3 tablespoons maraschino cherry syrup along with water and vanilla. Beat satin smooth. Fold in ¼ cup finely chopped California walnuts and ¼ cup finely chopped maraschino cherries, well drained. Fold yolk batter into egg whites as above. Bake in ungreased 9½x5x3-inch loaf pan in slow oven (325°) 50 to 55 minutes. Invert pan; cool.

Nut Bars—a quick fix-up

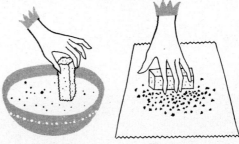

Cut Golden Lemon Chiffon Cake in oblong bars or squares. Dip in thin confectioners' sugar icing, then roll in chopped nuts.

Angel and sponge cakes

As for other cakes, read recipe carefully. Assemble all ingredients, use standard measuring utensils, and measure accurately.

Prepare pans according to directions in recipe. *Do not grease.* Spread mixed batter to sides of pan and fill all corners. Angel and sponge cakes are done when they spring back to the touch. Invert in pan; cool thoroughly. If cake falls away from the pan, it may be because pan was greased or because of insufficient baking.

Angel cakes

Angel cakes are leavened with just air. Whether or not you get a light, tender cake will depend on how much you beat the egg whites, the lightness with which you fold in the sugar-and-flour mixture, and the temperature at which you bake the cake.

Egg whites should be beaten till they are stiff enough to hold up in soft peaks, but are still moist and glossy.

Sponge cakes

Methods for making sponge cakes vary from recipe to recipe, but angel-cake rules for beating egg whites and folding in sugar and flour hold true with sponge cakes, too. It's important, also, to beat egg yolks till they're thick as whipped cream and lemon-colored. You may beat some or all of the sugar with the yolks, but remember to add sugar gradually. In some recipes, liquid is added to yolks and beaten till mixture is very light.

Angel Cake Supreme

1 cup sifted cake flour
1¼ cups sifted confectioners' sugar

• • •

1½ cups (12) egg whites
1½ teaspoons cream of tartar
¼ teaspoon salt
1½ teaspoons vanilla
¼ teaspoon almond extract
1 cup granulated sugar

Sift flour with confectioners' sugar 3 times. Beat egg whites with cream of tartar, salt, vanilla, and almond extract till stiff enough to hold up in soft peaks, but still moist and glossy. Beat in the granulated sugar, 2 tablespoons at a time, continuing to beat until meringue holds stiff peaks. Sift about ¼ of flour mixture over whites; fold in lightly with down-up-and-over motion, turning bowl. Fold in remaining flour by fourths. Bake in an *ungreased* 10-inch tube pan in moderate oven (375°) about 30 minutes or till done. Invert pan, cool thoroughly.

To match picture: Spoon strawberries over cake; add an avalanche of whipped cream.

Reasons for failures with angel cake and sponge cake

Tough cake
Too hot an oven
Not enough sugar
Overmixing

Coarse texture
Underbeaten egg whites
Insufficient blending of ingredients
Too slow an oven

Heavy sticky layer at bottom
Underbeaten egg yolks
Insufficient mixing of yolks with other ingredients

Cracks in crust
Overbeaten egg whites
Too much sugar
Too hot an oven

Sticky crust
Too much sugar
Underbaking

Undersized cake
Underbeaten, overbeaten whites
Overmixing
Too large a pan
Too hot an oven

Angel Cake

1 cup sifted cake flour
¾ cup sugar
1½ cups (12) egg whites
1½ teaspoons cream of tartar
¼ teaspoon salt
1½ teaspoons vanilla
¾ cup sugar

Sift flour with ¾ cup sugar 4 times. Beat egg whites with cream of tartar, salt, and vanilla till stiff enough to form soft peaks but still moist and glossy. Add the remaining ¾ cup sugar, 2 tablespoons at a time, continuing to beat until meringue holds stiff peaks. Sift ¼ of flour mixture over whites; fold in. Fold in remaining flour by fourths. Bake in *ungreased* 10-inch tube pan in moderate oven (375°) 35 to 40 minutes or till done. Invert pan, cool.

Chocolate Angel Cake: In Angel Cake recipe, substitute ¾ cup sifted cake flour and ¼ cup cocoa for 1 cup sifted cake flour. Sift cocoa with flour and sugar 4 times.

Daisy Marble Cake

Yellow and white, and beautiful! Angel cake and orange sponge from just one batter—

1 cup sifted cake flour
½ cup sugar
1⅜ cups (11) egg whites
1¼ teaspoons cream of tartar
¼ teaspoon salt
1 cup sugar
1 teaspoon grated orange peel
2 tablespoons orange juice
4 well-beaten egg yolks
2 tablespoons sifted cake flour
½ teaspoon vanilla

Sift 1 cup flour with ½ cup sugar. Beat egg whites with cream of tartar and salt till soft peaks form. Gradually add remaining 1 cup sugar to egg whites, beating till stiff peaks form. Sift about ¼ of flour mixture over whites; fold in lightly. Fold in remaining flour mixture by thirds. Divide batter in 2 parts. Add orange peel and juice to egg yolks; beat until very thick and lemon colored. Fold egg-yolk mixture and 2 tablespoons flour into *half* of the batter. Fold the vanilla into *other half* of batter. Spoon batters alternately into *ungreased* 10-inch tube pan. Bake in moderate oven (375°) about 35 minutes or till done. Invert pan; cool.

Orange Sponge Cake

6 eggs, separated
1 tablespoon grated orange peel
½ cup orange juice
1½ cups sugar
¼ teaspoon salt
1⅓ cups sifted cake flour
1 teaspoon cream of tartar

Beat egg yolks till thick and lemon-colored. Add peel and juice; beat till very thick. Gradually beat in *1 cup* sugar and the salt. Carefully fold in flour. Beat egg whites till foamy; add cream of tartar; beat till soft peaks form. Gradually add ½ *cup* sugar, beating till stiff peaks form. Thoroughly fold whites into yolk mixture. Bake in *ungreased* 10-inch tube pan at 325° about 55 minutes or till done. Invert pan; cool.

Butter Sponge

1 cup sifted cake flour
1 teaspoon baking powder
¼ cup butter, melted
½ teaspoon vanilla
½ cup milk, scalded
6 egg yolks
1 cup sugar

Sift together flour and baking powder. Add butter and vanilla to scalded milk and keep hot. Beat egg yolks till thick and lemon-colored; gradually beat in sugar. Quickly add flour mixture; stir just till mixed. Gently stir in the hot milk mixture. Bake in greased 9x9x2-inch pan in moderate oven (350°) 30 to 35 minutes or till done. Cool thoroughly (do not invert pan).

Pineapple Fluff Cake

6 eggs, separated
¼ teaspoon salt
1½ cups sugar
1 tablespoon lemon juice
½ cup unsweetened pineapple juice
1½ cups sifted cake flour
1 teaspoon baking powder

Beat egg whites with salt till soft peaks form. Gradually beat in ¾ *cup* sugar. Beat egg yolks with ¾ *cup* sugar till thick and lemon-colored. Add juices; beat till sugar dissolves. Sift flour with baking powder 3 times; add to yolk mixture. Fold in whites. Bake in *ungreased* 10-inch tube pan in slow oven (325°) about 1 hour. Invert, cool.

Bake a pair of festive
fruitcakes

Dark Fruitcake

3½ cups (1½ pounds) mixed diced fruits and peels for fruitcake
1¼ cups (8 ounces) dark seedless raisins
1¼ cups (8 ounces) light seedless raisins
1 cup (4 ounces) chopped California walnuts
1 cup (4 ounces) chopped pecans

• • •

3 cups sifted enriched flour
1 teaspoon baking powder
1 teaspoon salt
1 teaspoon cinnamon
1 teaspoon allspice
½ teaspoon nutmeg
½ teaspoon cloves

• • •

1 cup shortening
2 cups brown sugar
4 large eggs (1 cup)
¾ cup grape juice

Mix fruits and peels, raisins, and nuts. Sift together flour, baking powder, salt, and spices; sprinkle ¼ *cup* over fruit mixture, mixing well. Thoroughly cream shortening and sugar; beat in eggs, one at a time. Add dry ingredients to creamed mixture alternately with grape juice, beating smooth after each addition. Pour over fruits; mix well.

Line two 8½x4½x2½-inch loaf pans* with paper, allowing ½ inch to extend above all sides. Pour batter into pans, filling ¾ full; do not flatten. Bake in very slow oven (275°) 3 to 3½ hours or till done. (Have pan of water on bottom shelf of oven.) Cool in pans, then turn out. Makes 6 pounds.

If desired, wrap cakes in cheesecloth and moisten on all sides with brandy or wine. Wrap in foil and store in refrigerator or cool place for 3 to 4 weeks, moistening again once a week.

*Or bake in five 5½x3x2¼-inch loaf pans at 300° for 2 to 2½ hours or till done.

White Fruitcake

4 cups (1¾ pounds) mixed diced fruits and peels for fruitcake
½ cup pitted dates, cut up
½ cup dried apricots, cut up
½ cup dried figs, cut up
1¼ cups (8 ounces) light seedless raisins
2 cups (8 ounces) blanched almonds, slivered
2 cups flaked coconut

• • •

2 cups sifted enriched flour
1½ teaspoons baking powder
1 teaspoon salt
1 cup shortening
1 cup sugar
1 teaspoon rum flavoring
5 eggs
½ cup unsweetened pineapple juice

Mix fruits and peels, dates, apricots, figs, raisins, almonds, and coconut. Sift together flour, baking powder, and salt; sprinkle ½ *cup* over fruit mixture, mixing well. Thoroughly cream shortening, sugar, and flavoring; add eggs, one at a time, beating well after each. Add dry ingredients to creamed mixture alternately with pineapple juice, beating well after each addition. Add fruit mixture, stirring until well mixed. Line two 8½x4½x2½-inch loaf pans with paper, allowing ½ inch to extend above all sides of pan. (Or bake in smaller pans.) Pour batter into pans, filling ¾ full. Bake in very slow oven (275°) 2½ hours or till done. (Have pan of water on bottom shelf of oven while baking.) Makes about 5 pounds.

Note: You can mix your own candied fruits and peels if you prefer. We like 4 ounces each candied citron, orange peel, lemon peel, and cherries; and 12 ounces of candied pineapple. Buy them chopped or dice them yourself.

Pineapple Glaze

Combine ¼ cup canned unsweetened pineapple juice and ½ cup light corn syrup. Bring quickly to a rolling boil. Remove from heat. Immediately brush over cooled fruitcakes. Decorate top of cakes with blanched almonds, candied cherries, or candies. When set, brush on second coat of glaze. (Reheat glaze to boiling each time you use it.) Allow glaze to dry thoroughly before wrapping or storing cakes. Makes enough glaze to give double coat to 6 pounds of fruitcake.

Roll up a jelly roll

Pineapple Cake Roll

Thoroughly drain 1 No. 2½ can (3½ cups) crushed pineapple. (Use syrup in Pineapple Sauce.) Spread pineapple evenly in bottom of ungreased 15½x10½x1-inch jelly-roll pan; sprinkle with ⅔ cup brown sugar.

Mix batter as for Jelly Roll; spread evenly over pineapple in pan. Bake in moderate oven (375°) about 20 minutes or till done. Loosen sides; turn out on towel sprinkled with sifted confectioners' sugar. Let cool 2 or 3 minutes. Roll up, starting at narrow end. Wrap in the sugared towel; cool.

Take your pick from our jelly-roll jamboree!

Pineapple Sauce

Mix 2 tablespoons sugar and 1½ tablespoons cornstarch. Gradually stir in reserved pineapple syrup (about 1⅔ cups). Cook, stirring constantly, till thick and clear. Remove from heat; add 1 to 2 tablespoons lemon juice. Serve warm or chilled with slices of Pineapple Cake Roll.

Jelly Roll

4 egg yolks
¼ cup sugar
½ teaspoon vanilla
4 egg whites
½ cup sugar
¾ cup sifted enriched flour
1 teaspoon baking powder
½ teaspoon salt

Beat egg yolks till thick and lemon-colored; gradually beat in ¼ cup sugar and vanilla.

Beat egg whites till soft peaks form; gradually add ½ cup sugar and beat till stiff peaks form. Fold yolks into whites. Sift together flour, baking powder, and salt; fold into egg mixture. Bake in greased, waxed paper-lined 15½x10½x1-inch jelly-roll pan in moderate oven (375°) about 12 minutes. Loosen sides, turn out on towel sprinkled with sifted confectioners' sugar. Remove paper. Trim crusts. Roll quickly with fresh sheet paper on inside of roll. Wrap in sugared towel; cool. Unroll, remove paper; spread with favorite filling. Roll again.

Midget Cake Rolls: Turn warm Pineapple Cake Roll out of pan onto towel. Cut cake in half lengthwise. Then cut crosswise in fourths to make 8 rectangles. Quickly roll each piece, starting with narrow end. Top with whipped cream, tart jelly.

Pineapple Stack-ups: Cut rolled Pineapple Cake Roll in thin slices—two for each serving. Spoon Pineapple Sauce between and atop layers. Crown each serving with a fluff of whipped cream and chopped candied ginger. Serve warm or chilled.

Walnut Cream Roll

Light-and-airy cake filled with whipped cream—it's company best! Make it ahead and chill. Come dessert time, swirl top of roll with whipped cream and trim with California walnut halves.

Walnut Cream Roll

4 egg whites
½ teaspoon salt
1 teaspoon vanilla
½ cup sugar
4 egg yolks
¼ cup sifted enriched flour
½ cup chopped California walnuts
1 cup heavy cream, whipped, sweetened

Beat whites with salt and vanilla till soft peaks form. Gradually beat in sugar. Beat yolks till thick and lemon-colored. Fold yolks into whites; carefully fold in flour and nuts. Line bottom and sides of 15½x10½x1-inch jelly-roll pan with waxed paper. Spread batter evenly in pan. Bake in moderate oven (375°) 12 minutes or till cake springs back when lightly touched. Cool 5 minutes. Loosen sides of cake; turn out onto towel sprinkled with sifted confectioners' sugar. Peel off paper; cool to lukewarm. Starting at narrow end, roll cake and towel together; cool on rack. Unroll; spread with whipped cream. Reroll cake; chill.

Lincoln Log

Mix, bake, and cool Chocolate Roll-up. Spread with 1 cup heavy cream, whipped; roll up. Spread outside with Glossy Chocolate Frosting (page 59). Chill.

Chocolate Roll-up

5 eggs, separated
½ teaspoon cream of tartar
1 cup sugar
¼ cup sifted enriched flour
3 tablespoons cocoa
¼ teaspoon salt
1 teaspoon vanilla

Beat egg whites and cream of tartar till stiff but not dry. Gradually beat in ½ *cup* sugar. Beat egg yolks till thick and lemon-colored. Sift ½ *cup* sugar with flour, cocoa, and salt; fold into yolks till blended; add vanilla. Carefully fold yolk mixture into whites. Line bottom and sides of 15½x10½x1-inch pan with waxed paper; grease paper lightly. Spread batter evenly in pan. Bake in slow oven (325°) about 25 minutes. Cool 5 minutes; turn onto towel sprinkled with sifted confectioners' sugar. Peel off paper. Cool to lukewarm. Trim side crusts. Roll cake with towel. Cool. Unroll; spread with filling or whipped cream. Roll again.

Ice-cream Roll: Mix, bake, and cool Chocolate Roll-up. Stir 1 quart pink peppermint ice cream just to soften; gently spread on cake. Roll up. Wrap in waxed paper; freeze. Remove waxed paper, spread with Chocolate Glaze (page 59); dot with walnuts. Serve at once or freeze till serving time.

These small-size cakes meet

Coconut Chiffon Cupcakes

2¼ cups sifted cake flour
1 cup sugar
3 teaspoons baking powder
1 teaspoon salt
⅓ cup salad oil
1 cup milk
1½ teaspoons vanilla
2 eggs, separated
½ cup sugar
1 3½-ounce can flaked coconut

Sift together flour, 1 cup sugar, baking powder, and salt into mixing bowl; make a well in dry ingredients. Add salad oil, *half* of the milk, and the vanilla; mix to blend. Beat 1 minute at medium speed on mixer, scraping bowl constantly. Add remaining milk and the egg yolks. Beat 1 minute. Beat whites till soft peaks form; gradually add ½ cup sugar and beat till very stiff peaks form; fold into batter. Place paper bake cups in muffin pans; fill ½ full. Sprinkle coconut on tops. Bake in hot oven (400°) 12 to 15 minutes or till done. Makes about 3 dozen.

Apple Spice Cupcakes

½ cup shortening
1¼ cups sugar
1 teaspoon vanilla
2 eggs
2 cups sifted cake flour
2 teaspoons baking powder
½ teaspoon salt
¼ teaspoon soda
2 teaspoons instant coffee
1 teaspoon cinnamon
½ teaspoon nutmeg
½ teaspoon allspice
1 cup chopped tart apple
½ cup chopped California walnuts
¾ cup cold water

Thoroughly cream shortening and sugar. Add vanilla; beat in eggs, one at a time. Sift together dry ingredients; mix with apples and nuts. Add to creamed mixture alternately with water. Place paper bake cups in muffin pans; fill ½ full. Bake at 375° about 25 minutes. Makes 2 dozen.

Praline Cupcakes

⅓ cup butter, margarine, or shortening
2 cups sifted cake flour
1 cup sugar
2 teaspoons baking powder
½ teaspoon salt
¾ cup milk
1 egg
1 teaspoon lemon extract
½ cup chopped California walnuts
1 recipe Praline Topping

Stir butter to soften. Sift in dry ingredients. Add *half* the milk and the egg; mix until all flour is dampened. Then beat vigorously 2 minutes. Add remaining milk and extract; beat 1 minute longer. Stir in nuts. Place paper bake cups in muffin pans and fill ½ full. Bake in moderate oven (375°) 25 minutes or till done.

Praline Topping: Combine ¼ cup melted butter or margarine and ¾ cup brown sugar; quickly spoon over hot cakes. Center each with walnut half. Continue baking 5 minutes longer. Makes 18 medium cupcakes.

Peanut-butter Cupcakes

Tops for a small-fry party—

½ cup peanut butter
⅓ cup shortening
1 teaspoon vanilla
1½ cups brown sugar
2 eggs
2 cups sifted enriched flour
2 teaspoons baking powder
½ teaspoon salt
¾ cup milk

Cream together peanut butter, shortening, and vanilla. Gradually add brown sugar, beating till light and fluffy. Add eggs one at a time, beating well after each. Sift together dry ingredients; add alternately with milk. Place paper bake cups in muffin pans; fill ½ full. Bake in moderate oven (375°) 20 minutes or till done. "Frost" with peanut butter. Sift a small dot of confectioners' sugar atop each. Makes about 2 dozen.

big occasions

Fruitcake-ettes

Combine one package spice cake mix, ¼ cup shortening, and ½ cup boiling water. Mix till well moistened. Let stand 30 minutes.

Mix at medium speed on mixer for 2 minutes. Add 2 eggs and ¼ cup cooking sherry; beat 2 minutes. Stir in 3½ cups chopped mixed candied fruits, 1 cup raisins, and 2 cups coarsely chopped walnuts. Line 2-inch muffin pans with paper bake cups; fill ¾ full. Bake at 300° for 45 minutes. Makes 7 dozen.

Petits Fours

¼ cup butter or margarine
¼ cup shortening
1 cup sugar
½ teaspoon vanilla
¼ teaspoon almond extract

• • •

2 cups sifted cake flour
3 teaspoons baking powder
¼ teaspoon salt
⅔ cup milk
⅞ cup (6) egg whites
¼ cup sugar

Cream butter and shortening thoroughly. Gradually add 1 cup sugar, and cream together until light and fluffy. Add extracts. Sift together flour, baking powder, and salt; add to creamed mixture alternately with milk, beating after each addition. Beat egg whites until foamy; gradually add remaining ¼ cup sugar and beat until mixture forms soft peaks. Fold into batter. Bake in paper-lined 13x9½x2-inch pan in moderate oven (350°) about 40 minutes or till done.

Cool cake 5 minutes before removing from pan. When thoroughly cool, cut in 1½-inch squares or in diamonds. Or cut in rounds with tiny biscuit cutter. Line cakes up on rack with cooky sheet below. Spoon Petits Fours Icing over cakes, coating evenly. (Keep icing over hot water.) For pretty glaze, give cake two coats icing. If icing gets too thick, add few drops hot water. With pastry tube, pipe frosting rose on each cake or trim with candy decoration.

Serve Petits Fours for coffee go-with or a dainty dessert

Bake one big cake, cut in bite-size pieces, pour icing over. Presto—tiny party cakes!

Petits Fours Icing: Cook 3 cups sugar, ¼ teaspoon cream of tartar, and 1½ cups hot water to thin syrup (226°). Cool to lukewarm (110°). Add 1 teaspoon vanilla. Stir in sifted confectioners' sugar (about 2¼ cups) till frosting is of consistency to pour. If you like, tint frosting with few drops food coloring.

Start with a ready-baked cake

Viennese Torte

1 6-ounce package (1 cup) semisweet
   chocolate pieces
½ cup butter or margarine
¼ cup water
4 slightly beaten egg yolks
2 tablespoons sifted confectioners' sugar
1 teaspoon vanilla
1 12-ounce loaf pound cake

In heavy saucepan, heat chocolate, butter, and water over medium heat, stirring till blended. Cool slightly. Add egg yolks, sugar, and vanilla; stir till smooth. Chill till mixture is of spreading consistency, about 45 minutes. Slice cake horizontally in 6 layers. Spread chocolate between layers, then frost top and sides. Chill at least 45 minutes before serving. Cut in ¼-inch slices.

Coffee Ribbon Loaf

Combine 2 cups heavy cream, ⅔ cup sugar, and 2 to 3 tablespoons instant coffee. Whip till stiff. Rub brown crumbs from one 10x4x2-inch loaf angel cake; cut lengthwise in 4 even layers. Add ½ cup chopped California walnuts to half of whipped cream; spread between cake layers. Cover top and sides of loaf with remaining whipped cream. Sprinkle with 1¼ cups toasted flaked coconut. Chill. Makes 10 servings.

Easy blender method

No cooking necessary!
Combine all ingredients for torte frosting in blender, using *soft* butter and *warm* water. Blend on high speed till mixture is smooth. Chill till of spreading consistency. Fill, frost, chill pound cake as above.

Elegant Viennese Torte An easy version of a fabulous European creation! You may assemble the layered cake ahead, then tuck it away in your freezer. Fancy dessert needed? It's ready to serve in an hour.

Daffodil Layers

½ envelope (1½ teaspoons) unflavored
  gelatin
½ cup sugar
3 beaten egg yolks
¾ teaspoon grated lemon peel
⅓ cup lemon juice
3 egg whites
¼ cup sugar
Few drops yellow food coloring
1 10-inch tube angel cake

Combine gelatin and ½ cup sugar in top of
double boiler; add yolks, lemon peel and
juice. Cook over *hot, not boiling*, water, stirring constantly until slightly thick and gelatin is completely dissolved, about 5 to 8 minutes. Cool until partially set. Beat egg whites
till soft peaks form; gradually add ¼ cup
sugar, beating to stiff peaks. Fold into gelatin mixture. Tint with few drops yellow food
coloring. Trim or brush crusts from cake.
Cut crosswise in 3 equal layers. Spread bottom layer with half the gelatin mixture;
add second cake layer and spread with remaining gelatin; top with third cake layer.
Chill well. Frost with whipped cream.
Makes 10 servings.

...el Ring

¼ ...aspo...
¾ cup ...ar
... (1 tablespoon) unflavored
¼ cup ...
...on salt
1¼ cups milk
2 1-ounce squares unsweetened chocolate
3 beaten egg yolks
1 teaspoon vanilla
3 egg whites
¼ cup sugar
1 cup heavy cream, whipped
1 10- or 10½-ounce loaf angel cake

Thoroughly mix ½ cup sugar, the gelatin,
and salt. Add milk, chocolate. Heat and stir
over low heat till chocolate melts and gelatin dissolves; gradually add to yolks, mixing
well. Add vanilla. Chill, stirring occasionally, till partially set. Beat whites till soft
peaks form; gradually add ¼ cup sugar,
beating to stiff peaks. Fold in chocolate
mixture, then whipped cream.

Remove brown crumbs from cake; tear
cake in bite-size pieces; fold into chocolate
mixture. Turn into 9-inch spring-form pan
or tube pan. (Line bottom of tube pan with
foil.) Chill several hours or overnight. Unmold. Trim with whipped cream, shaved
chocolate. Makes 10 servings.

Lemonade Angel Dessert

1 envelope unflavored gelatin
½ cup sugar
2 beaten eggs
½ cup water
1 6-ounce can frozen lemonade
  concentrate
1 14½-ounce can evaporated milk,
  chilled *icy cold* and whipped
1 10-inch tube angel cake

Mix gelatin, sugar, and *dash salt;* add eggs,
water. Cook and stir till gelatin dissolves and
mixture thickens slightly; remove from heat.
Stir in concentrate. Chill till partially set;
fold into whipped milk.

Add few drops *yellow food coloring*. Rub
brown crumbs off cake; tear cake in bite-
size pieces. Cover bottom of 10-inch tube
pan with thin layer of gelatin mixture.
Loosely arrange ⅓ of cake on top. Pour ⅓
of remaining gelatin over. Repeat. Chill till
firm. Unmold. Makes 12 servings.

Frozen Maple Loaf

1 10x4x2-inch loaf angel cake
6 fig-bar cookies, crumbled
¾ cup maple-flavored syrup
1 tablespoon butter or margarine
1 quart maple-nut ice cream
1 cup heavy cream, whipped

Rub brown crumbs off cake, then cut loaf
lengthwise in 3 even slices. Line bottom and
sides of buttered 8½x4½x2½-inch loaf pan
with cake slices; chill. In saucepan combine
cookies, syrup, and butter; cook and stir
till slightly thick and well blended (about 5
minutes). Cool. Stir ice cream just to soften.
Swirl sauce through ice cream; spoon into
cake lined pan. Cover and freeze 12 hours or
overnight. To serve, unmold by dipping
quickly in warm water. Invert on chilled platter; frost with whipped cream. Trim with
walnut halves. Makes 6 to 8 servings.

Raspberry Ring

Dissolve 1 package raspberry-flavored gelatin and dash salt in 1¼ cups boiling water.
Add one 10-ounce package frozen raspberries and stir till thawed. Chill till partially
set. Whip till fluffy; fold in 1 cup heavy
cream, whipped. Rub brown crumbs from
one 10x4x2-inch loaf angel cake; tear cake
in 1½ to 2-inch pieces. Loosely arrange
half of cake in bottom of 10-inch tube pan.
Pour half of gelatin mixture over. Repeat.
Chill firm. Unmold. Makes 8 servings.

Frostings, fillings, and sauces

Crown your cake with frosting

Favorite fillings, plain and fancy

Cake decorating—it's a snap!

Top dessert with a delicious sauce

Sauce up a spectacular sundae!

Frost with a flourish, add a speedy trim

← Chocolate cake gets a party look with Peppermint-stick Frosting. Fill between layers, then cover sides, spreading high enough to hide top edge. Swirl remaining frosting over top. Decorate cake with crushed peppermint-stick candy.

Crown your cake with frosting

Fluffy Frosting

1 cup sugar
¼ teaspoon cream of tartar
Dash salt
⅓ cup water

. . .

1 egg white
¼ teaspoon vanilla

Bring sugar, cream of tartar, salt, and water to a boil; cook until sugar dissolves. Slowly add to unbeaten egg white, beating constantly with rotary or electric beater until frosting is of spreading consistency. Add vanilla. Frosts tops, sides of two 8- or 9-inch layers or one 10-inch tube cake.

Boiled Frosting

2 cups sugar
¾ cup water
1 tablespoon light corn syrup
  or ¼ teaspoon cream of tartar
Dash salt

. . .

2 stiff-beaten egg whites
1 teaspoon vanilla

Cook sugar, water, corn syrup and salt over low heat, stirring until sugar dissolves. Cover saucepan 2 to 3 minutes to dissolve sugar crystals on sides of pan. Uncover; continue cooking to soft-ball stage (236°). Gradually add hot syrup to egg whites, beating constantly. Add vanilla and beat till frosting is of spreading consistency. Frosts tops and sides of two 8- or 9-inch layers.

Mocha Chip Fluff

1 package fluffy instant-
  frosting mix
3 to 4 teaspoons instant coffee

. . .

1 6-ounce package (1 cup) semisweet
  chocolate pieces

Combine frosting mix and instant coffee. Prepare frosting according to package directions. Fold in chocolate pieces. Frosts top and sides of one 10-inch tube cake.

Seven-minute Frosting

2 unbeaten egg whites
1½ cups sugar
1½ teaspoons light corn syrup
  or ¼ teaspoon cream of tartar
⅓ cup cold water
Dash salt
1 teaspoon vanilla

Place all ingredients except vanilla in top of double boiler (not over heat); beat 1 minute with electric or rotary beater to blend. Place over boiling water and cook, beating constantly till frosting forms stiff peaks, *about* 7 minutes (*don't overcook*). Remove from boiling water. Pour into mixing bowl, if you wish. Add vanilla, beat till of spreading consistency, about 2 minutes. Frosts tops and sides of two 8- or 9-inch layers or one 10-inch tube cake.

Burnt-sugar Frosting: Decrease sugar to 1¼ cups and the water to ¼ cup; substitute 3 to 4 tablespoons Burnt-sugar Syrup (page 32) for the corn syrup called for.

Peppermint-stick Frosting: Add vanilla to Seven-minute Frosting. Then tint frosting a delicate pink with few drops red food coloring. Beat till of spreading consistency, about 2 minutes. Sprinkle top and sides of frosted cake with crushed peppermint-stick candy.

Brown-sugar Frosting: Substitute ¾ cup brown sugar for ¾ cup of the granulated sugar in Seven-minute Frosting recipe.

Chocolate Fluff Frosting: Add two 1-ounce squares unsweetened chocolate, melted and cooled, to Seven-minute Frosting just before spreading on cake. Fold in; do not beat.

Cream-cheese Whip: Add vanilla to Seven-minute Frosting. Stir one 3-ounce package cream cheese till *soft;* beat in small amount of frosting, then fold cream cheese mixture into the frosting, blending thoroughly (*do not beat*).

Pineapple Frosting: Substitute syrup from canned pineapple for water in Seven-minute Frosting. Omit vanilla; add 1 teaspoon grated lemon peel. Garnish frosted cake with pineapple cubes.

Caramel Seven-minute Frosting—delectable! All you do is follow recipe for Seven-minute Frosting, but use brown sugar instead of granulated sugar. Substitute ½ teaspoon maple flavoring for the vanilla. Swirl frosting on the cake, sprinkle sides with broken California walnuts.

Here are the tricks for perfect Seven-minute Frosting

Seven-minute cooking tips: Boiling water should not touch top pan of double boiler. Beat frosting about 7 minutes. Remove from water when stiff peaks form as shown. Don't overcook.

Crumbs behave if you cover sides and top edge of cooled cake with thin frosting layer. Then spread on more—crumbs won't mix with second coat. For a fine finish, frost top last.

Butter Frosting

⅓ cup butter
4 cups sifted confectioners' sugar
1 egg yolk
1½ teaspoons vanilla
About 2 tablespoons light cream

Cream butter; gradually add about *half* the sugar, blending well. Beat in egg yolk and vanilla. Gradually blend in remaining sugar. Add enough cream to make of spreading consistency. Frosts two 8- or 9-inch layers.

Orange Frosting: Add 2 teaspoons grated orange peel to butter in Butter Frosting. Stir in orange juice instead of cream to make of spreading consistency.

Mocha Frosting: Add ¼ cup cocoa and ½ teaspoon instant coffee to butter in Butter Frosting.

Chocolate Butter Frosting: In Butter Frosting, add two 1-ounce squares unsweetened chocolate, melted and cooled, with the egg yolk and vanilla; blend well.

Butter-cream Frosting

Here's a "not-so-sweet" frosting—

¼ cup butter or margarine
3 tablespoons enriched flour
¾ cup milk
1½ teaspoons vanilla
½ cup butter or margarine
¾ cup sugar

Melt ¼ cup butter in saucepan over low heat. Blend in flour. Gradually stir in milk. Cook and stir till mixture thickens and comes to boiling. Cool to room temperature. Add vanilla. Cream remaining butter with sugar till fluffy; gradually add milk mixture, beating till frosting is fluffy and of spreading consistency, about 5 minutes. Frosts tops and sides of two 9-inch layers.

Note: In hot weather, chill frosting before spreading on cake.

Confectioners' Icing

No icing could be simpler—

Add sufficient top milk or cream to 2 cups sifted confectioners' sugar to make of spreading consistency (or add only enough milk to make of consistency to pipe through tube). Add dash salt and 1 teaspoon vanilla.

Note: Or use Ornamental Frosting (page 63) for pastry-tube art.

Caramel Butter Frosting

Melt ½ cup butter; add 1 cup brown sugar. Bring to a boil; stir 1 minute or until slightly thick. Cool slightly. Add ¼ cup milk; beat smooth. Beat in about 3¼ cups sifted confectioners' sugar till of spreading consistency. Frosts tops and sides of two 8-inch layers.

Broiled Coconut Frosting

⅔ cup brown sugar
⅓ cup melted butter or margarine
¼ cup light cream
1 3½-ounce can (1¼ cups) flaked coconut
½ teaspoon vanilla

Thoroughly combine ingredients; spread over warm cake. Brown lightly in broiler. Frosts one 9-inch square cake.

Rich Chocolate Icing

An easy recipe from California's Nut Tree—

3 egg whites
1½ cups sifted confectioners' sugar
¾ cup soft butter
⅓ cup cocoa
½ teaspoon vanilla
⅓ cup halved almonds, toasted

In small bowl of mixer beat egg whites to soft peaks; gradually add ¾ *cup* of the confectioners' sugar, beating till stiff peaks form. Set this meringue aside. Using same beater in large bowl, beat butter till creamy. Mix remaining sugar with cocoa; gradually beat into butter mixture. Fold in vanilla and meringue until well blended. Use to fill and frost cooled cake. Sprinkle toasted almonds or chopped walnuts lightly over frosting.

Chocolate-Cream Cheese Fluff

2 3-ounce packages cream cheese
1 egg
1 teaspoon vanilla
Dash salt
5 cups sifted confectioners' sugar
3 1-ounce squares unsweetened chocolate, melted

Have cheese at room temperature. Blend in egg, vanilla, and salt; gradually beat in sugar. Blend in slightly cooled chocolate. Frosts tops and sides of two 9-inch layers.

Chocolate Satin Frosting

3½ 1-ounce squares unsweetened
 chocolate
3 cups sifted confectioners' sugar
4½ tablespoons hot water

. . .

1 egg
½ cup soft butter or margarine
1½ teaspoons vanilla

Melt chocolate in mixing bowl over hot water. Remove from heat. With electric mixer blend in sugar and water. Beat in egg, then butter and vanilla. Frosting will be thin at this point, so place bowl in ice water; beat till of spreading consistency. Frosts tops and sides of two 9-inch layers.

Glossy Chocolate Frosting

Mix ½ cup sugar and 1½ tablespoons cornstarch; add one 1-ounce square unsweetened chocolate, dash salt, and ½ cup boiling water. Cook and stir till blended and mixture thickens. Remove from heat; add 1½ tablespoons butter and ½ teaspoon vanilla. Spread on cake while hot. Frosts one 9-inch square cake or one loaf cake.

Chocolate Glaze

In small saucepan combine one 6-ounce package (1 cup) semisweet chocolate pieces and one 6-ounce can (⅔ cup) evaporated milk. Cook and stir over low heat till blended and mixture comes to a boil. Lower heat; cook gently and stir 3 to 5 minutes till thick. Cool, stirring occasionally.

Fudge Frosting

2 1-ounce squares unsweetened chocolate
3 cups sugar
3 tablespoons light corn syrup
¼ teaspoon salt
1 cup milk
¼ cup butter or margarine
1 teaspoon vanilla

Combine chocolate, sugar, syrup, salt, and milk in a 3-quart saucepan. Cook over low heat, stirring until sugar dissolves and chocolate melts. Cook to soft-ball stage (234°). Remove from heat; add butter and cool till just warm (110°). Add vanilla and beat till mixture is of spreading consistency. Frosts tops and sides of two 9-inch layers.

You'll like this No-cook Fudge Frosting—mix it in a saucepan!

Melt two 1-ounce squares chocolate over hot water; cool. In small saucepan, thoroughly mix 1 cup sifted confectioners' sugar, 3 tablespoons milk, 1 egg, and 1 teaspoon vanilla.

Stir in chocolate. Add 3 tablespoons soft (not melted) butter or margarine, one at a time, beating well after each addition.

Chill frosting 10 minutes in refrigerator. Then place pan in bowl of ice water. (Why the pan? It gives you a handle to hold while beating. And metal speeds the transfer of cold from the ice to the frosting.)

Beat frosting over ice water till just right to spread. Frosts one 8-inch square cake.

Swirl cupcakes with this easy-to-make Jelly Frosting. Spoonful of preserves makes topknots.

Jelly Frosting: Combine ½ cup tart jelly, 1 egg white, and dash salt in top of double boiler. Cook over hot water, beating constantly with electric or rotary beater till jelly disappears, 3 to 4 minutes.

Remove from heat; beat till mixture stands in peaks. Frosts 14 medium cupcakes or two 9-inch layers.

Caramel Candy Frosting

½ pound (28) caramels
½ cup water
½ cup butter or margarine
Dash salt
4 cups sifted confectioners' sugar
¼ cup chopped California walnuts

Melt caramels in water in top of double boiler over boiling water, stirring now and then. Cool sauce to room temperature. Thoroughly cream the butter; add salt. Add sugar alternately with the caramel sauce, blending till frosting is smooth and creamy. Add nuts. Chill till of spreading consistency. Frosts two 8- or 9-inch layers.

Coconut Frosting

1 6-ounce can (⅔ cup) evaporated milk
⅔ cup sugar
¼ cup butter or margarine
1 slightly beaten egg
Dash salt
1 teaspoon vanilla
1 3½-ounce can (1¼ cups) flaked coconut
½ cup chopped pecans

In saucepan combine milk, sugar, butter, egg, and salt. Cook and stir over medium heat till mixture thickens and begins to boil, 12 to 15 minutes. Remove from heat. Add vanilla, coconut, and pecans. Cool thoroughly. Frosts two 8- or 9-inch layers.

Chocolate-Nut Fluff

Cook ½ cup halved, blanched almonds in 1½ tablespoons butter till golden; cool. Melt ½ cup semisweet chocolate pieces over hot water. Cool. Fold chocolate and almonds into 1 cup heavy cream, whipped, allowing chocolate to harden in flecks. Use to frost angel or sponge cake.

Apple Candy Frosting

In top of double boiler, combine 1 egg white, ¾ cup sugar, 2 tablespoons red cinnamon candies, dash salt, ½ cup applesauce, and 1 teaspoon light corn syrup. Beat 1 minute with electric or rotary beater. Place over boiling water; beat till peaks form, *about* 4 minutes (don't overcook). Remove from boiling water. Beat till of spreading consistency. Frosts tops of 12 cupcakes.

Rocky-road Frosting

2 1-ounce squares unsweetened chocolate
2 cups tiny marshmallows
¼ cup water
¼ cup butter or margarine
2 cups sifted confectioners' sugar
1 teaspoon vanilla
½ cup broken California walnuts

In small saucepan, place chocolate, *1 cup* marshmallows, water, and butter. Heat over low heat, stirring till blended. Cool slightly. Add sugar and vanilla; beat till smooth and slightly thick, about 2 minutes. Stir in remaining marshmallows and walnuts. Frosts top of one 13x9x2-inch cake.

Plain and fancy fillings

Cream Filling

½ cup sugar
⅓ cup enriched flour
½ teaspoon salt
2 cups milk
2 slightly beaten eggs
1 teaspoon vanilla

Mix sugar, flour, salt; slowly stir in milk. Cook and stir over medium heat till mixture boils and thickens; cook 2 minutes longer. Stir a little of hot mixture into eggs; stir into remaining hot mixture; stirring constantly, bring just to boiling. Add vanilla; cover surface with waxed paper; cool. Makes 2⅓ cups.

Butterscotch Filling: In above recipe, use ⅔ cup brown sugar in place of granulated sugar. Add ¼ cup butter with vanilla.

Chocolate Filling: In Cream Filling, add 1½ 1-ounce squares unsweetened chocolate, cut up, with milk; increase sugar to ¾ cup.

French Custard Filling

⅓ cup sugar
1 tablespoon enriched flour
1 tablespoon cornstarch
¼ teaspoon salt
1½ cups milk
1 beaten egg yolk
1 teaspoon vanilla
½ cup heavy cream, whipped

Combine sugar, flour, cornstarch, and salt. Gradually stir in milk. Cook and stir till mixture thickens and boils; cook and stir 2 to 3 minutes longer. Stir a little of hot mixture into egg yolk; return to hot mixture. Stirring constantly, bring just to boiling. Add vanilla. Cover entire surface with clear plastic wrap or waxed paper; cool. Beat smooth; fold in whipped cream. Makes 2 cups.

Date-Nut Filling

In saucepan, combine one 8-ounce package (1½ cups) pitted dates, cut up, with ½ cup orange juice. Cook and stir till dates are almost tender and mixture is thick, about 2 to 3 minutes. Add 1 teaspoon grated orange peel. Cool. Add ¼ cup broken California walnuts. Makes about 1¼ cups.

Orange Filling

¾ cup sugar
2 tablespoons cornstarch
Dash salt
1 teaspoon grated orange peel
¾ cup orange juice
1 tablespoon lemon juice
1 to 2 beaten egg yolks
1 tablespoon butter or margarine

Combine sugar, cornstarch, and salt. Add peel and juices gradually; blend well. Cook over medium heat, stirring constantly till thick and clear.

Add small amount of hot mixture to egg yolks, stir into remaining hot mixture. Cook about 2 minutes longer. Remove from heat; add butter. Cool. Makes about 1 cup.

Lemon Filling

¾ cup sugar
2 tablespoons cornstarch
Dash salt
1 slightly beaten egg yolk
¾ cup water
3 tablespoons lemon juice
• • •
1 teaspoon grated lemon peel
1 tablespoon butter or margarine

Mix sugar, cornstarch, and salt; add egg yolk, water, and lemon juice; cook in double boiler till thick, stirring occasionally.

Remove from heat and add lemon peel and butter. Cool. Makes 1½ cups.

Lemonade Filling

Melt 2 tablespoons butter or margarine; blend in ¼ cup sugar, 2 tablespoons cornstarch, and ¼ teaspoon salt. Gradually stir in ¾ cup water. Cook, stirring constantly, till mixture thickens.

Combine 2 beaten egg yolks with ⅓ cup frozen lemonade concentrate. Stir a small amount of hot mixture into yolk mixture; return to hot mixture and, stirring constantly, bring just to a boil. Tint with a few drops yellow food coloring, if desired. Cool. Makes about 1 cup.

Cake decorating—easy!

Use what's on the shelf for simple, spectacular trims

Here's quick glamour for the cake you're cooling—these trims make it a Cinderella!

Doll-ups with chocolate

Chocolate Leaves: You'll need real leaves—rose leaves, ivy, philodendron, or other sturdy, smooth leaves.

Leave a little of stem for handle. Rinse leaves; dry. Melt chocolate (candy-making chocolate or semisweet chocolate pieces) over hot water till partly melted; remove from heat, stir till smooth.

With water-color brush (new), paint the underside of leaves with smooth, thick coat of chocolate, spreading just to edge. Refrigerate to set and firm up chocolate.

Insert point of paring knife at tip of leaf, then peel real leaf from chocolate one. Now onto waxed paper—be quick but gentle. Chill till ready to trim cake. After decorating, refrigerate cake till party time so leaves will be fresh and perky.

Finishing touch:
Drizzle on
Chocolate Icicles

Chocolate Icicles: Melt one 1-ounce square unsweetened chocolate with ½ teaspoon shortening. Using a teaspoon, pour chocolate from the tip in a steady stream along edge of frosted cake, letting chocolate run down sides in icicles, as above.

Curlicues: Shave off thin curls of chocolate with vegetable parer or sharp knife. Arrange curls on frosted cake.

Polka-dot: Sprinkle semisweet chocolate pieces over frosted cake. Or cover sides of cake with chocolate-mint candy wafers.

Sprinkle chocolate decorettes on frosted cake. Or spoon decorettes in diagonal stripes or in a spiral atop frosted cake.

Easy artistry with candy

Mint Candleholders: Fasten flat sides of two chocolate-mint wafers together with frosting; stack two of the double candies with frosting between. Melt candle wax to hold candle on candy. Place around cake.

Top cake with
coconut and
Gumdrop Tulips

Gumdrop Tulips: Roll out big red gumdrops between sheets of waxed paper—sprinkle sugar over bottom sheet of waxed paper and top of candy. Cut with tulip cutter; press in toothpick stems. Perch atop frosted cake sprinkled with coconut.

Roll out green jelly strings; with scissors, snip leaves; press into frosting.

Rocket Cake: Decorate chocolate-frosted cake with candy peanuts. To make them stand up, rocket-fashion, "drill" hole in one end with metal skewer; insert one end of toothpick in candy, other end in cake.

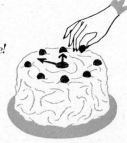

Happy New Year Cake!
Make clock face
from fat gumdrops

Clock: Swirl frosting on sides of cake, but smooth frosting over top. For clock face, use fat black gumdrops as numbers (try eight to give the effect without overcrowding). Cut up a penny licorice whip for the hands and set at a few minutes before midnight. Center with big fat licorice drop.

Tricks with nuts

Brazil-nut Blossoms: Cover unshelled Brazils with cold water; simmer 3 minutes; drain. Let stand in cold water 1 minute; drain, shell. Cover nuts with cold water; simmer 3 minutes; drain. Cut paper-thin, lengthwise petals with vegetable parer. Place petals around candied-cherry centers.

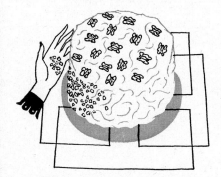

Walnuts add a party-going look to cake

Walnut Topper: Dot top of frosted cake with California walnut halves. Press broken walnuts against side of cake—speed the job along with palm of hand.

To catch spills: Before frosting cake, place 4 strips waxed paper so they cover edges of plate (not center). Frost cake. Then pull out paper—plate is neat.

Almond Stick-up: Poke toasted slivered almonds into top and sides of frosted cake, porcupine style.

Decorations with fruit

The possibilities are endless! Use fresh, dried, canned, or candied fruit. The flavor of the cake, filling, or frosting can be your guide. Pineapple cake? Trim with daisies of pineapple tidbits; use maraschino-cherry centers. For date-filled cake, arrange streamers of thin-cut dates atop.

Coconut capers

To tint, place flaked coconut in jar; add few drops food coloring. Cover and shake till coconut is uniform in color. Sprinkle tinted coconut on frosted cake.

Coconut-Mallow Candleholders: Dip marshmallows in hot light cream, roll in tinted flaked coconut. Insert a little birthday candle in each. Arrange around base of cake. You're all set for a celebration!

Pipe on a frosting frill!

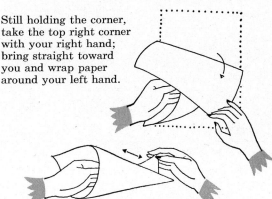

To make paper cone, place sheet of typing paper or a rectangular piece of parchment or freezing paper so short side is toward you. With left hand, bring lower corner to center of paper. Do not fold.

Still holding the corner, take the top right corner with your right hand; bring straight toward you and wrap paper around your left hand.

Adjust size of opening at point of cone by pulling up or down on outside corner with right hand. Tape outer corner in place.

To decorate: Fill paper cone ⅔ full of Ornamental Frosting, pushing it into point. Flatten top and fold side edges toward center, then fold top down several times or till there's no space above frosting.

Hold cone in right hand, with fingers around cone and thumb over top; squeeze to force frosting through. Guide tip of cone with left hand. As cone empties, fold top.

Ornamental Frosting

With pastry blender, cut ¼ cup butter into 4 cups sifted confectioners' sugar till like corn meal. Add 2 unbeaten egg whites, 1 teaspoon vanilla, and ¼ teaspoon cream of tartar. Beat thoroughly. Stir in 1 to 2 teaspoons light cream till frosting is a little stiffer than spreading consistency. Add few drops food coloring, if desired.

Speedy Ornamental Frosting: For each cup fluffy white frosting (from mix), measure about 1½ cups sifted confectioners' sugar and 1 tablespoon butter. Add sugar to frosting till of piping consistency. Blend in the butter.

Spoon on a sauce!

Custard Sauce

4 beaten egg yolks
Dash salt
¼ cup sugar
2 cups milk, scalded
1 teaspoon vanilla

In top of double boiler combine egg yolks, salt, and sugar. Gradually stir in slightly cooled milk. Cook over *hot, not boiling*, water, stirring constantly till custard coats metal spoon; remove from heat. Cool at once. Add vanilla. Chill. Makes 2 cups.

Yankee Sauce

A mite sweet, a mite tangy—and rich!—

½ cup butter or margarine
1 cup sifted confectioners' sugar
1 cup cold water
1 tablespoon cornstarch
1 teaspoon vinegar
1½ teaspoons vanilla

Cream butter; gradually add sugar, creaming till light and fluffy. Stir water into cornstarch; cook and stir until clear and thick. Stir hot mixture into creamed mixture. Add vinegar and vanilla. Serve warm.

Makes about 1⅔ cups.

Top dessert with one of these delicious sauces—such sweet things will happen!

Butter Sauce

¼ cup butter or margarine
2 tablespoons enriched flour
2 tablespoons sugar
1 cup boiling water or fruit juice
• • •
½ teaspoon vanilla

Melt butter; blend in flour and sugar. Add liquid; bring to a boil over low heat, stirring constantly. Cover; place over hot water. When ready to serve, add vanilla *or* 2 teaspoons lemon juice. Makes 1⅓ cups.

Foamy Sauce

3 egg yolks
¾ cup sifted confectioners' sugar
½ teaspoon vanilla
Dash salt
• • •
1 cup heavy cream, whipped

Beat egg yolks, sugar, vanilla, and salt; fold in whipped cream. Chill. Stir before using. Makes about 3 cups sauce.

Hard Sauce

½ cup butter or margarine
2 cups sifted confectioners' sugar
1 teaspoon vanilla

Thoroughly cream butter and sugar; add vanilla. Vary flavor with lemon or orange juice and grated peel. Makes 1⅔ cups.

Fluffy Hard Sauce

½ cup butter or margarine
1 egg yolk
2 cups sifted confectioners' sugar
1 teaspoon vanilla
1 stiff-beaten egg white

Cream the butter; stir in egg yolk; gradually beat in sugar till fluffy and light. Add vanilla. Fold in egg white. Vary flavor with lemon or orange juice and grated peel, or rum or brandy flavoring.

Makes about 1⅔ cups sauce.

**Rosy Cherry Sauce—
a luscious topper**

Tasty-tart Cherry Sauce is easy to make and so good ladled over angel or sponge cake or cottage pudding. Perfect for a buffet dinner—keep sauce hot atop candle warmer, let guests help themselves to dessert and cups of steaming coffee.

Cherry Sauce

1 No. 2 can (2½ cups) canned pitted
   tart red cherries*
½ cup sugar*

· · ·

1½ tablespoons cornstarch
Few drops red food coloring

Drain cherries, reserving juice. Combine ¾ cup of the cherry juice and the sugar; heat to boiling. Add cherries; cook 10 minutes. Mix cornstarch with remaining cold cherry juice; add to hot mixture. Cook, stirring constantly, till thick and clear. If desired, add few drops red food coloring. Serve warm with cake or cottage pudding.

   Makes 6 to 8 servings.

   *Or use one No. 2 can (2½ cups) frozen pitted tart red cherries, thawed, decreasing the sugar to ¼ cup.

Quick Cherry Sauce

   Chop drained maraschino cherries. Add light corn syrup and a little lemon juice to taste; add dash of salt. Spoon over ice cream.

Butterscotch Sauce

1 slightly beaten egg yolk
¼ cup butter or margarine
¼ cup water
⅔ cup brown sugar
⅓ cup light corn syrup

Combine all ingredients and mix well; cook in double boiler until thick, stirring frequently. Stir before using. Makes 1 cup.

Fudge Sauce

Bittersweet and fudge-y—

½ cup light corn syrup
1 cup sugar
1 cup water
3 1-ounce squares unsweetened
   chocolate
1 teaspoon vanilla
½ cup evaporated milk

Combine corn syrup, sugar, and water; cook to the soft-ball stage (236°). Remove from heat; add chocolate and stir till chocolate melts. Add vanilla. Slowly stir in evaporated milk; mix thoroughly. Serve warm or cool. Makes 2 cups.

Lemon Sauce

½ cup sugar
1 tablespoon cornstarch
Dash salt
Dash nutmeg
1 cup water

· · ·

2 tablespoons butter or margarine
1½ tablespoons lemon juice

Mix sugar, cornstarch, salt, and nutmeg; gradually stir in water. Cook over low heat, stirring constantly, until thick and clear. Add butter and lemon juice; blend thoroughly. Makes 1⅓ cups sauce.

Speedy Raspberry Sauce

   Stir a jar of red-raspberry preserves to make it of just right spooning consistency to ladle over ice cream. That's all!

Sauce up a sundae!

Fudge Sundae

Mondae Sauce

A lush chocolate sauce that's thick and fudge-y! And see how easy! —

1 6-ounce package (1 cup) semisweet
   chocolate pieces
½ cup evaporated milk

In small heavy saucepan, heat chocolate and evaporated milk over medium heat, stirring constantly till blended. Serve warm or at room temperature. Makes 1 cup sauce.

Fudge Sundae: Start out with enough Mondae Sauce in each serving dish to cover the bottom generously. In the center place hub of chocolate or vanilla ice cream. Then overlap 4 big spoonfuls of ice cream around it, alternating light and dark for a harlequin effect—see picture above.

Drizzle more sundae sauce over top. Sprinkle with broken California walnuts or toasted slivered almonds. Pass sugar wafers.

Butterscotch Sauce

1½ cups brown sugar
⅔ cup corn syrup
Dash salt
1 6-ounce can (⅔ cup)
   evaporated milk

Combine brown sugar, corn syrup, and salt. Heat, stirring occasionally, till the mixture comes to a full rolling boil. Remove from heat; cool slightly. Gradually stir in evaporated milk. Serve sauce warm or cool. Makes 2 cups sauce.

Crunchy Butterscotch Sundaes: Mix 1½ cups sugar-coated crisp rice or wheat cereal with ½ cup flaked coconut. Form 1 quart vanilla ice cream in 10 balls. Coat with cereal mixture, pressing it on. Place in freezer till serving time. (To keep coating crisp, store only 1 to 4 hours.) Serve with Butterscotch Sauce. Makes 10 servings.

Praline Sundae Sauce

1¼ cups brown sugar
1 cup light cream
¼ pound (about 16) marshmallows
¼ cup butter or margarine
1 teaspoon vanilla
⅓ cup broken California walnuts

Combine brown sugar, cream, marshmallows, and dash salt in a 2-quart saucepan. Heat and stir until brown sugar dissolves and mixture comes to boiling. Then cook over medium heat 8 to 10 minutes (or till candy thermometer reaches 224°). Remove from heat; add butter. Cool slightly; add vanilla and walnuts. Serve warm. Makes 2 cups.

Minty Pineapple Sauce

1 9-ounce can (1 cup) crushed pineapple
¼ teaspoon mint extract
2 drops green food coloring
½ cup light corn syrup

Combine the pineapple, extract, and food coloring. Blend in corn syrup; chill. Serve over ice cream. Makes 1½ cups.

Crimson Raspberry Sauce

1 10-ounce package frozen red raspberries, thawed and crushed
1½ teaspoons cornstarch
½ cup currant jelly

Thoroughly combine the raspberries and cornstarch; add jelly. Bring to boiling. Cook and stir until clear and the mixture thickens slightly. Strain; cool.

Peach Sundae Melba: Spoon sauce over peach halves filled with vanilla ice cream.

Mocha Butterscotch Sauce

1 cup sugar
2 tablespoons instant coffee
1½ cups water
2 tablespoons cornstarch
3 tablespoons cold water
2 tablespoons butter or margarine
¼ teaspoon salt
½ cup broken California walnuts

In heavy skillet, melt sugar slowly over low heat, stirring constantly, till medium brown and smooth. Combine coffee with 1½ cups water; slowly add to sugar, stirring to blend. Combine cornstarch and 3 tablespoons water; stir into syrup mixture. Cook, stirring constantly, till thick. Add butter, salt, and nuts. Makes 1¾ cups.

Speedy Sauces

Caramel Topping: Combine ½ pound (28) caramels with ½ cup hot water in top of double boiler. Heat over hot water, stirring occasionally till caramels melt. Serve warm or cool over maple-nut or vanilla ice cream. Makes 1 cup.

Hot Fudge Sauce: Melt 2 squares unsweetened chocolate with ½ cup honey over hot water. Add dash salt; stir till smooth. Spoon hot sauce over ice cream.

Choco-Mint Sauce: Melt 12 chocolate-covered mint patties (about 1½ inches in diameter) over hot water. Stir in 2 tablespoons light cream. Serve warm over ice cream. Makes ½ cup sauce.

Mintmallow Sauce: Combine about ½ cup marshmallow creme and 3 tablespoons water. With electric or rotary beater, whip till fluffy. Add ¼ cup mint jelly and beat smooth. Tint with few drops green food coloring. Spoon over vanilla or chocolate ice cream. Makes about 2 cups sauce.

Top Banana Split

Just let yourself go and live it up!—

Fully ripe, flecked-with-brown bananas
Canned pineapple slices, chilled
Three flavors of ice cream or sherbet—strawberry, vanilla, and orange
Three sundae sauces—Raspberry Sauce (page 65), Mondae Sauce or chocolate syrup, and marshmallow creme
Bing cherries or maraschino cherries with stems on

Count on 1 banana, halved lengthwise and peeled, for each split. Drain pineapple, and dip bananas in the pineapple syrup to keep color bright. Place a pineapple ring in center of each *long* dish. Now add a banana runner on each side—the pineapple ring makes the banana ride high, gives the whole split a boost in the air.

Top pineapple ring with scoop of orange sherbet; add scoop of vanilla ice cream on one side, scoop of strawberry on the other. Cut a pineapple ring in half and tuck in, like wings, between scoops. Ladle Raspberry Sauce over vanilla ice cream, Mondae Sauce over strawberry, marshmallow creme over sherbet. Then flood dish with all three sauces. Trim with cherries.

Top Banana Split

Pies

Out of this world!

All the tricks for wonderful pastry

Trims for one-crust pies

Easy steps for a lattice top

How to make perfect meringue

Fruit pies—your favorites!

Custard pie—and kin!

Magnificent meringue pies

Pies—light as a cloud!

Luscious pies from Mother's recipe scrapbook

← Folks who think they can't eat another bite will change
their minds when they see these pies! There's Mince
Pie, pleasantly tart with apples and lemon. The Pumpkin
Pie is the spicy, smooth-as-velvet, traditional kind.
Coconut Cream Pie is chock-full of coconut—delectable!

How to make perfect pastry

Plain Pastry

For single-crust pie:

    1 cup sifted enriched flour
    ½ teaspoon salt
    ⅓ cup shortening
    2 to 3 tablespoons cold water

Note: You need a generous amount of pastry for a beautiful edge on a pastry shell. For one 9- or 10-inch pie shell, you'll want to use the larger pastry recipe below that calls for 1½ cups flour.

For 8-inch double-crust pie or 4 to 6 tart shells:

    1½ cups sifted enriched flour
    ½ teaspoon salt
    ½ cup shortening
    4 to 5 tablespoons cold water

For one 9- or 10-inch double-crust pie, one 8- or 9-inch lattice-top pie, or 6 to 8 tart shells:

    2 cups sifted enriched flour
    1 teaspoon salt
    ⅔ cup shortening
    5 to 7 tablespoons cold water

To bake pie shell for single-crust pie:

Fit pastry loosely onto bottom and sides of pie plate and trim ½ to 1 inch beyond edge; fold under and flute.

If *baked* pie shell is needed, prick bottom and sides well with a fork—no puffing as shell bakes. Bake in very hot oven (450°) till pastry is golden, 10 to 12 minutes. (Make cutouts from extra dough to trim filled pie. Bake on cooky sheet.)

If filling and crust are to be baked together, *do not prick pastry.* Pour in filling; bake as directed in pie recipe.

Wrap any extra dough in aluminum foil or several thicknesses of waxed paper; store in refrigerator till needed.

Tart Shells

Mix pastry; roll to ⅛ inch. Cut in 5- or 6-inch circles. Fit pastry into tart pans, pressing out air bubbles. Trim pastry ½ inch beyond edge; turn under and flute. Prick bottom and sides well. (Or fit pastry circles over inverted custard cups; pinch together 4 corners; prick well.)

Bake in very hot oven (450°) about 10 to 12 minutes or till pastry is golden.

Note: More tart shells, page 124.

Follow these three steps for mixing and rolling Plain Pastry

Sift together the flour and salt. Cut in the shortening with pastry-blender or blending fork till pieces are the size of small peas.

For extra tender and flaky pastry, cut in *half* of shortening till mixture looks like corn meal. Then cut in remaining half till like small peas.

Sprinkle 1 tablespoon of the water over part of mixture. Gently toss with fork; push to one side of bowl.

Sprinkle next tablespoon of water over dry part; mix lightly; push to moistened part at side. Repeat till all is moistened. Gather up with fingers and form into a ball.

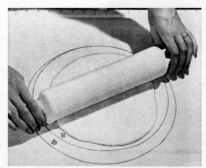

Two-crust pie: Divide dough for lower, upper crust. Form each into ball.

On lightly floured surface, flatten slightly, smoothing edges. Roll ⅛ inch thick. Roll from center; use light strokes. Roll pastry over rolling pin; unroll over pie plate, fitting loosely onto bottom and sides.

Orange Pastry

Substitute orange juice for the water in recipe for Plain Pastry.

Hot-water Pastry

Pour ⅓ cup boiling water over ⅔ cup shortening; beat till creamy. Cool. Sift 2 cups sifted enriched flour with ¾ teaspoon salt; add to shortening mixture. Mix to a soft dough with fork. Wrap in waxed paper; chill before rolling. Makes pastry for one 8-inch double-crust pie.

Pat-a-pie Oil Pastry

2 cups sifted enriched flour
2 teaspoons sugar
1¼ teaspoons salt
⅔ cup salad oil
3 tablespoons milk

Into 8- or 9-inch pie plate, sift together flour, sugar, and salt. With fork, whip together salad oil and milk; pour over flour mixture. Mix with fork till all flour is dampened. Reserve about ⅓ of dough for top "crust." Press remaining dough evenly against bottom and sides of pie plate. Crimp edges. Fill with favorite fruit filling.

For top "crust," crumble reserved dough in small pieces. Sprinkle over filling. Bake as directed in fruit-pie recipe.

Graham-cracker Crust: Combine 1½ cups (18 crackers) fine graham-cracker crumbs, ¼ cup sugar, and ½ cup melted butter or margarine. Mix well. Press firmly in unbuttered 9-inch pie plate. Bake in moderate oven (375°) about 8 minutes or till edge is lightly browned. Cool.

If you prefer an unbaked crust, chill crust till set, about 45 minutes, before filling.

Gingersnap Crust: Mix 1½ cups fine gingersnap crumbs (about 24 gingersnaps) and ¼ cup soft butter until well mixed. Press into bottom and sides of buttered 9-inch pie plate. Bake in moderate oven (375°) about 8 minutes. Cool.

Vanilla-wafer Crust: Combine 1¼ cups fine vanilla- or chocolate-wafer crumbs (about 38 wafers) with ⅓ cup melted butter or margarine. Press firmly in buttered 9-inch pie plate. Chill until set.

Corn-flake Crust: Combine 1 cup crushed corn flakes or crisp rice cereal, or corn-flake crumbs, with ¼ cup sugar and ⅓ cup melted butter or margarine. Press firmly in 9-inch pie plate. Chill.

Coconut Crust: Toast one 3½-ounce can (1¼ cups) flaked coconut at 350° about 10 minutes, stirring frequently for even browning. Cool. Generously butter bottom and sides of 9-inch pie plate; sprinkle with coconut and press.

These pictures show you how to make Oil Pastry—it's simple, speedy!

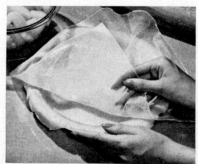

Oil Pastry: For 8- or 9-inch double-crust pie, sift 2 cups sifted enriched flour with 1½ teaspoons salt.

Pour ¼ cup cold milk and ½ cup salad oil into a measuring cup (but do not stir). Add all at once to the flour mixture. Stir lightly with a fork. Now on to step two—the rolling!

Form dough in a ball; divide in half; flatten each slightly.

Roll each piece between two 12-inch squares of waxed paper. (First dampen table slightly so the paper won't slip.) When dough is rolled to the edges of paper, it will be the right thickness for the pie crust.

Peel off top sheet of paper and fit dough, paper side up, into pie plate. Remove remaining piece of paper. Trim edges even with rim of pie plate.

Place top crust over the filled pie; trim off pastry edge even with rim. Seal edges with fork, or flute. Cut slits or cutouts in top crust.

Pretty edges for one-crust pies

Crisscross edge: Trim crust even with edge of pie plate. Moisten rim.

Loosely interlace two ½-inch strips of pastry around edge of pie; at each crossing, press the part of the strip that's *underneath* against rim.

Keep strips flat—don't twist or turn over and be careful not to stretch.

Fluted edge: Trim pastry ½ inch beyond rim; fold under for double edge.

Use a knife handle or your index finger to make the indentations. Thumb and index finger of other hand are a wedge to push against to make the scallop around knife handle.

If desired, pinch curved edges into definite points.

Zigzag edge: Trim pastry ½ to 1 inch beyond edge of pie plate; fold under to make plump pastry rim.

Press dough between thumb and bent finger, pushing slightly forward on slant with finger and pulling back with thumb.

Place thumb in dent left by finger; repeat around edge of pie shell.

Spiral edge: Trim pastry even with the edge of the pie plate. Moisten rim.

With a sharp knife, cut long strips of pastry ¾ inch wide—use ruler edge for straight lines.

Press end of strip to rim; hold in place with left hand and twist with right. Press spiral to rim each place they touch.

Tips for weaving a lattice crust

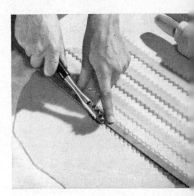

First, cut uniform pastry strips. Make a cardboard guide, 12 inches long and ½ to ¾ inch wide.

Cut along guide with pastry wheel (for a zig-zag edge) or sharp knife.

Speedy spiral: Cut long ¾-inch-wide strips; moisten ends; join. Twist strip; swirl from center in spiral, covering pie.

Woven lattice: Trim lower crust ½ inch beyond rim. Lay strips lengthwise atop pie at 1-inch intervals. Fold back alternate strips to help you weave cross-strips over and under. Trim lattice even with outer rim of pie plate. Dampen edge of pastry; fold lower crust over strips. Seal; crimp.

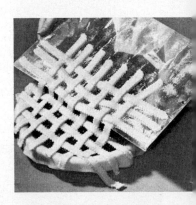

Slip-on lattice: If you prefer to weave a lattice on "dry land," try this: Sprinkle cooky sheet generously with sugar; weave lattice on it. Tilt cooky sheet over far edge of pie and move toward you.

Lattice top slides onto filling—sugar acts as rollers. Trim strips; fold crust over; seal, crimp.

Pretty brown: Your pie will have a beautiful golden-brown edge if protected with aluminum foil for part of the baking time. Foil will help keep the juices in pie, too.

Cut a strip of aluminum foil 2½ inches wide. Fold around rim of pie, making certain that foil covers all crimped edge.

Toppers for two-crust pies

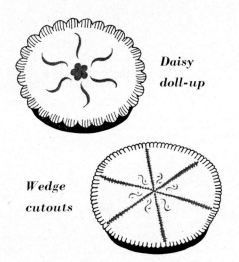

Daisy doll-up

Wedge cutouts

Daisy doll-up: Trim bottom crust ½ inch beyond rim of pie plate. Roll top crust so edges will match lower crust; make design with cooky cutter, slits with knife. Place on pie: pinch edges together. For scallops, cut with tip of teaspoon, bowl side down; mark with fork.

Wedge cutouts: Serving's a snap! Trim bottom crust even with rim of pie plate. Roll top crust in circle; cut in wedges with pastry cutter. Cut small design in each piece to prevent puffing. Place on pie. Seal edges with tines of fork or handle of wooden spoon.

Meringue Shell

3 egg whites
1 teaspoon vanilla
¼ teaspoon cream of tartar
Dash salt
· · ·
1 cup sugar

Have egg whites at room temperature. Add vanilla, cream of tartar, and salt. Beat till frothy. Gradually add sugar, a small amount at a time, beating till very stiff peaks form and sugar is dissolved.

Cover cooky sheet with plain ungreased paper. Using a 9-inch round cake pan as guide, draw a circle on the paper. Spread meringue over circle; shape into shell with back of spoon, making bottom ½ inch thick and mounding around edge to make sides 1¾ inches high. Bake in very slow oven (275°) 1 hour. Turn off heat and let dry in oven (door closed) at least 2 hours.

Individual Meringue Shells

Make meringue as above. Cover cooky sheet with plain ungreased paper. Draw eight 3½-inch circles; spread each with about ⅓ cup meringue. Shape with back of spoon to make shells. Bake in very slow oven (275°) 1 hour. Turn off heat; let dry in oven (door closed) 1½ hours.

Swirl billowy Meringue atop creamy pie, brown to perfection

1 For 9-inch pie, separate 3 eggs. Whites will whip fluffier if at room temperature. Use yolks in pie filling or sauce.

Beat egg whites with ½ teaspoon vanilla and ¼ teaspoon cream of tartar till soft peaks form. Now add sugar.

2 Gradually add 6 tablespoons sugar, beating till stiff and glossy and *all* sugar is dissolved (test with fingers).

For an 8-inch pie, use 2 egg whites, ¼ teaspoon cream of tartar, ½ teaspoon vanilla, and 4 tablespoons sugar.

3 Spread meringue over filling (room temperature), *sealing* meringue to edges of pastry all around—this prevents shrinking.

Bake in moderate oven (350°) 12 to 15 minutes, or till peaks of meringue are golden brown. Get ready for compliments!

Favorite fruit pies

Perfect Apple Pie

5 to 7 tart apples*
¾ to 1 cup sugar
2 tablespoons enriched flour
1 teaspoon cinnamon
¼ teaspoon nutmeg
Dash salt
Pastry for 2-crust 9-inch pie
2 tablespoons butter or
   margarine

Pare apples and slice thin. Combine sugar, flour, spices, and salt; mix with apples. Line 9-inch pie plate with pastry, fill with apple mixture; dot with butter. Adjust top crust; sprinkle with sugar for sparkle. Bake in hot oven (400°) 50 minutes or till done.

*Or save time by using two No. 2 cans (5 cups) sliced pie apples, drained.

Red-hot Apple Pie: Omit cinnamon and nutmeg in Perfect Apple Pie recipe above. Combine 3 tablespoons red cinnamon candies with sugar, flour, and salt.

Open-face Apple Pie

A specialty at Nieman-Marcus—

1 10-inch unbaked pastry shell*
11 cups quartered pared apples (about
   11 large apples—Winesaps, Rome
   Beauties, or Greenings are best)
2 cups sugar
4 tablespoons enriched flour
1 teaspoon salt
⅓ cup light cream
¼ cup milk
⅛ teaspoon cinnamon

Heap unbaked pie shell with the quartered apples. Thoroughly combine sugar, flour, and salt; add cream and milk; beat. Pour over apples. Sprinkle with cinnamon.

Bake in moderate oven (375°) 1½ to 2 hours or till apples are soft. (Cover pie loosely with aluminum foil for first hour of baking, then remove foil.) Serve warm with scoops of aged Cheddar.

*Use an extra-deep 10-inch pie plate. Place sheet of aluminum foil on oven rack to catch any wayward juices.

Apple Crumb Pie

5 to 7 tart apples *or* 2 No. 2 cans
   (5 cups) sliced pie apples,
   drained
1 9-inch unbaked pastry shell
½ cup sugar
1 teaspoon cinnamon
½ cup sugar
¾ cup enriched flour
⅓ cup butter or margarine

Pare apples and cut in eighths; arrange in unbaked pie shell. Combine ½ cup sugar with the cinnamon; sprinkle over apples.

Combine ½ cup sugar with the flour; cut in butter till crumbly. Sprinkle over apples.

Bake in hot oven (400°) 40 minutes, or till done. Cool. Spoon whipped cream atop; sprinkle with a cinnamon-sugar mixture.

Pear-tree Mince Pie

½ cup seedless raisins
1 cup chopped pared tart apples
¾ cup brown sugar
¼ cup slivered blanched almonds
¼ cup orange marmalade
¼ cup lemon juice
2 tablespoons enriched flour
1 teaspoon cinnamon
½ teaspoon nutmeg
¼ teaspoon cloves
¼ teaspoon salt
    . . .
Pastry for 2-crust 9-inch pie
1 No. 2½ can (3½ cups) pear halves,
   drained and sliced, *or* 3 fresh pears,
   pared and sliced (2½ to 3 cups)
1 tablespoon butter or margarine

Simmer raisins in water to cover, about 5 minutes; drain. Combine raisins, apples, brown sugar, nuts, marmalade, lemon juice, flour, spices, and salt.

Line 9-inch pie plate with pastry; top with *half* the pear slices. Cover with mince-meat mixture; top with remaining pears. Dot with butter. Adjust top crust, crimping edges. With cooky cutter or knife, make cut-out in center of top crust. Bake in hot oven (400°) 45 minutes or till done.

Perfect Apple Pie

Juicy apple slices bubble and bake with sugar and spice inside their flaky pastry coverlet. Top the warm pie wedges with cheese cornucopias: Roll up process cheese slices; peg with cloves.

Mincemeat Pie

1¾ cups prepared mincemeat
  or 1 9-ounce package
2 cups thinly sliced apples
½ teaspoon grated lemon peel
2 tablespoons lemon juice

• • •

Pastry for 2-crust 8-inch pie

If using packaged mincemeat, prepare according to package directions.

Combine mincemeat with apples, lemon peel, and lemon juice. Line 8-inch pie plate with pastry; pour in filling. Adjust top crust and crimp edges. With cooky cutter or knife, cut design in crust. Sprinkle lightly with sugar for sparkle. Bake in hot oven (400°) about 35 minutes. Serve warm. Pass brandy-flavored Hard Sauce, (page 64), if desired.

Cranberry Mince Pie

1⅓ cups sugar
½ teaspoon salt
½ teaspoon *each* ginger and cloves
1 teaspoon cinnamon
1⅓ cups seedless raisins
⅓ cup chopped California
  walnuts
1 tablespoon grated orange peel
2 teaspoons grated lemon peel
⅓ cup lemon juice
¾ cup canned jellied cranberry
  sauce, crushed
1⅓ cups finely chopped apple
Pastry for 2-crust 9-inch pie

Combine sugar, salt, and spices. Add remaining filling ingredients; mix well. Line 9-inch pie plate with pastry; fill. Top with lattice crust. Bake at 400° about 35 minutes.

Basic Berry Pie

Pastry for 2-crust 9-inch pie
3 cups fresh berries
⅔ to 1 cup sugar
2 tablespoons cornstarch
or 4 tablespoons flour
1 tablespoon butter or margarine

Line 9-inch pie plate with pastry; fill with berries. Mix sugar, cornstarch, and dash salt; sprinkle over. Dot with butter; adjust top crust. Bake at 400° 40 to 50 minutes.

Blueberry Pie

Line 9-inch pie plate with pastry. Combine 4 cups fresh blueberries with ¾ to 1 cup sugar, 3 tablespoons flour, ½ teaspoon grated lemon peel, and dash salt. (Like spice? Add ½ teaspoon *each* cinnamon and nutmeg.) Fill pie shell. Sprinkle with 1 to 2 teaspoons lemon juice; dot with 1 tablespoon butter. Adjust top crust. Bake in hot oven (400°) 35 to 40 minutes. Serve warm.

Glazed Blueberry Pie

1 3-ounce package cream cheese
1 9-inch baked pastry shell
3 cups fresh blueberries

• • •

1 cup fresh blueberries
½ cup water
¾ cup sugar
2 tablespoons cornstarch
2 tablespoons lemon juice

Soften cream cheese; spread in bottom of cooled pie shell. Fill with 3 cups berries.

Combine 1 cup blueberries and the water; bring just to boiling, reduce heat, and simmer 2 minutes. Strain, reserving juice (about ½ cup). Combine sugar and cornstarch; gradually add reserved juice. Cook, stirring constantly, till thick and clear. Cool slightly; add lemon juice. Pour over berries in pastry shell. Chill. Trim with pastry daisies.* Serve with whipped cream.

*Cut daisies from pastry scraps; bake in very hot oven (450°) 3 to 4 minutes.

Strawberry Cream Pie

This pie is a miracle of luscious eating — strawberries and cream plus! The pastry is lined with toasted almonds, filled with creamy French custard, crowned with glazed strawberries.

Red Raspberry-Cherry Pie

2 cups fresh red raspberries
1 cup pitted sour cherries
3 tablespoons quick-cooking tapioca
1½ cups sugar
1 teaspoon lemon juice
Pastry for 2-crust 9-inch pie
1 tablespoon butter or margarine

Mix raspberries and cherries. Combine tapioca, sugar, and lemon juice; add to fruits. Let stand 1 hour. Line 9-inch pie plate with pastry; pour in filling. Dot with butter. Adjust top crust and flute edge. Bake in hot oven (400°) 40 to 50 minutes.

Strawberry Cream Pie

1 9-inch baked pastry shell
½ cup slivered blanched almonds, toasted
1 recipe Cream Filling (below)
2½ cups fresh strawberries
½ cup water
¼ cup sugar
2 teaspoons cornstarch
Few drops red food coloring

Cover bottom of cooled pastry shell with nuts. Fill with chilled Cream Filling. Halve 2 cups of the strawberries. Pile atop filling.

Glaze: Crush remaining ½ cup berries; add water; cook 2 minutes; sieve. Mix sugar and cornstarch; gradually stir in berry juice. Cook, and stir till thick and clear. Tint to desired color with food coloring. Cool slightly; pour over halved strawberries. Keep refrigerated till serving time. Pass whipped cream, if desired.

Cream Filling

(*for Strawberry Cream Pie*)

½ cup sugar
3 tablespoons cornstarch
3 tablespoons enriched flour
½ teaspoon salt
2 cups milk
1 slightly beaten egg
½ cup heavy cream, whipped
1 teaspoon vanilla

Mix first 4 ingredients. Gradually stir in milk. Stirring constantly, bring to a boil; reduce heat and cook and stir till thick. Stir a little of hot mixture into egg; return to remaining hot mixture. Bring just to boiling, stirring constantly. Cool, then chill. Beat well; fold in whipped cream and vanilla.

Strawberry-Rhubarb Pie

A flavor-duo, refreshing as spring—

3 beaten eggs
1¼ cups sugar
¼ cup enriched flour
¼ teaspoon salt
½ teaspoon nutmeg
2½ cups 1-inch slices pink rhubarb
1½ cups sliced fresh strawberries
Pastry for 9-inch lattice-top pie
1 tablespoon butter or margarine

Combine eggs, sugar, flour, salt, and nutmeg; mix well. Combine rhubarb and strawberries. Line 9-inch pie plate with pastry; fill with fruits. Pour egg mixture over. Dot with butter. Top with lattice crust, crimping edge high. Bake in hot oven (400°) about 40 minutes. Fill openings in lattice crust with whole strawberries. Serve warm.

Strawberry Fluff Pie

½ cup butter or margarine
1½ cups sifted confectioners' sugar
2 beaten eggs
1 9-inch Vanilla-wafer Crust, page 71
1½ cups drained sweetened sliced strawberries
1 to 2 cups heavy cream, whipped

Cream butter; gradually stir in confectioners' sugar. Add eggs; beat till fluffy. Spoon into Vanilla-wafer Crust; smooth top.

Fold strawberries into whipped cream (for extra-rich pie, use 2 cups). Spread over butter mixture; trim with additional crumbs. Chill till firm, 6 to 8 hours or overnight.

Fresh Gooseberry Pie

3 cups fresh gooseberries
1½ cups sugar
3 tablespoons quick-cooking tapioca
¼ teaspoon salt
Pastry for 9-inch 2-crust pie
2 tablespoons butter or margarine

Stem, wash, and drain gooseberries. Crush ½ cup of the berries and combine with sugar, tapioca, and salt. Add the whole berries. Cook and stir till mixture thickens. Line 9-inch pie plate with pastry; fill. Dot with butter. Adjust top crust.

Bake in very hot oven (450°) 10 minutes; reduce temperature to 350° and bake about 30 minutes longer or till crust is done. Serve slightly warm.

Fruit-pie praise winners

Cherry Pie Supreme

½ to ¾ cup sugar
2½ tablespoons cornstarch
Dash salt
1 cup juice from cherries
1 tablespoon butter
6 to 8 drops almond extract
4 cups thawed, drained, frozen pitted
 tart red cherries
Pastry for 9-inch lattice-top pie

In saucepan, combine sugar, cornstarch, and dash salt. Gradually add cherry juice, stirring smooth. Cook and stir till thick and clear. Add butter and extract. Cool.

Line 9-inch pie plate with pastry. Add cherries to cornstarch mixture; pour into pastry. Top with lattice crust. Crimp edges high and cover with foil strip. Bake in hot oven (425°) 35 to 45 minutes. Remove foil 10 minutes before end of baking time.

For fresh cherries: Combine 3 cups pitted sour cherries, 1 to 1½ cups sugar, ¼ cup enriched flour, and dash salt. Put in 8-inch pastry-lined pie plate. Dot with 2 tablespoons butter or margarine. Adjust lattice top; flute; bake as in Cherry Pie Supreme.

Bake a cherry pie! Serve faintly
warm, cut big wedges. So good!

Red Cherry Pie

¾ cup juice from cherries
¾ cup sugar
1½ tablespoons quick-cooking tapioca
2½ cups drained, canned, pitted
 tart red cherries
Few drops red food coloring
1 tablespoon butter or margarine
Pastry for 9-inch lattice-top pie

Combine juice, sugar, tapioca, cherries, food coloring, and dash salt; let stand 20 minutes. Line 9-inch pie plate with pastry; fill with cherry mixture. Dot with butter. Adjust lattice crust; crimp edge high. Bake in very hot oven (450°) 10 minutes. Reduce heat to 350°; bake about 30 minutes more.

Old-fashioned Cherry Pie

1 cup sugar
¼ cup sifted enriched flour
¼ teaspoon salt
½ cup juice from cherries
3 cups drained, canned, pitted tart
 red cherries
1 tablespoon soft butter
4 drops almond extract
Pastry for 9-inch lattice-top pie

Combine sugar, flour, and salt; stir in juice. Cook and stir over medium heat till thick; cook 1 minute longer. Add cherries, butter, extract, and 10 drops red food coloring. Let stand; make pastry.

Line 9-inch pie plate with pastry; fill. Top with lattice crust. Flute edges. Bake in very hot oven (450°) 10 minutes. Reduce heat to 350° and bake about 45 minutes more.

Peach Angel Pie

Beat 3 egg whites and dash salt till foamy; gradually add ¾ cup sugar, beating to stiff peaks. Fold in 1 cup toasted flaked coconut and ⅓ cup chopped toasted blanched almonds. Spread in well-buttered 9-inch pie plate; build up sides. Bake at 350° about 30 minutes or till lightly browned and dry along edge. Cool.

At serving time, fill cooled meringue crust with 2½ to 3 cups drained thinly sliced peaches (sweeten if fresh). Top with whipped cream and ¼ cup toasted flaked coconut.

Easy, delicious
Red Cherry Pie

Downright good
eating! Filling is
tart yet sweet,
crust golden and
flaky; cherries peek
through lattice top.

The easy no-cook
filling is made
with tapioca. If
you prefer to
precook filling,
try our cornstarch
or flour version.
Short on time?
Use cherry-pie
filling from a can.

Peach Pie

Pastry for 9-inch lattice-top pie
¾ cup sugar
3 tablespoons enriched flour
¼ teaspoon nutmeg or cinnamon
Dash salt
5 cups sliced fresh peaches
2 tablespoons butter or margarine

Line 9-inch pie plate with pastry. Combine sugar, flour, spice, and salt. Add to peaches; mix lightly. Fill pastry. Dot with butter. (Sprinkle with extra spice, if desired.)

Adjust lattice crust; crimp edges. Bake in hot oven (400°) 40 to 45 minutes or till done. Serve warm with cream or ice cream.

Butterscotch Peach Pie

Pastry for 9-inch lattice-top pie
1 No. 2½ can (3½ cups) sliced peaches
½ cup brown sugar
2 tablespoons enriched flour
¼ cup butter or margarine
2 teaspoons lemon juice

Line 9-inch pie plate with pastry. Drain peaches, reserving ¼ cup syrup. Arrange peaches in pastry-lined pie plate.

Combine sugar, flour, dash salt, and reserved peach syrup; add butter; cook and stir till thick. Remove from heat; add lemon juice; pour over peaches. Top with lattice crust; flute edges. Bake in hot oven (425°) 30 minutes or till done.

Apricot Pie

2 cups dried apricots
1 cup sugar
1½ cups water
2 tablespoons quick-cooking tapioca
½ teaspoon salt
1 teaspoon cinnamon
Pastry for 9-inch 2-crust pie

Put apricots through food chopper, using coarse blade. Add next 5 ingredients. Bring to boil; reduce heat, cook and stir 2 or 3 minutes. Line 9-inch pie plate with pastry; fill; dot with butter. Adjust top crust. Bake in hot oven (400°) about 30 minutes.

Spicy Raisin Tarts

2 cups seedless raisins
2 cups cider
½ cup brown sugar
2 tablespoons cornstarch
½ teaspoon cinnamon
¼ teaspoon nutmeg
½ cup chopped California walnuts
1 tablespoon butter or margarine
4 to 6 unbaked tart shells

Cook raisins in cider till plump, about 10 minutes. Combine sugar, cornstarch, and spices; stir in a little of hot cider; add to remaining hot mixture. Cook and stir till thick, about 5 minutes. Remove from heat, stir in nuts and butter. Fill shells. Bake in hot oven (400°) 20 to 25 minutes.

Pear Cheese Pie

Pears bake under a smooth golden custard capped with fluffy meringue—

1 1-pound can (2 cups) pear halves, well drained
1 9-inch Graham-cracker Crust, page 71
2 well-beaten egg yolks
1 8-ounce package cream cheese
1 cup dairy sour cream
½ teaspoon grated lemon peel
1 teaspoon lemon juice
½ cup sugar
1 tablespoon enriched flour
½ teaspoon salt
½ teaspoon nutmeg

. . .

2 egg whites
¼ teaspoon cream of tartar
¼ cup sugar

Slice pears into Graham-cracker Crust. Combine egg yolks and softened cream cheese; beat smooth. Blend in sour cream, lemon peel, and juice. Combine ½ cup sugar, flour, salt, nutmeg; add to cheese mixture; mix well. Pour over pears. Bake in moderate oven (375°) 25 minutes or till just set.

Meanwhile beat egg whites with cream of tartar until frothy. Gradually add ¼ cup sugar, beating till stiff peaks form. Spread meringue over filling, sealing to edges of crust. Continue baking 10 minutes longer or until meringue is golden brown.

Marmalade Plum Pie

2 pounds fresh Italian prunes, quartered and pitted (3 cups)
⅓ cup water
¾ cup sugar
2 tablespoons cornstarch
¼ teaspoon salt
⅓ cup chopped California walnuts
2 tablespoons butter or margarine
Pastry for 9-inch 2-crust pie
⅓ cup orange marmalade

Combine prunes and water; bring to boiling and cook 3 to 4 minutes. Combine sugar, cornstarch, and salt; stir into prune mixture. Cook slowly till thick and clear, stirring constantly. Remove from heat. Stir in nuts and butter; cool.

Line 9-inch pie plate with pastry; spread bottom with orange marmalade. Fill with prune mixture. Adjust top crust; flute edge. Bake in hot oven (425°) 30 to 35 minutes.

Glazed-plum Cheese Pie

Luscious, easy cream-cheese filling, tart topper of fresh Italian prunes—

Filling:

1 8-ounce package cream cheese
½ cup sweetened condensed milk
2 tablespoons lemon juice
½ cup heavy cream, whipped
1 9-inch Graham-cracker Crust, page 71

Glazed-plum Topping:

1 cup sugar
¾ cup water
1 pound fresh Italian prunes, halved and pitted (2 cups)
1½ teaspoons cornstarch

Filling: Soften cream cheese, blend in condensed milk and lemon juice. Fold in whipped cream; pour into crust; chill well.

Glazed-plum Topping: Combine sugar and water; bring to boiling, stirring constantly, and simmer 5 minutes. Add prunes to syrup; simmer till just tender, about 10 minutes. Cool in syrup. Drain prunes well, reserving syrup. Gradually stir ½ cup of cooled prune syrup into cornstarch; cook, stirring constantly, till thick and clear. Cool.

Arrange prunes, rounded side up, on chilled filling; spoon glaze over. Chill 4 hours.

Concord-grape Pie

1½ pounds (4 cups) Concord grapes
1 cup sugar
¼ cup enriched flour
¼ teaspoon salt
1 tablespoon lemon juice
1½ tablespoons butter, melted
1 9-inch unbaked pastry shell

Slip skins from grapes; set skins aside. Bring pulp to boiling point; reduce heat, and simmer 5 minutes. Press through sieve to remove seeds. Add skins.

Combine sugar, flour, salt. Add lemon juice, butter, and grape pulp. Pour into shell. Top with *Crumb Topping:* Sift ½ cup enriched flour with ¼ cup sugar. Cut in ⅓ cup butter till crumbly. Sprinkle over pie. Bake in hot oven (400°) about 40 minutes.

For grape-leaf garnish, cut leaf design from pastry with sharp knife. Mark leaf veins with tip of knife. Bake on cooky sheet at 450° about 10 minutes. Cool; sprinkle with sugar. Place on baked pie.

Rhubarb Cream Pie

1½ cups sugar
¼ cup enriched flour
¾ teaspoon nutmeg
3 slightly beaten eggs
4 cups 1-inch slices rhubarb (1 pound)
Pastry for 9-inch lattice-top pie
2 tablespoons butter or margarine

Blend sugar, flour, nutmeg. Beat into eggs. Add rhubarb. Line 9-inch pie plate with pastry; fill; dot with butter. Top with lattice crust. Bake at 400° 50 to 60 minutes. Cool.

Rhubarb Pie

Combine 3 cups 1-inch slices rhubarb, 1 cup sugar, ½ teaspoon grated orange peel, 3 tablespoons flour, and a dash salt.

Line 9-inch pie plate with Orange Pastry (page 71). Fill with rhubarb mixture and dot with 2 tablespoons butter or margarine.

Top with lattice crust. Bake in hot oven (400°) 40 to 50 minutes.

Orange-blossom Pie

3 cups orange sections, white membrane removed (7 to 10 oranges)
½ cup sugar
1 3-ounce package cream cheese
1 9-inch Gingersnap Crust, page 71
1 recipe Orange Glaze
½ cup heavy cream, whipped

Sprinkle *2 cups* orange sections with sugar; set aside for ½ hour. Spread softened cream cheese over bottom of Gingersnap Crust.

Place drained sweetened orange sections atop cream cheese. Pour ½ *cup* glaze over. Spiral remaining 1 cup orange sections (drained) around edge of pie. Cover with remaining glaze. Chill till top is set, about 1 hour. Pile whipped cream atop pie.

Orange Glaze: In saucepan blend 2½ tablespoons cornstarch with ⅓ cup sugar. Drain syrup from sweetened orange sections and add orange juice to make 1 cup; stir into sugar mixture. Cook, stirring constantly, till thick and clear. Cool.

So refreshing—
Orange-blossom Pie

This sunny pie brings a touch of gold to your table! For a pretty edge, press crust only halfway up sides of pie plate. Arrange first layer of orange sections over the rich cream cheese; then place halved gingersnaps around edge of pie plate to match picture.

Custard pie—and kin

Custard Pie

1 9-inch unbaked pastry shell
4 slightly beaten eggs
½ cup sugar
¼ teaspoon salt
½ teaspoon vanilla
⅛ teaspoon almond extract
2½ cups milk, scalded
Nutmeg

Chill pie shell while making filling. Blend eggs, sugar, salt, vanilla, and almond extract. Gradually stir in scalded milk. Pour into pie shell. Sprinkle with nutmeg.

Bake in hot oven (400°) 25 to 30 minutes or till knife inserted halfway between outside and center of custard comes out clean. Cool on cooling rack 15 to 30 minutes; then chill in refrigerator.

Honey Tarts

Beat 2 eggs. Blend in ½ cup honey, ¼ cup sugar, ¼ teaspoon salt, 1 teaspoon vanilla, and ⅔ cup broken pecans.

Pour into 4 to 6 unbaked pastry tart shells. Bake in hot oven (400°) 15 to 18 minutes or till filling is set.

Neat way to fill pie shell—

To avoid spilling a custard-type filling and to keep the crust free of spatters, fill your pie shell at the oven. We mixed the filling in a pitcher-bowl for easy pouring.

Coconut Custard Pie

4 eggs
½ cup granulated sugar
¼ teaspoon salt
1 teaspoon vanilla
2½ cups milk, scalded
1 3½-ounce can flaked coconut
1 9-inch unbaked pastry shell, chilled
¼ cup brown sugar
2 tablespoons soft butter or margarine

Beat eggs slightly; stir in granulated sugar, salt, and vanilla. Gradually stir in milk. Reserve ½ cup coconut; add remainder to custard. Pour into pie shell. Bake in hot oven (400°) 25 to 30 minutes or till knife inserted halfway between edge and center comes out clean. Cool. At serving time, mix reserved coconut, brown sugar, and butter; sprinkle on top of pie. Broil 3 to 4 inches from heat 2 to 4 minutes or till lightly browned.

Pumpkin Pie

1½ cups canned or mashed
  cooked pumpkin
¾ cup sugar
½ teaspoon salt
1 to 1¼ teaspoons cinnamon
½ to 1 teaspoon ginger
¼ to ½ teaspoon nutmeg
¼ to ½ teaspoon cloves
3 slightly beaten eggs
1¼ cups milk
1 6-ounce can (⅔ cup) evaporated milk
1 9-inch unbaked pastry shell

Thoroughly combine pumpkin, sugar, salt, spices. Blend in eggs, milk, and evaporated milk. Pour into pastry shell (crimp edges high—filling is generous). Bake at 400° 50 minutes, or till knife inserted halfway between center and edge comes out clean. Cool.

Southern classic—Pecan Pie

A compliment winner from way back! And pecan pie is easier than you'd think. We give recipes for both the rich, rich traditional pie and for a delectable but less sweet version.

Southern Pecan Pie

The real thing—rich and sweet, with plenty of pecans. Ready for the oven as fast as you can say "y'all"!—

3 eggs
⅔ cup sugar
Dash salt
1 cup dark corn syrup
⅓ cup melted butter or margarine

· · ·

1 cup pecan halves

· · ·

1 9-inch unbaked pastry shell

Beat eggs thoroughly with sugar, salt, corn syrup, and melted butter. Add pecans. Pour into unbaked pastry shell.

Bake in moderate oven (350°) 50 minutes or till knife inserted halfway between outside and center of filling comes out clean. Cool pie before serving.

Pecan Pie

A not-so-sweet version of this all-time favorite. The mixer does the work!—

¼ cup butter or margarine
½ cup sugar
1 cup dark corn syrup
¼ teaspoon salt
3 eggs
1 cup pecan halves

· · ·

1 9-inch unbaked pastry shell

Cream butter to soften. Add sugar gradually and cream till fluffy. Add syrup and salt; beat well. Add eggs one at a time, beating thoroughly after each. Stir in pecans. Pour into unbaked pastry shell.

Bake in moderate oven (350°) 50 minutes. Pie is done when knife inserted halfway between outside and center of filling comes out clean. Cool before serving.

Meringue pies

Grandma's Raisin Pie

¾ cup sugar
1 tablespoon cornstarch
¼ teaspoon salt
1 teaspoon cinnamon
½ teaspoon nutmeg
¼ teaspoon cloves
1 cup dairy sour cream
1 tablespoon lemon juice
1 cup seedless raisins
2 beaten egg yolks
½ cup broken California walnuts
1 8-inch baked pastry shell
1 recipe Meringue

In heavy saucepan, combine first 6 ingredients. Stir in sour cream and lemon juice. Add raisins. Bring to boil over medium heat, stirring constantly; cook and stir till thick.

Remove from heat; stir small amount hot mixture into egg yolks, then return to hot mixture. Cook and stir 1 minute. Cool to lukewarm. Add nuts. Pour into cooled shell.

Meringue: Beat 2 egg whites with ¼ teaspoon cream of tartar to soft peaks. Gradually add ¼ cup sugar, beating till stiff peaks form and all sugar is dissolved. Spread meringue atop pie, *sealing* to edges. Bake in moderate oven (350°) 12 to 15 minutes.

A quick way to a reputation as a good cook: Make a luscious pie!

Lemon Meringue Pie (*9-inch*)

1½ cups sugar
7 tablespoons cornstarch
Dash salt
1½ cups water
3 beaten egg yolks
1 teaspoon grated lemon peel
2 tablespoons butter or margarine
½ cup lemon juice
1 9-inch baked pastry shell
3 egg whites
1 teaspoon lemon juice
6 tablespoons sugar

In saucepan, mix first 3 ingredients; stir in water. Bring to boil over medium heat, stirring; cook and stir till thick, about 5 minutes. Remove from heat; stir small amount hot mixture into egg yolks, then return to hot mixture. Bring to boiling and cook 1 minute, stirring constantly. Remove from heat. Add lemon peel and butter. Slowly stir in ½ cup lemon juice. Cool to lukewarm, stirring frequently to prevent "film." Pour into cooled pastry shell.

Beat egg whites with 1 teaspoon lemon juice to soft peaks. Gradually add 6 tablespoons sugar, beating till stiff peaks form and *all* sugar has dissolved (test with fingers). Spread meringue over filling, *sealing* to edges of pastry to avoid shrinking.

Bake in moderate oven (350°) 12 to 15 minutes or till meringue is golden brown. Cool pie thoroughly before serving.

Lemon Meringue Pie (*8-inch*)

1¼ cups sugar
⅓ cup cornstarch
Dash salt
1¼ cups water
2 beaten egg yolks
1 teaspoon grated lemon peel
1 tablespoon butter or margarine
⅓ cup lemon juice
1 8-inch baked pastry shell
2 egg whites
1 teaspoon lemon juice
¼ cup sugar

Follow method for 9-inch pie above.

Lemon Meringue Pie
to do you proud

As you cut each pretty wedge, the yellow filling "stands alone," yet is quivery and creamy. The meringue billows atop, snow white with browned peaks. Taste! Lemon-fresh flavor, tart and sweet. Serving tip: For neat wedges, cool pie thoroughly before cutting.

Vanilla Cream Pie

¾ cup sugar
⅓ cup enriched flour
   or 3 tablespoons cornstarch
¼ teaspoon salt
2 cups milk
3 slightly beaten egg yolks
2 tablespoons butter or margarine
1 teaspoon vanilla
1 9-inch baked pastry shell
1 recipe Meringue

In saucepan, combine sugar, flour, and salt; gradually stir in milk. Cook and stir over medium heat till mixture boils. Cook 2 minutes longer; remove from heat. Stir small amount hot mixture into yolks; return to hot mixture; cook and stir 2 minutes. Remove from heat. Add butter, vanilla; cool to room temperature. Pour into pastry shell.

Meringue: Beat 3 egg whites with ½ teaspoon vanilla and ¼ teaspoon cream of tartar till soft peaks form. Gradually add 6 tablespoons sugar, beating to stiff peaks. Spread over filling, *sealing* to pastry. Bake at 350° about 12 to 15 minutes. Cool.

Banana Cream Pie

Slice 3 bananas into cooled 9-inch pastry shell; top with Vanilla Cream Pie filling and Meringue. Bake as directed.

Butterscotch Pie

Substitute brown sugar for granulated sugar in recipe for Vanilla Cream Pie. Increase butter to 3 tablespoons.

Chocolate Cream Pie

In Vanilla Cream Pie recipe, increase sugar to 1 cup. Chop two 1-ounce squares unsweetened chocolate; add with milk.

Coconut Cream Pie

Add 1 cup flaked coconut to Vanilla Cream Pie filling. Sprinkle ¼ cup coconut over meringue before browning.

Note. See step-by-step picture directions for making meringue on page 73.
Recipes for pastry are on pages 70 and 71.

Pies– light as a cloud!

Americana Key Lime Pie

A spectacular from the famous Miami hotel! See it on our cover!—

1 tablespoon (1 envelope)
  unflavored gelatin
½ cup sugar
¼ teaspoon salt
4 egg yolks
½ cup lime juice
¼ cup water
1 teaspoon grated lime peel
Few drops green food coloring
. . .
4 egg whites
½ cup sugar
1 cup heavy cream, whipped
1 9-inch baked pastry shell

Thoroughly mix gelatin, ½ cup sugar, and salt in saucepan. Beat together egg yolks, lime juice, and water; stir into gelatin mixture. Cook and stir over medium heat just till mixture comes to boiling. Remove from heat; stir in grated peel. Add food coloring sparingly to tint pale green.

Chill, stirring occasionally, until the mixture mounds slightly when dropped from a spoon. Beat egg whites till soft peaks form; gradually add ½ cup sugar, beating to stiff peaks. Fold gelatin mixture into egg whites. Fold in whipped cream. Pile into cooled baked pastry shell. Chill till firm. Spread with more whipped cream; edge with grated lime peel. Center with grated pistachio nuts. Trim with lime wedges.

Citrus Chiffon Pie

1 envelope (1 tablespoon) unflavored
  gelatin
½ cup sugar
Dash salt
4 egg yolks
½ cup lemon juice
½ cup orange juice
¼ cup water
½ teaspoon grated lemon peel
½ teaspoon grated orange peel
. . .
4 egg whites
⅓ cup sugar
1 9-inch baked pastry shell

Thoroughly mix gelatin, ½ cup sugar, and salt in saucepan. Beat together egg yolks, fruit juices, and water; stir into gelatin mixture. Cook and stir over medium heat just till mixture comes to boiling. Remove from heat; stir in peels. Chill, stirring occasionally, till mixture mounds slightly when dropped from a spoon. Beat egg whites till soft peaks form. Gradually add ⅓ cup sugar, beating to stiff peaks; fold in gelatin mixture. Pile into cooled baked pastry shell. Chill till firm. Trim with whipped cream and thin orange slices cut in fourths.

Pumpkin Chiffon Pie

¾ cup brown sugar
1 envelope unflavored gelatin
½ teaspoon salt
1 teaspoon cinnamon
½ teaspoon nutmeg
¼ teaspoon ginger
3 slightly beaten egg yolks
¾ cup milk
1¼ cups canned or mashed
  cooked pumpkin
3 egg whites
⅓ cup granulated sugar
1 9-inch Graham-cracker Crust, page 71

In saucepan, combine brown sugar, gelatin, salt, and spices. Combine egg yolks and milk; stir into brown-sugar mixture. Cook and stir till mixture comes to a boil. Remove from heat; stir in pumpkin.

Chill till mixture mounds slightly when spooned. (Test every now and then—don't let it get too stiff.) Beat egg whites till soft peaks form; gradually add granulated sugar, beating to stiff peaks. Fold pumpkin mixture thoroughly into egg whites. Turn into crust. Chill firm. Garnish with whipped cream; drizzle with vanilla caramel sauce.

Strawberry Chiffon Pie

1 pint fresh strawberries
½ cup sugar
1 envelope (1 tablespoon)
  unflavored gelatin
¼ cup cold water
½ cup hot water
1 tablespoon lemon juice
½ cup heavy cream, whipped
2 egg whites
¼ cup sugar
1 9-inch Graham-cracker Crust, page 71

Crush strawberries (makes 1¼ cups); cover with ½ cup sugar; let stand 30 minutes. Soften gelatin in cold water; dissolve in hot water. Cool. Add strawberries, lemon juice, and dash salt. Chill till mixture mounds when spooned. Fold in whipped cream.

Beat egg whites to soft peaks; gradually add ¼ cup sugar, beating till stiff peaks form. Fold into strawberry mixture. Pour into crust. Chill firm. Top with more whipped cream and berries.

Raspberry Chiffon Pie

1 10-ounce package frozen red
  raspberries, thawed
1 package raspberry-flavored gelatin
¾ cup hot water
2 tablespoons lemon juice
½ cup heavy cream, whipped
Dash salt
2 egg whites
¼ cup sugar
1 9-inch baked pastry shell

Drain raspberries and add water to syrup to make ⅔ cup. Dissolve gelatin in ¾ cup hot water; add lemon juice and raspberry syrup. Chill till partially set. Beat mixture till soft peaks form.

Fold in raspberries and whipped cream. Add salt to egg whites; beat till soft peaks form. Add sugar gradually, beating till stiff peaks form. Fold egg whites into raspberry mixture. Pour into cooled baked pastry shell (have edges crimped high—filling is generous). Chill till set.

Mile-high Citrus Chiffon Pie

Perfection! Tart and sweet, orange-y and lemon-y — no wonder this pie rates as one of our most popular recipes!

This delicious pie deserves a pretty trim. Spoon on daisy-petal dollops of whipped cream. Tuck in quarters of a thin orange slice. Add an orange twist in the center.

Eggnog Pie with Blueberries

⅓ cup sugar
1 envelope (1 tablespoon) unflavored
   gelatin
¼ teaspoon salt
3 beaten egg yolks
1½ cups milk
1 teaspoon vanilla
3 egg whites
¼ cup sugar
½ cup heavy cream, whipped
1 9-inch baked pastry shell
Sugared blueberries or blueberry sauce

In top of double boiler, mix the ⅓ cup sugar, the gelatin, and salt. Add egg yolks and milk. Cook and stir over *hot, not boiling*, water till mixture is slightly thick. Remove from heat; add vanilla. Chill, stirring occasionally, till mixture mounds slightly when spooned.

Beat egg whites to soft peaks. Gradually add ¼ cup sugar, beating to stiff peaks. Beat gelatin mixture just till smooth; fold into egg whites. Fold in whipped cream. Pile into cooled pastry shell (have edges crimped high). Chill firm. Serve with blueberries.

Nesselrode Pie

3 egg whites
¼ cup granulated sugar
¾ cup coarsely chopped
   blanched almonds, toasted
⅓ cup maraschino cherries,
   cut in fourths
2 tablespoons maraschino-cherry syrup
1 teaspoon vanilla
   . . .
⅓ cup sifted confectioners' sugar
1½ cups heavy cream, whipped
1 9-inch Vanilla-wafer Crust, page 71

Beat egg whites till foamy; add granulated sugar gradually and beat till stiff. Fold in almonds, cherries, cherry syrup, and vanilla. Fold confectioners' sugar into whipped cream; fold into first mixture. Pour into Vanilla-wafer Crust and freeze firm.

Holiday trim: Top pie with maraschino-cherry poinsettias and gumdrop holly leaves.

Hold cherry at stem end; snip almost through from opposite end into 6 petals; spread.

Roll green gumdrops ⅛ inch thick on sugared waxed paper; snip out leaves.

Caramel Fluff Pie

½ pound (28) vanilla caramels
1 cup milk

• • •

Dash salt
1 envelope (1 tablespoon)
  unflavored gelatin
¼ cup cold water
1 cup heavy cream, whipped
½ cup chopped pecans
1 teaspoon vanilla
1 9-inch Gingersnap Crust, page 71
Pecan halves

Melt caramels in milk in top of double boiler over boiling water, stirring occasionally. (Or heat over low heat, stirring constantly.) Add salt. Soften gelatin in cold water; add to caramels; stir to dissolve. Chill till mixture mounds slightly when dropped from spoon. Fold in whipped cream, chopped nuts, and vanilla. Fill crust; trim top with pecans. Chill 2 to 3 hours or till firm.

Peach Parfait Pie

3½ cups sliced peaches, sweetened,
  or 1 No. 2½ can
1 package lemon-flavored gelatin
½ cup cold water
1 pint vanilla ice cream

• • •

1 9-inch baked pastry shell
½ cup heavy cream, whipped

If using fresh peaches, let stand about 15 minutes after mixing with sugar. Drain peaches (fresh *or* canned), reserving syrup.

Add water to syrup to make 1 cup; heat to boiling. Add gelatin; stir till dissolved. Add cold water. Cut ice cream in 6 pieces; add to hot liquid. Stir till melted. Chill till mixture mounds slightly when dropped from a spoon (15 to 20 minutes). Fold in peach slices. Pour into cooled pastry shell.

Chill till firm, 45 minutes (filling will resemble cream pie) to several hours (filling will be firmer like a gelatin pie). Trim with whipped cream and peaches.

A peach of a parfait pie!

Elegant and quick is this Peach Parfait Pie. Ice cream speeds the setting, makes it fluffy and rich. Garnish pie with a mound of whipped cream and a swirl of peach slices.

Strawberry Parfait Pie

Dissolve 1 package strawberry-flavored gelatin in 1 cup hot water. Add ½ cup cold water; stir. Cut 1 pint of vanilla ice cream in 6 chunks; add to gelatin mixture. Stir till ice cream melts. Chill till mixture mounds slightly when dropped from spoon (20 to 30 minutes).

Gently fold in 1 cup sliced fresh strawberries. Pour into cooled 9-inch Coconut Crust. Chill till firm, about 20 to 25 minutes. Trim with whipped cream and berries.

Grape Parfait Pie

1 package grape-flavored gelatin
1 cup hot grape juice
⅔ cup cold water
2 tablespoons lemon juice
1 pint vanilla ice cream
2 medium *fully ripe* bananas
1 9-inch baked pastry shell

Dissolve gelatin in hot grape juice. Add water and lemon juice. Cut ice cream in 6 chunks; add to gelatin mixture and stir till melted. Chill till mixture mounds slightly when spooned (about 45 minutes).

Slice one banana over bottom of cooled pastry shell; top with layer of filling. Slice second banana over; add remaining filling. Chill till set (1½ to 2 hours). Trim with whipped cream and banana slices, if desired.

Cranberry Parfait Pie

1 package lemon-flavored gelatin
1 cup hot cranberry-juice cocktail
½ cup cold water
1 pint vanilla ice cream
1 teaspoon grated lemon peel
3 tablespoons lemon juice
1 1-pound can (2 cups) whole
  cranberry sauce
1 9-inch baked pastry shell

Dissolve gelatin in hot cranberry cocktail. Add cold water. Cut ice cream in 6 chunks; add to gelatin mixture and stir till melted. Chill till mixture mounds slightly when dropped from spoon (about 20 to 30 minutes). Stir lemon peel and lemon juice into cranberry sauce; fold into gelatin mixture.

Chill again till mixture mounds when spooned (20 to 30 minutes). Pile into cooled pastry shell. Garnish with whipped cream and cranberry sauce, if desired.

Chocolate Chiffon Pie

1 envelope unflavored gelatin
¼ cup cold water
½ cup boiling water
2 1-ounce squares unsweetened
  chocolate
3 egg yolks
⅓ cup sugar
¼ teaspoon salt
1 teaspoon vanilla
3 egg whites
½ cup sugar
1 9-inch Coconut Crust, page 71

Soften gelatin in cold water. In saucepan, combine boiling water and chocolate. Stir over low heat till blended; remove from heat. Add softened gelatin and stir till dissolved. Beat egg yolks till thick and light. Gradually beat in ⅓ cup sugar; add salt and vanilla. Gradually stir in chocolate mixture. Chill till mixture mounds when spooned. Stir until smooth.

Beat egg white till soft peaks form. Gradually add ½ cup sugar, beating till stiff peaks form. Fold into chocolate mixture. Pile into Coconut Crust. Chill till firm. Top with whipped cream; drizzle with *Syrup Trim:* Stir 1½ tablespoons light corn syrup and one-half 1-ounce square unsweetened chocolate over low heat till blended.

Coffee Chiffon Pie

Omit chocolate in Chocolate Chiffon Pie. Dissolve 2 tablespoons instant coffee in the boiling water; add softened gelatin and stir till completely dissolved. Gradually add to egg-yolk mixture and proceed as above. Trim with fluffs of whipped cream and chocolate curls.

Peppermint Pie in Chocolate Shell

1 package strawberry-flavored gelatin
1 cup hot water
· · ·
2 cups heavy cream, whipped
1 cup crushed peppermint-stick candy
Chocolate Shell

Dissolve gelatin in hot water; chill till partially set. Fold whipped cream and *½ cup* of candy into gelatin mixture. Spoon into Chocolate Shell. Chill till set, about 4 hours. Just before serving, sprinkle top with remaining ½ cup candy.

Chocolate Shell

12-inch square of aluminum foil
· · ·
1 6-ounce package (1 cup)
  semisweet chocolate pieces
2 tablespoons shortening

Line 9-inch pie plate with 12-inch square of foil, pressing over bottom, sides, and rim. Remove foil, place on ungreased baking sheet.

Put chocolate pieces and shortening in foil pan and heat in moderate oven (350°) about 5 minutes. Remove from oven and replace foil in pie plate. Gently blend chocolate and shortening; spread over bottom of foil. Chill 8 to 10 minutes, or till chocolate is of spreading consistency. With back of spoon, swirl chocolate evenly over sides, forming a scalloped edge around rim. Chill about ½ hour.

Remove from plate. Carefully tear off foil. Return shell to pie plate; keep chilled.

Black-bottom Pie

½ cup sugar
1 tablespoon cornstarch
2 cups milk, scalded
4 beaten egg yolks
1 teaspoon vanilla
1 6-ounce package (1 cup) semisweet
  chocolate pieces
1 9-inch baked pastry shell
· · ·
1 envelope (1 tablespoon)
  unflavored gelatin
¼ cup cold water
4 egg whites
½ cup sugar

Combine sugar and cornstarch. Slowly add milk to beaten egg yolks. Stir in sugar mixture. Cook and stir in top of double boiler over *hot, not boiling* water till custard coats a spoon. Remove from heat; add vanilla. To *1 cup* of the custard, add the chocolate and stir till melted. Pour into bottom of cooled, baked pastry shell. Chill.

Meanwhile soften gelatin in cold water; add to remaining hot custard. Stir until dissolved. Chill until slightly thick. Beat egg whites till soft peaks form. Gradually beat in sugar and continue beating till stiff peaks form. Fold in custard-gelatin mixture. Pile over chocolate layer, chill till set.

Trim with shaved unsweetened-chocolate curls and bias-cut banana slices.

High, handsome
Chocolate
Chiffon Pie —
company best!

Frosty Chocolate Pie

1 6-ounce package (1 cup) semisweet
   chocolate pieces
¼ cup water
1 tablespoon instant coffee
Dash salt
2 beaten egg yolks
1 7½- or 8-ounce jar marshmallow creme
1 teaspoon vanilla
⅛ teaspoon almond extract
2 stiff-beaten egg whites
1 cup heavy cream, whipped
1 9-inch baked pastry shell

In top of double boiler combine chocolate,
water, instant coffee, and dash salt; heat
over *hot, not boiling* water just till chocolate
melts, stirring occasionally. Pour small
amount of mixture into egg yolks; return to
hot mixture. Cook and stir 3 minutes; remove from heat. Stir in marshmallow creme
and flavorings. Chill. Fold in egg whites,
then whipped cream. Pour into pastry shell.

Freeze firm, 10 hours or overnight. Trim
with whipped cream sprinkled with crushed
peppermint candy. Serve promptly.

Coffee 'n Cream Pie

1 tablespoon unflavored gelatin
¼ cup cold water
3 tablespoons instant coffee
⅓ cup sugar
2 egg yolks
1½ cups milk
1 teaspoon vanilla
2 egg whites
¼ teaspoon salt
¼ cup sugar
½ cup heavy cream, whipped
1 9-inch baked pastry shell

Soften gelatin in cold water. Combine instant coffee, ⅓ cup sugar, and yolks; stir in
milk gradually. Cook and stir over *hot, not
boiling* water, until mixture thickens slightly.
Remove from heat immediately. Add gelatin and stir till dissolved. Add vanilla. Chill
till partially set, then beat until fluffy. Beat
egg whites and salt till foamy; gradually
add ¼ cup sugar, beating to soft peaks.
Fold into gelatin mixture. Fold in whipped
cream. Turn into pie shell. Chill firm. Trim
with walnut halves, if desired.

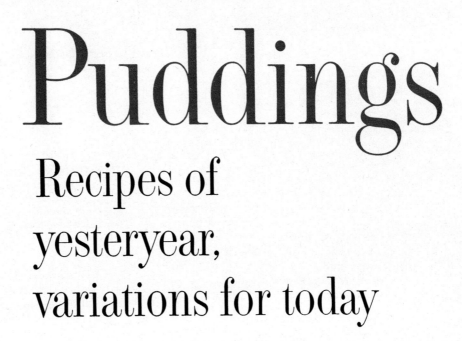

Puddings

Recipes of yesteryear, variations for today

Pudding specials for top of the range

How to make perfect custard, baked and stirred

Homespun baked and steamed puddings

Luscious puddings just right for a party!

What's for dessert? Old-fashioned puddings

← For Strawberry Floating Island, sail snowy meringue puffs on a golden custard sauce and polka-dot with strawberries; pass crisp cookies. Caramel-trimmed Custards get a lacy burnt-sugar topping when they come from the oven. Above is Custard Pie.

Top-of-range puddings

Chocolate Pudding

½ cup sugar
⅓ cup cocoa*
3 tablespoons cornstarch
¼ teaspoon salt
• • •
2½ cups milk
1½ teaspoons vanilla

In saucepan, mix sugar, cocoa, cornstarch, and salt. Gradually blend in milk. Cook over medium heat, stirring constantly, till mixture thickens. Cook 2 to 3 minutes more. Add vanilla. Pour into 5 or 6 sherbets; chill. Or pour into individual molds, rinsed with cold water; chill till firm. Unmold in chilled dessert dishes. Serve with cream.

*Or add two 1-ounce squares unsweetened chocolate, cut up, along with milk.

Vanilla pudding (*Blancmange*)

Follow directions for Chocolate Pudding, but omit cocoa and decrease the sugar to ⅓ cup. Pour mixture into individual molds; chill. Unmold and serve with fruit, cream, or dessert sauce.

Caramel Pudding

Melt ¼ cup sugar in heavy skillet over low heat, stirring constantly, till rich medium brown. Remove from heat. Slowly add ½ cup boiling water. Return to heat and stir till lumps dissolve.

In saucepan combine ¼ cup sugar, 3 tablespoons cornstarch, and ¼ teaspoon salt; blend in 2 cups milk. Stir in caramel syrup. Cook and stir over medium heat till thick. Cook 2 minutes more. Add 1½ teaspoons vanilla. Pour into 5 rinsed molds; chill.

Rennet Custard

Crush 1 rennet tablet in 1 tablespoon cold water; dissolve thoroughly. Add 3 tablespoons sugar and 1 teaspoon vanilla to 2 cups fresh milk; warm slowly to lukewarm. Add dissolved tablet; stir quickly for a few seconds. Pour at once into sherbets. Let stand 10 minutes; when set, chill.

Speedy Pudding

Whip up a smoothie dessert in no time! Use packaged pudding, follow the easy directions on the box. Take a look at page 125, too—fancy puddings from a package!

Tapioca Cream

1 quart milk
¼ cup quick-cooking tapioca
½ cup sugar
¼ teaspoon salt
3 slightly beaten egg yolks
1½ teaspoons vanilla
3 egg whites

Combine milk, tapioca, sugar, and salt. Let stand 5 minutes. Add egg yolks. Bring quickly to boiling, stirring constantly. Remove from heat (mixture will be thin); add vanilla.

Beat egg whites till soft peaks form. Put about ⅓ of the beaten egg whites in large bowl; slowly stir in hot mixture. Fold in remaining egg white, leaving little "pillows" of egg white. Chill. Pile into sherbets. Top with currant jelly. Makes 8 to 10 servings.

Spoon over fresh or canned peaches, or other fruit, if desired.

Date Tapioca: In recipe for Tapioca Cream, stir ½ cup chopped dates into hot mixture before adding to beaten egg whites.

Pots de Creme

1 6-ounce package (1 cup)
 semisweet chocolate pieces
1¼ cups light cream
• • •
2 egg yolks
Dash salt

In heavy saucepan, combine chocolate pieces and cream. Stir over low heat till blended and *satin-smooth*. Mixture should be *slightly thick*—but don't let it boil. Beat egg yolks with salt till thick and light. Gradually stir in chocolate mixture.

Spoon mixture into 6 or 7 traditional cups or into small sherbets, filling ⅔ full. Cover and chill at least 3 hours or till mixture is like pudding.

A frankly fancy dessert Rich, smooth, chocolate-good! That's Pots de Creme—pronounced "poh-deh-krem". The French cook it like a custard, but this version takes almost no cooking, tastes wonderful!

Caramel Dumplings

You're missing out if you haven't tried these old-style dessert dumplings. They are easier than Grandma's—you use a mix—

Caramel Syrup:

¾ cup sugar

• • •

2½ cups hot water
¾ cup sugar
¼ teaspoon salt
1 teaspoon vanilla

Dumplings:

1 cup packaged biscuit mix
2 tablespoons sugar
⅓ cup milk
⅓ cup chopped California walnuts

Caramel Syrup: In electric skillet, melt ¾ cup sugar at high heat (about 420°), stirring until amber-colored. Turn off heat; stir until liquid thickens and cools slightly. Slowly stir in water; add ¾ cup sugar, salt, and vanilla; mix well.

Dumplings: With fork, combine biscuit mix, 2 tablespoons sugar, milk, and nuts, stirring until just moistened.

Heat syrup to simmering; then drop batter in by rounded teaspoon, making 8 dumplings. Cover and cook at low heat (about 260°) 6 to 8 minutes, or till done. Cool slightly. Makes 8 servings.

Strawberry Floating Island

2 egg whites
Dash salt
¼ cup sugar
3 cups milk
3 eggs
2 egg yolks
½ cup sugar
Dash salt
Milk
1½ teaspoons vanilla
2 cups hulled strawberries

Poached Meringues: Beat egg whites with a dash salt till soft peaks form. Gradually add ¼ cup sugar, beating till stiff peaks form. In skillet, heat 3 cups milk to simmering. Drop meringue in by tablespoons to make 6 meringues. Cook slowly, uncovered, till firm, about 5 minutes. Lift from milk (reserve milk for the custard); drain on paper towels.

Custard: Beat eggs and yolks slightly; add ½ cup sugar and dash salt. Stir in 3 cups slightly cooled milk (from meringues plus extra if needed).

Cook in double boiler over *hot, not boiling* water, stirring constantly till mixture coats metal spoon. At once, remove from heat; cool slightly. Add vanilla.

Place strawberries in serving dish, pour custard over. Top with meringues. Chill. Garnish with more berries. Makes 6 servings.

How to make perfect custard

Turn out smooth, velvety Stirred Custard—a cook's triumph!

Smooth custard sauce starts here: Add a small amount of scalded milk to slightly beaten egg-sugar mixture (blended but not foamy). Now stir egg mixture into remaining hot liquid. No lumps!

Cook in double boiler over *hot, not boiling,* water. (Be sure that water in the bottom of your double boiler doesn't touch the top pan.) Stir all the time you cook the custard—a wooden spoon does a nice silent job, keeps a cool handle.

Is your Stirred Custard done? Test with a metal spoon. (Remember to use a *clean* spoon for each test.) When it comes out wearing a velvet coat, you know it's time to stop cooking.

Hurry the pan from hot water to a cool-off bath in sink or bowl of cold water. Stir the custard a minute or two to hasten cooling, then add vanilla. Chill before serving over fresh fruits, wedges of angel cake, or cottage pudding.

Try these baking tips for tender, delicate Baked Custard

No spills here! The custard cups in their handy rack go into a shallow pan on the oven shelf. (Or use a casserole for a larger, one-dish custard.) For even baking, pour hot water, about an inch deep around the custard cups.

Next pour in the custard mixture. (This is easy if the mixing was done in a quart measuring cup. Fewer dishes for the cook to wash, too.) Filling the pan and cups at the oven saves you performing a tricky, cross-kitchen balancing act.

Know "when" for Baked Custard? Insert a thin-bladed knife halfway between center and edge of custard. Hold the knife straight up, making the cut short and only about ½ inch deep. Clean knife means the custard is done.

Remove from pan of hot water and serve warm, or chill. Add a topping, if you wish.

Make knife test a little ahead of time to avoid overbaking. The same test works for little cup custards as for a family size like this one.

Baked Custard

    3 slightly beaten eggs
    ¼ cup sugar
    ¼ teaspoon salt
    2 cups milk, scalded
    ½ to 1 teaspoon vanilla

Combine eggs, sugar, and salt. Slowly stir in slightly cooled milk and vanilla. Set six 5-ounce custard cups* in shallow pan on oven rack. Pour hot water around them, 1 inch deep. Pour in custard.

Bake in slow oven (325°) 40 to 45 minutes, or till knife inserted off-center comes out clean. Serve warm or chilled.

*For one large custard, bake in a 1-quart casserole about 60 minutes or till done.

Skillet Custards: Mix ingredients as for Baked Custard. Pour into six 5-ounce custard cups; sprinkle with nutmeg. Place cups on rack in preheated electric skillet. Cover and bake at 380° about 25 to 30 minutes or till mixture doesn't adhere to knife. (Or follow manufacturer's directions as to temperature.) Serve warm or chilled.

Coconut Custard Topping

Combine ¼ cup flaked coconut, 2 tablespoons brown sugar, and 1 tablespoon soft butter or margarine. Sprinkle atop warm or chilled Baked Custards. Place cups on cooky sheet. Broil 3 to 4 inches from heat, about 5 minutes, till tops are brown.

Caramel Custard Cups

Melt 12 caramels in ¼ cup milk in top of double boiler over boiling water, stirring now and then. Divide the caramel sauce among six 5-ounce custard cups.

Combine ingredients as for Baked Custard; pour over caramel sauce in cups. Bake as for Baked Custard. Serve warm in cups. Or chill and invert cups to unmold—baked-in sauce covers each custard.

Caramel-trimmed Custards

Melt ½ cup sugar in a heavy skillet over low heat, stirring constantly. When the syrup turns a pretty golden brown, remove from heat. Immediately drizzle syrup over warm or chilled Baked Custards in a free-hand design. The syrup will harden into crackly candy. See picture, page 92.

Beauty tip for baked custard

This trick does away with knife slits in the top of baked custard. With practice, you can tell when custard is done by the way it shakes. Jiggle custard very gently. If top quivers like a bowl of jelly, custard's done. If surface shakes like a bowl of milk, custard needs to bake a little longer.

The first few times you'll want to double-check with the knife test. After that, you'll be in the advanced class of custard makers!

Cup custard turn-out: To unmold chilled cup custards, first loosen edge; then slip point of knife down side to let air in. Invert on dessert plate.

Stirred Custard

Combine same ingredients as for Baked Custards, except vanilla. Cook in double boiler, over *hot, not boiling,* water, stirring constantly. As soon as custard coats metal spoon, remove from heat.

Cool at once—place pan in sink or bowl of cold water and stir a minute or two; add vanilla. Chill. Makes 5 or 6 servings.

Creme Brulee

Here's an elegant dessert—rich custard with a broiled brown-sugar crust atop—

    3 slightly beaten eggs
    ¼ cup sugar
    ¼ teaspoon salt
    2 cups light cream, scalded
    1 teaspoon vanilla
       • • •
    ½ cup brown sugar

Combine eggs, sugar, and salt in top of double boiler. Slowly stir in cream. Cook over *hot, not boiling* water till custard coats spoon, about 8 minutes. Continue cooking about 2 minutes longer or till custard thickens slightly. Pour into 8-inch round baking dish or creme brulee dish. Chill.

Sift brown sugar evenly over custard. Set in shallow pan; surround dish with ice cubes and a little cold water.

Broil 8 inches from heat about 5 minutes, till custard has bubbly brown crust. Serve immediately—or chill, being careful not to break crust. Serve as is, or spoon over peaches or other fruit. Makes 4 or 5 servings.

Puddings—baked and steamed

Cottage Pudding

1 cup sifted cake flour
⅔ cup sugar
1¼ teaspoons baking powder
¼ teaspoon salt
⅓ cup milk
¼ cup soft shortening
½ teaspoon vanilla
1 egg

Sift dry ingredients into mixing bowl; add milk, shortening, and vanilla. Beat vigorously 2 minutes. Add egg; beat 2 minutes longer. Pour into paper-lined 8x8x2-inch pan. Bake in hot oven (400°) about 20 minutes. Serve warm with a dessert sauce or fruit spooned atop. Makes 6 servings.

Baked Indian Pudding

From New England's Abner Wheeler House—

4 cups milk
½ cup yellow corn meal
½ teaspoon salt
½ teaspoon mace or cinnamon
¼ teaspoon ginger
¼ teaspoon cloves (optional)
¼ teaspoon nutmeg (optional)
2 tablespoons butter
¾ cup light molasses
1 beaten egg
2 cups milk

Put 4 cups milk in top of double boiler; gradually stir in corn meal. Cook over boiling water, stirring frequently, till thick—10 to 15 minutes. Add remaining ingredients; mix well. Pour into 2-quart casserole; bake in very slow oven (250°) 5 hours. Cool till slightly warm. Top with ice-cream curls: Scrape tip of teaspoon ⅛ inch deep across vanilla ice cream. Makes 8 servings.

Upside-down Date Pudding

Like brownie pudding, but it's date-nut cake atop, a butterscotch-y sauce beneath!—

1 cup pitted dates, cut up
1 cup boiling water

• • •

½ cup granulated sugar
½ cup brown sugar
1 egg
2 tablespoons butter
 or margarine, melted
1½ cups sifted enriched flour
1 teaspoon soda
½ teaspoon baking powder
½ teaspoon salt
1 cup chopped California walnuts

• • •

1 recipe Brown-sugar Sauce

Combine dates and water. Blend sugars, egg, and butter. Sift together flour, soda, baking powder, and salt; add to sugar mixture. Stir in nuts and cooled date mixture. Pour into 11x7x1½-inch baking dish.

Top with *Brown-sugar Sauce:* Combine 1½ cups brown sugar, 1 tablespoon butter or margarine, and 1½ cups boiling water. Bake in moderate oven (375°) about 40 minutes. Cut in squares; invert on plates. Serve warm with whipped cream. Makes 9 servings.

Fragrant puddings—m-m-m!
The compliments are all for the cook!

An all-in-one dessert! For Lemon Cups, you whip up only one mixture, but see what happens in the oven! A fluffy sponge cake bobs to top with tangy sauce beneath. A favorite for the whole family!

Lemon Cups

1 cup sugar
¼ cup sifted enriched flour
2 tablespoons salad oil
2 teaspoons grated lemon peel
⅓ cup lemon juice
1½ cups milk, scalded
3 beaten egg yolks
3 stiff-beaten egg whites

Combine sugar, flour, salad oil, dash salt. Add lemon peel, juice. Stir milk into egg yolks; add to lemon mixture. Fold in egg whites. Pour into eight 5-ounce custard cups. Set custard cups in shallow pan. Pour hot water around them, 1 inch deep. Bake at 325° 40 minutes, or till cake part is done.

Brownie Pudding

1 cup sifted enriched flour
¾ cup granulated sugar
2 tablespoons cocoa
2 teaspoons baking powder
½ teaspoon salt
½ cup milk
2 tablespoons salad oil
1 teaspoon vanilla
¾ to 1 cup chopped walnuts
¾ cup brown sugar
¼ cup cocoa
1¾ cups hot water

Sift together first five ingredients. Add milk, salad oil, vanilla; mix smooth. Add nuts. Pour into greased 8x8x2-inch pan. Mix brown sugar, and ¼ cup cocoa; sprinkle over batter. Pour hot water over entire batter. Bake at 350° about 45 minutes.

Pineapple Cheesecake Cups

⅓ cup sugar
2 tablespoons cornstarch
¼ teaspoon salt
1½ cups unsweetened pineapple juice
¼ teaspoon grated lemon peel
1 tablespoon lemon juice
1 8-ounce package cream cheese, softened
2 eggs
½ cup sugar
¼ teaspoon salt
½ cup milk
½ teaspoon vanilla
⅓ cup sliced pecans

Pineapple Layer: Mix first 3 ingredients in saucepan; add pineapple juice. Cook and stir till thick and clear. Add peel and lemon juice. Pour into six 6-ounce custard cups.

Cheesecake Layer: To cream cheese, add eggs, one at a time, beating smooth after each. Add sugar and salt. Stir in milk and vanilla. Spoon over Pineapple Layer. Sprinkle with pecans. Bake in slow oven (325°) 25 minutes or till set around edge. Cool.

Date-Nut Dessert

Add ¾ cup sugar gradually to 3 beaten eggs, beating till thick and light.

Sift together ¼ cup sifted enriched flour, 1 teaspoon baking powder, and ¼ teaspoon salt; fold into egg mixture. Fold in 1 cup *each* chopped dates and chopped walnuts. Turn into greased 8x8x2-inch pan. Bake at 350° about 40 minutes or till done. Cut in 8 squares; serve warm with ice cream.

Baked Date Pudding

¾ cup boiling water
1 cup pitted dates, cut up
2 tablespoons butter or margarine
1 beaten egg
½ cup brown sugar
1 cup orange marmalade
1¾ cups sifted enriched flour
1 teaspoon salt
1 teaspoon soda
½ cup chopped California walnuts

Pour water over dates and butter. Combine egg, brown sugar, and marmalade; stir into date mixture. Sift together dry ingredients; stir into date mixture till just moistened. Add nuts. Pour into greased 11x7x1½-inch baking dish. Bake in moderate oven (350°) about 30 minutes. Cut in 9 or 10 squares; serve warm with Hard Sauce (page 64).

Steamed Brazil-nut Pudding

½ cup orange juice
1 cup chopped pared apple
1¾ cups seedless raisins
⅓ cup chopped candied citron
1 tablespoon grated orange peel
2 slightly beaten eggs
½ cup light molasses
1 cup coarsely chopped Brazil nuts
½ cup (2 ounces) coarsely ground suet
¾ cup fine dry bread crumbs
½ cup sifted enriched flour
¼ cup sugar
1 teaspoon baking powder
½ teaspoon soda
½ teaspoon salt
½ teaspoon cinnamon
¼ teaspoon allspice
¼ teaspoon cloves

Pour orange juice over fruits, peel; let stand 1 hour. Combine eggs, molasses, nuts, suet, bread crumbs. Sift together dry ingredients; blend into egg mixture. Mix in fruits.

Pour into greased 1½-quart mold with tight cover (or cover with foil; tie tightly).

Place on rack in deep kettle;* pour in boiling water to half the depth of the mold. Cover; steam 3 hours, adding more boiling water if needed. Uncover pudding, place in moderate oven (350°) 10 minutes. Cool 30 minutes; unmold. Serve warm with Fluffy Hard Sauce (page 64). Makes 10 servings.

*Or steam in pressure cooker at 10 to 15 pounds pressure. Cover mold, exhaust, and steam, following manufacturer's directions.

Perfect Bread Pudding

Wonderfully old-fashioned—the thrifty way to use the last of the loaf—

2¼ cups milk
2 slightly beaten eggs
2 cups 1-inch day-old bread cubes
½ cup brown sugar
1 teaspoon cinnamon
1 teaspoon vanilla
¼ teaspoon salt
½ cup seedless raisins,
    dark or light

Combine milk and eggs; pour over bread cubes. Add remaining ingredients; toss lightly to blend. Spread mixture in greased 8x8x2-inch baking dish. Set dish in shallow pan on oven rack. Pour hot water around it 1 inch deep.

Bake in moderate oven (350°) about 35 to 40 minutes or till knife inserted halfway between center and outside edge comes out clean. Makes 9 servings.

Raisin-Meringue Bread Pudding

Tangy orange meringue gives bread pudding fancy flavor, a pretty topping—

2 cups milk
2 cups 1-inch day-old bread cubes
¼ cup brown sugar
¼ teaspoon salt
2 tablespoons melted butter
    or margarine
1 teaspoon vanilla
2 beaten egg yolks
2 cups seedless raisins,
    dark or light

• • •

2 egg whites
3 tablespoons granulated sugar
¾ teaspoon grated orange peel

Pour milk over bread cubes. Add next 6 ingredients; toss lightly to blend. Spread in greased 8x8x2-inch baking dish. Set dish in shallow pan on oven rack. Pour hot water around dish 1 inch deep.

Bake in moderate oven (350°) 50 minutes. Remove from oven; spread with Orange Meringue. Then bake 10 minutes longer, or till meringue is lightly browned. Makes 8 servings.

Orange Meringue: Beat egg whites till fluffy. Gradually add the granulated sugar; beat till soft peaks form. Fold in grated orange peel. Spread on baked pudding.

Party-going puddings

Snowy Coconut Pudding

1 cup sugar
1 envelope (1 tablespoon)
  unflavored gelatin
½ teaspoon salt
1¼ cups milk
 . . .
1 teaspoon vanilla
1 3½-ounce can (1¼ cups)
  flaked coconut
2 cups heavy cream, whipped
Crimson Raspberry Sauce

Thoroughly mix sugar, gelatin, and salt; add milk. Stir over medium heat till gelatin and sugar dissolve. Chill till partially set.

Add vanilla. Fold in coconut, then whipped cream. Pile into 1½-quart mold; chill till firm, at least 4 hours. Unmold. Serve with Crimson Raspberry Sauce, (page 67). Makes 8 servings.

Frozen Yuletide Pudding

1 9-ounce can (1 cup)
  crushed pineapple
1 4-ounce jar (½ cup)
  maraschino cherries
½ cup light raisins
2 cups tiny marshmallows
⅓ cup chopped blanched
  almonds, toasted
1 tablespoon grated lemon peel
2 tablespoons lemon juice
2 teaspoons rum flavoring
 . . .
2 egg whites
¼ teaspoon salt
⅓ cup sugar
 . . .
1 cup heavy cream, whipped

Drain pineapple and cherries, reserving syrups. Chop cherries. Combine syrups, and raisins; heat to boiling. Add marshmallows; stir till dissolved. Cool; add pineapple, cherries, toasted almonds, lemon peel, lemon juice, and rum flavoring.

Beat egg whites and salt till foamy; gradually add sugar, beating to stiff peaks. Fold into mixture. Fold in cream. Freeze firm in refrigerator tray. Makes 8 servings.

Glorified Rice

1 9-ounce can crushed pineapple
⅔ cup packaged precooked rice
⅔ cup water
½ teaspoon salt
1½ cups tiny marshmallows
1 fully ripe banana, diced
2 teaspoons lemon juice
1 cup heavy cream, whipped

Drain pineapple, reserving syrup. In saucepan, combine rice, water, pineapple syrup, and salt; mix just to moisten rice. Bring quickly to boiling; reduce heat, cover and simmer 5 minutes. Remove from heat and let stand 5 minutes. Add marshmallows, pineapple, banana, and lemon juice. Cool. Fold in cream. Chill. Makes 8 to 10 servings.

Americana Rice Pudding

A great hotel in Miami bows to the homey perfection of this rice pudding—

1 quart milk
1 orange
½ cup long-grain rice
½ cup sugar
¾ teaspoon salt
1 cup light cream
2 egg yolks
½ teaspoon vanilla
Cinnamon-sugar mixture

Scald milk in double boiler. Pare orange like an apple, going round and round so peel is in one long spiral. (Use peel only.)

To scalded milk add peel, rice, sugar, and salt. Cook covered in double boiler till rice is tender, about 45 minutes; stir occasionally during first part of cooking.

Remove orange peel. Mix cream, egg yolks; stir in small amount of hot rice mixture. Stir into remainder of rice. Continue cooking covered till mixture thickens, about 20 minutes; stir now and then. Add vanilla.

Pour into custard cups and cool; chill, if desired. Sprinkle with cinnamon-sugar mixture (1 part sugar and 1 part cinnamon). Garnish with whipped cream and maraschino cherries. Makes 8 servings.

Cookies and candies

Wonderful drop cookies, shaped cookies

Refrigerator-cooky rounds—oh, so good!

Bar cookies—the best you ever ate!

Cooky-cutter treats to fill or frost

Your favorite candies—fudge, pralines, brittle

Which to make first? They're all delicious!

← Top row: Date Pinwheels, Sugar Cooky, Brownies, Coconut Kiss;
Second row: Creamy Praline Patty, Gingersnaps, Sandies,
Jam Shortbread Cooky; Third row: Sugar Cooky, Apricot Pastries,
Sugar Cooky, Peanut Brittle; Fourth row: Cherry Divinity,
Brown-eyed Susan, Chocolate Crinkles, Ginger Cream;
Bottom row: Toffee Bars, Sugar Cooky, Cherry Wink, Sandies.

Drop cookies

Cherry Winks

⅓ cup shortening
½ cup sugar
1 teaspoon grated lemon peel
1 teaspoon vanilla
1 egg
2 tablespoons milk
• • •
1 cup sifted enriched flour
½ teaspoon baking powder
¼ teaspoon soda
¼ teaspoon salt
½ cup seedless raisins
½ cup chopped California walnuts
• • •
1½ cups wheat flakes, slightly crushed
Candied cherries

Thoroughly cream together shortening, sugar, lemon peel, and vanilla. Add egg and milk; beat thoroughly. Sift dry ingredients together; add to creamed mixture, mixing well. Stir in raisins and nuts. Drop by teaspoons onto crushed wheat flakes; toss lightly to coat. Place on greased cooky sheet about 2 inches apart. Top each with a candied-cherry half. Bake in hot oven (400°) about 12 minutes. Cool slightly before removing from pan. Makes about 3 dozen.

Crunchy Date Rounds

½ cup shortening
½ cup granulated sugar
¼ cup brown sugar
1 egg
1 teaspoon vanilla
1¼ cups sifted enriched flour
½ teaspoon soda
½ teaspoon salt
½ cup broken California walnuts
½ cup chopped pitted dates
1½ cups sugared cereal flakes, coarsely crushed

Thoroughly cream shortening and sugars. Add egg and vanilla; beat well. Sift together dry ingredients; gradually add to creamed mixture, blending well. Stir in nuts and dates. Drop from teaspoon into crushed flakes, rolling to coat well. Place 2 inches apart on ungreased cooky sheet. Top with walnut halves, if desired. Bake in moderate oven (375°) 12 to 15 minutes, or till top springs back when lightly touched. Cool before removing from pan. Makes 3 dozen.

Hermits

1 cup shortening
2 cups brown sugar
2 eggs
3½ cups sifted enriched flour
1 teaspoon baking powder
1 teaspoon soda
½ teaspoon salt
2 teaspoons cinnamon
1 teaspoon nutmeg
½ cup sour milk* or buttermilk
1 cup broken California walnuts
2 cups seeded raisins
1 cup dates, cut up

Thoroughly cream shortening and sugar; add eggs and beat well. Sift dry ingredients together; add to creamed mixture alternately with sour milk. Add nuts and fruits; drop by heaping teaspoons onto greased cooky sheet. Bake in moderate oven (375°) 10 to 12 minutes. Makes about 6 dozen.

*Add 2 teaspoons vinegar to ½ cup milk.

Good drop cookies—a cooky-jar raider's dream come true!

Crunchy Date Rounds

Bound to be a rush to the cooky jar or lunch box that holds these delicious cookies! They're full of dates and walnuts, have crisp cereal jackets. California walnut halves make the trim.

Oatmeal Cookies

These are just as you remember them from childhood days—wonderful!—

    1 cup shortening
    1½ cups brown sugar
    2 eggs
    ½ cup buttermilk*
    1¾ cups sifted enriched flour
    1 teaspoon soda*
    1 teaspoon baking powder*
    1 teaspoon salt
    1 teaspoon cinnamon
    1 teaspoon nutmeg
    3 cups quick-cooking rolled oats
    ½ cup raisins
    ½ cup chopped California walnuts

Cream together shortening, brown sugar, and eggs till light and fluffy. Stir in buttermilk. Sift together flour, soda, baking powder, salt, and spices; stir into creamed mixture. Stir in rolled oats, raisins, and nuts.

Drop from tablespoon 2 inches apart on greased cooky sheet. Top each with walnut half, if desired. Bake in hot oven (400°) about 8 minutes or till lightly browned. Cool slightly and remove from pan. Makes about 5 dozen.

*Or use ½ cup sweet milk; reduce soda to ¼ teaspoon and increase measure of baking powder to 2 teaspoons.

Coconut Kisses

Beat 2 egg whites with dash salt till soft peaks form; gradually add 1 cup sugar, beating to stiff peaks. Add ½ teaspoon vanilla. Fold in 2 cups corn flakes, one 3½-ounce can (1¼ cups) flaked coconut, and ½ cup chopped walnuts. Drop from teaspoon onto well-greased cooky sheet. Bake at 350° about 20 minutes. Remove cookies immediately. (If cookies stick, return to oven to soften.) Trim with spiral of melted chocolate, if desired. Makes 1½ dozen.

Speedy Coconut Macaroons

Mix one 8-ounce package shredded coconut and ⅔ cup sweetened condensed milk; add 1 teaspoon vanilla. Drop from teaspoon onto *well-greased* baking sheet about 1 inch apart. Bake at 350° 8 to 10 minutes. Let cool slightly; remove to rack. Makes about 24.

Caramel Chews

Melt 36 vanilla caramels in 3 tablespoons light cream over simmering water; stir occasionally. Toss together 1 cup *each* corn flakes, crisp rice cereal, flaked coconut, and chopped pecans; pour caramel mixture over. Mix with buttered spoon. Drop from teaspoon onto waxed paper. Makes 24.

Ginger Creams

¼ cup shortening
½ cup sugar
1 egg
⅓ cup molasses
2 cups sifted enriched flour
½ teaspoon soda
½ teaspoon salt
1 teaspoon ginger
½ teaspoon cinnamon
½ teaspoon cloves
½ cup water

Cream together shortening and sugar; beat in egg. Stir in molasses. Sift dry ingredients; add alternately with water. Drop from teaspoon 2 inches apart on greased cooky sheet. Bake at 400° about 8 minutes. While slightly warm, frost with Confectioners' Icing. Top with pecan halves. Makes 3 dozen.

Chocolate Chippers

Cream together ½ cup shortening, ½ cup granulated sugar, ¼ cup brown sugar, 1 egg, and 1 teaspoon vanilla till fluffy.

Sift together 1 cup sifted enriched flour, ¾ teaspoon salt, and ½ teaspoon soda; stir into creamed mixture, blending well.

Stir in one 6-ounce package (1 cup) semi-sweet chocolate pieces, ½ cup crushed peppermint-stick candy (optional), and ½ cup broken walnuts. Drop from teaspoon 2 inches apart on greased cooky sheet. Bake at 375° 10 to 12 minutes. Remove from pan immediately. Makes about 4 dozen.

Chocolate Crinkles

½ cup shortening
1⅔ cups granulated sugar
2 teaspoons vanilla
2 eggs
2 1-ounce squares unsweetened chocolate, melted
2 cups sifted enriched flour
2 teaspoons baking powder
½ teaspoon salt
⅓ cup milk
½ cup chopped walnuts
Sifted confectioners' sugar

Thoroughly cream shortening, sugar, and vanilla. Beat in eggs, then chocolate. Sift together dry ingredients; blend in alternately with milk. Add nuts. Chill 3 hours. Form in 1-inch balls. Roll in confectioners' sugar. Place on greased cooky sheet 2 to 3 inches apart. Bake at 350° about 15 minutes. Cool slightly; remove from pan. Makes 4 dozen.

Gingersnaps

¾ cup shortening
1 cup brown sugar
¼ cup molasses
1 egg
2¼ cups sifted enriched flour
2 teaspoons soda
½ teaspoon salt
1 teaspoon ginger
1 teaspoon cinnamon
½ teaspoon cloves

Cream together first 4 ingredients till fluffy. Sift together dry ingredients; stir into molasses mixture. Form in small balls. Roll in granulated sugar and place 2 inches apart on greased cooky sheet. Bake in moderate oven (375°) about 10 minutes. Cool slightly; remove from pan. Makes about 5 dozen.

Peanut-butter Cookies

Thoroughly cream together 1 cup shortening, 1 cup granulated sugar, 1 cup brown sugar, 2 eggs, and 1 teaspoon vanilla. Stir in 1 cup peanut butter.

Sift together 3 cups sifted enriched flour,* 2 teaspoons soda, and ½ teaspoon salt. Stir into creamed mixture. Drop by rounded teaspoons on ungreased cooky sheet. Press with back of floured fork to make crisscross. Bake at 350° about 10 minutes or till light brown. Makes about 5 dozen.

*For richer cookies, use 2 cups flour.

Sandies

Cream 1 cup butter or margarine and ⅓ cup sugar; add 2 teaspoons vanilla and 2 teaspoons water. Add 2 cups sifted enriched flour; mix well. Stir in 1 cup chopped pecans. Shape into small balls or "fingers." Bake on ungreased cooky sheet in slow oven (325°) about 20 minutes. Remove to rack.

Cool slightly. Roll in confectioners' sugar. If desired, dip one end of each "finger" in thin chocolate icing. Makes 3 dozen.

Brown-eyed Susans

Cream ¾ cup soft butter, ½ cup sugar, 1 egg, 1 teaspoon vanilla, and ¼ teaspoon salt. Stir in 1¾ cups sifted enriched flour. Chill 1 hour. Shape in 1-inch balls.

Place on ungreased cooky sheet. Top each with a chocolate-mint candy wafer (not cream-filled)—takes one 7-ounce package.

Bake in hot oven (400°) 8 to 10 minutes. Remove from pan. Makes 4 dozen.

Refrigerator cookies

Oatmeal Crisps

Calling all kids! You'll love these good cookies with a mug of milk—

1 cup shortening
1 cup brown sugar
1 cup granulated sugar
2 eggs
1 teaspoon vanilla
. . .
1½ cups sifted enriched flour
1 teaspoon salt
1 teaspoon soda
3 cups quick-cooking rolled oats
½ cup chopped California walnuts

Thoroughly cream shortening and sugars. Add eggs and vanilla. Beat well. Sift together flour, salt, and soda; add to creamed mixture. Stir in rolled oats and nuts. Mix well.

Form dough in rolls, 1 to 1½ inches in diameter. Wrap in waxed paper, aluminum foil, or saran wrapping. Chill thoroughly.

With sharp knife, slice cookies about ¼ inch thick. Bake on ungreased cooky sheet in moderate oven (350°) 10 minutes or till lightly browned. Makes about 5 dozen.

Spicy Refrigerator Thins

1 cup shortening
½ cup granulated sugar
½ cup brown sugar
1 egg
. . .
2¼ cups sifted enriched flour
½ teaspoon soda
½ teaspoon salt
2 teaspoons cinnamon
¼ teaspoon nutmeg
¼ teaspoon cloves
½ cup finely chopped walnuts

Cream together shortening and sugars; add egg and beat well. Sift together dry ingredients; stir into creamed mixture. Add nuts. Shape in rolls about 2½ inches across. Wrap in waxed paper; chill thoroughly.

Slice *very thin*, ⅛ inch or less. Bake 1 inch apart on lightly greased cooky sheet in moderate oven (375°) 5 to 7 minutes or till delicately browned. Remove at once to rack. Makes 5 to 6 dozen.

Date Pinwheels

½ cup butter or margarine
½ cup brown sugar
½ cup granulated sugar
1 egg
½ teaspoon vanilla
2 cups sifted enriched flour
½ teaspoon soda
½ teaspoon salt
1 recipe Date Filling

Thoroughly cream together butter and sugars. Add egg and vanilla; beat well. Sift together dry ingredients; stir into creamed mixture. Chill. Divide dough in half.

On lightly floured surface, roll one part in 12x8-inch rectangle, about ¼ inch thick. Spread half of Date Filling evenly over dough. Begin at long edge, roll like jelly roll. Repeat with remaining dough. Wrap rolls in waxed paper. Chill several hours. Slice ¼ inch thick. Bake on greased cooky sheet at 400° about 8 minutes. Makes 5 dozen.

Date Filling: In saucepan, combine 1 pound pitted dates, cut up, ½ cup sugar, and ½ cup water. Cook and stir till mixture boils and thickens slightly. Cool. Just before using, add ½ cup finely chopped walnuts.

Lemon-Pecan Dainties

⅔ cup shortening
1 cup sugar
1 egg
1 tablespoon grated lemon peel
1 tablespoon lemon juice
. . .
2 cups sifted enriched flour
1 teaspoon baking powder
½ teaspoon salt
. . .
1 cup finely chopped pecans

Thoroughly cream shortening and sugar; add egg, lemon peel, and lemon juice; beat well. Sift together dry ingredients; add to creamed mixture; mix well. Stir in nuts.

Shape in rolls 2 inches across. Chill thoroughly. Slice very thin. Bake on greased cooky sheet in moderate oven (350°) 12 to 15 minutes. Cool slightly before removing from pan. Makes 5 dozen cookies.

Best-ever bar cookies

Brownies (*Fudge-type*)

½ cup butter or margarine
1 cup sugar
2 eggs
2 1-ounce squares unsweetened chocolate, melted
1 teaspoon vanilla
½ cup sifted enriched flour
½ cup chopped California walnuts

Cream butter and sugar; beat in eggs. Blend in chocolate, vanilla, and flour. Add walnuts. Bake in greased 8x8x2-inch pan at 325° about 35 minutes. Cool. Cut in 16 squares.

Brownies (*Cake-type*)

½ cup shortening
2 1-ounce squares unsweetened chocolate
¾ cup sifted enriched flour
½ teaspoon baking powder
½ teaspoon salt
2 eggs
1 cup sugar
1 teaspoon vanilla
1 cup broken California walnuts

Melt shortening and chocolate together over hot water; cool. Sift together flour, baking powder, and salt. Beat eggs till light; stir in sugar, then blend in chocolate mixture; stir in flour mixture, vanilla, and nuts. Pour into greased 8x8x2-inch pan. Bake at 350° for 30 to 35 minutes. Cool; cut in 16 squares.

Butterscotch Brownies

1 cup brown sugar
1 teaspoon vanilla
1 well-beaten egg
½ cup sifted enriched flour
¼ teaspoon salt
¼ teaspoon soda
1 cup chopped California walnuts

Add sugar, vanilla to egg; mix well. Sift flour, salt, and soda; stir in. Add nuts. Spread batter in greased 8x8x2-inch pan. Bake at 350° about 20 minutes. While warm, cut in 16 squares. Cool; remove from pan.

Toffee Bars

Almost like old-fashioned toffee candy—

1 cup butter or margarine
1 cup brown sugar
1 teaspoon vanilla
. . .
2 cups sifted enriched flour
1 6-ounce package (1 cup) semisweet chocolate pieces
1 cup chopped California walnuts

Thoroughly cream together butter, sugar, and vanilla. Add flour, mix well. Stir in chocolate and walnuts. Press mixture into ungreased 15½x10½x1-inch jelly-roll pan. Bake in moderate oven (350°) 25 minutes or until browned. While warm, cut in bars or squares. Cool before removing from pan. Makes about 5 dozen.

Coconut Diamonds

½ cup soft butter or margarine
½ cup brown sugar
½ teaspoon salt
1 cup sifted enriched flour
. . .
2 eggs
1 teaspoon vanilla
1 cup brown sugar
2 tablespoons enriched flour
½ teaspoon salt
1 3½-ounce can (1¼ cups) flaked coconut
1 cup broken California walnuts

Layer I. Cream together butter, ½ cup brown sugar, and ½ teaspoon salt. Stir in 1 cup flour. Pat dough into ungreased 13x9x2-inch pan. Bake in moderate oven (350°) 12 to 15 minutes or till lightly browned.

Layer II. Meanwhile, beat egg slightly; add vanilla. Gradually add 1 cup brown sugar, beating just till blended. Add 2 tablespoons flour and ½ teaspoon salt. Stir in coconut and walnuts. Spread over baked layer. Bake 20 to 25 minutes longer or till toothpick comes out clean. Cool. If desired, frost with lemon confectioners' icing. Cut in diamonds or squares. Makes 2 dozen.

Oatmeal Squares

1 beaten egg
½ cup granulated sugar
½ cup brown sugar
1 teaspoon vanilla or
   ½ teaspoon lemon extract
. . .
½ cup sifted enriched flour
½ teaspoon salt
½ teaspoon soda
½ teaspoon nutmeg
. . .
⅓ cup shortening, melted
1 cup quick-cooking rolled oats
½ cup chopped California walnuts

Combine egg, sugars, and extract; beat well. Sift together dry ingredients; gradually add to egg mixture, beating well. Stir in shortening, oats, and nuts. Chill dough about 1 hour. Spread ¼ inch thick on greased cooky sheet, leaving 1-inch space around edges of sheet. Bake in moderate oven (350°) till golden brown and flat in center, about 15 minutes. At once cut in squares; remove from pan and cool on rack. Makes 3 dozen.

Spicy Orange Bars

Full of spice, raisins, and nuts—

⅔ cup shortening
1½ cups brown sugar
2 eggs
2 tablespoons grated orange peel
3 tablespoons orange juice
. . .
2 cups sifted enriched flour
1 teaspoon soda
½ teaspoon salt
1 teaspoon cinnamon
½ teaspoon nutmeg
¼ teaspoon cloves
. . .
1 cup seedless raisins,
   dark or light
1 cup chopped California walnuts

Cream together shortening, sugar, and eggs. Stir in orange peel and juice. Sift together flour, soda, salt, and spices; add to creamed mixture and mix well. Stir in raisins and nuts. Spread in greased 15½x10½x1-inch jelly-roll pan. Bake in moderate oven (350°) about 30 minutes or till done. Cool. Cut in bars or diamonds. If you like, sift confectioners' sugar over tops. Makes 4 dozen.

Date-Nut Cutups

½ cup shortening
1 cup sugar
1 teaspoon vanilla
2 eggs
2 cups sifted enriched flour
2 teaspoons baking powder
½ teaspoon salt
1 teaspoon cinnamon
½ teaspoon cloves
½ teaspoon nutmeg
1 cup pitted dates, cut up, or 1 cup
   seedless raisins
½ cup chopped California walnuts

Cream first 3 ingredients. Add eggs; beat well. Sift together dry ingredients; stir in. Add dates and nuts. Divide in 4 portions.

On greased cooky sheets, spread each in 12x2½x½-inch strip (3 inches apart). Bake at 375° about 15 minutes. While warm, cut in bars; remove to rack. Makes 3 dozen.

Date Torte Cookies

Beat 2 eggs till fluffy; gradually add 1 cup sifted confectioners' sugar, beating till thick. Sift 2 tablespoons *unsifted* enriched flour, ½ teaspoon salt, and 1 teaspoon baking powder; mix in 1 cup pitted dates, cut up, and 1 cup broken walnuts. Fold into egg mixture. Spread in greased 9x9x2-inch pan.

Bake at 350° 30 to 35 minutes. Cool. Cut in 16 squares. Roll in confectioners' sugar.

Some cookies! The lunch-box crowd will love them—better watch Dad, too!

Roll 'n cut cookies

Sugar Cookies

⅔ cup shortening
¾ cup sugar
½ teaspoon grated orange peel
½ teaspoon vanilla
1 egg
4 teaspoons milk
2 cups sifted enriched flour
1½ teaspoons baking powder
¼ teaspoon salt

Thoroughly cream shortening, sugar, orange peel, and vanilla. Add egg, beat till light and fluffy. Stir in milk. Sift together dry ingredients; blend into creamed mixture. Divide dough in half. Chill 1 hour.

On lightly floured surface, roll to ⅛ inch. Cut in desired shapes with cutters. Bake on greased cooky sheet at 375° about 6 to 8 minutes. Cool slightly; remove from pan. Cool on rack. Decorate. Makes 2 dozen.

Swedish Ginger Cookies

1 cup butter or margarine
1½ cups sugar
1 egg
1½ tablespoons grated orange peel
2 tablespoons dark corn syrup
1 tablespoon water
3¼ cups sifted enriched flour
2 teaspoons soda
2 teaspoons cinnamon
1 teaspoon ginger
½ teaspoon cloves
Blanched almonds

Thoroughly cream butter and sugar. Add egg; beat till light and fluffy. Add orange peel, corn syrup, and water; mix well.

Sift dry ingredients; stir into creamed mixture. Chill dough thoroughly. On lightly floured surface, roll to ⅛ inch. Sprinkle dough with sugar; press in lightly with rolling pin. Cut in desired shapes. Place 1 inch apart on ungreased baking sheet. Top each with blanched almond half. Bake at 375° about 8 to 10 minutes. Makes 8 dozen.

Apricot Pastries

2 cups dried apricots
2 cups water
3 cups sifted enriched flour
1 tablespoon sugar
½ teaspoon salt
1 cup shortening
½ cup milk
1 package active dry yeast
1 slightly beaten egg
½ teaspoon vanilla
Confectioners' sugar

Simmer apricots in water till tender. Cool. Sift together flour, sugar, and salt; cut in shortening till mixture resembles coarse crumbs. Scald milk; cool to *warm;* add yeast and let soften. Add egg and vanilla. Add to flour mixture; mix well.

Divide dough in 4 parts. On a surface well dusted with confectioners' sugar, roll one part at a time, to 10-inch square. Cut each in sixteen 2½-inch squares; place heaping teaspoon of apricots in center of each. Pinch two opposite corners together. Place 2 inches apart on greased cooky sheet. Let stand 10 minutes. Bake in moderate oven (350°) 10 to 12 minutes. Remove immediately from pan; roll in confectioners' sugar. Cool on rack. Makes about 5 dozen.

Jam Shortbread Cookies

1 cup shortening
½ cup granulated sugar
½ cup brown sugar
2 egg yolks
3 tablespoons milk
2 teaspoons vanilla
2⅔ cups sifted enriched flour
2 teaspoons cream of tartar
1 teaspoon soda
½ teaspoon salt
½ cup commercial red-raspberry preserves or jam

Thoroughly cream shortening and sugars; add egg yolks, milk, and vanilla; beat well. Sift together dry ingredients; add to creamed mixture. Chill dough 1 hour.

On *well-floured* pastry cloth, roll *half* the dough at a time to ⅛ inch. Cut with 2-inch round cutter. Cut small hole in center of *half* the cookies. Place ½ teaspoon preserves on each plain cooky; top with cutout cooky; press edges with inverted spoon to seal. Bake, 1 inch apart, on ungreased cooky sheet at 350° 10 to 12 minutes. Makes 3½ dozen.

Make a batch of candy!

Old-time Fudge

2 cups sugar
¾ cup milk
2 1-ounce squares unsweetened chocolate
Dash salt
1 teaspoon corn syrup, light or dark

• • •

2 tablespoons butter or margarine
1 teaspoon vanilla

Butter sides of heavy 2-quart saucepan. In it combine sugar, milk, chocolate, salt, and corn syrup. Heat over medium heat, stirring constantly till sugar dissolves, chocolate melts, and mixture comes to boiling. Then cook to soft-ball stage (234°), stirring only if necessary. Immediately remove from heat; add butter and cool to lukewarm (110°) without stirring. (To speed cooling, set pan in sink of cold, *but not icy*, water.) Add vanilla.

Beat vigorously till fudge becomes very thick and starts to lose its gloss. (If you like, stir in 1 cup broken walnuts at this point.) Quickly spread in buttered shallow pan or small platter. Score in squares while warm and, if desired, top each with perfect walnut half; cut when firm.

Fudge repair: If fudge doesn't set, it was poured too soon or not cooked enough. Add ¼ cup milk, stir and recook; beat.

If fudge is smooth but becomes too stiff before pouring, knead with your hands till softened; press into buttered pan.

Old-time Fudge (*large recipe*)

Even experienced home candymakers are wary of batches larger than this—they take longer to beat, are more likely to go wrong—

3 cups sugar
1 cup milk
3 1-ounce squares unsweetened chocolate
Dash salt
2 teaspoons corn syrup, light or dark
3 tablespoons butter or margarine
1½ teaspoons vanilla

Follow the method given above, but use a heavy 3-quart saucepan.

Remarkable Fudge

4 cups sugar
1 14½-ounce can (1⅔ cups) evaporated milk
1 cup butter or margarine
1 12-ounce package (2 cups) semisweet chocolate pieces
1 pint marshmallow creme
1 teaspoon vanilla
1 cup broken California walnuts

Butter sides of heavy 3-quart saucepan. In it combine sugar, milk, and butter. Cook over medium heat to soft-ball stage (236°) stirring frequently. Remove from heat; add chocolate, marshmallow creme, vanilla, and nuts. Beat till chocolate is melted and blended. Pour into buttered 9x9x2-inch pan.* Score in squares while warm; top each with a walnut half, if desired. Cut when firm. Makes 3 dozen 1½-inch pieces.

*For thinner pieces of fudge, pour mixture into 13x9½x2-inch pan.

Opera Fudge

It's blond fudge with red cherry polka dots—

2 cups sugar
1 cup milk
½ teaspoon salt
1 tablespoon butter or margarine
1 teaspoon vanilla
½ cup marshmallow creme
½ cup chopped candied cherries

Butter sides of heavy 2-quart saucepan. In it combine sugar, milk, and salt. Heat over medium heat, stirring constantly till sugar dissolves and mixture comes to boiling. Then cook to soft-ball stage (238°), stirring only if necessary. Immediately remove from heat. Add butter and cool to lukewarm (110°) without stirring. Add vanilla. Beat vigorously until mixture begins to hold its shape. Add marshmallow creme; beat till fudge becomes very thick and starts to lose its gloss. Quickly stir in cherries and spread in buttered shallow pan or small platter. Score in squares while warm; cut when firm.

Panocha

Butter sides of heavy 2-quart saucepan. In it combine 1½ cups granulated sugar, 1 cup brown sugar, ⅓ cup light cream, ⅓ cup milk, and 2 tablespoons butter.

Heat and stir over medium heat till sugars dissolve and mixture comes to boil. Then cook to soft-ball stage (238°), stirring only if necessary. Immediately remove from heat and cool to lukewarm (110°) without stirring.

Add 1 teaspoon vanilla. Beat vigorously till fudge becomes very thick and starts to lose its gloss. Quickly stir in ½ cup broken California walnuts or pecans. Spread in buttered shallow pan or small platter. Score in squares while warm. Cut when firm.

Divinity

2 cups sugar
½ cup light corn syrup
½ cup hot water
¼ teaspoon salt
2 stiff-beaten egg whites
1 teaspoon vanilla

In heavy 2-quart saucepan combine sugar, corn syrup, water, and salt. Cook and stir till sugar dissolves and mixture comes to boiling. Then cook to hard-ball stage (250°) without stirring. Wipe crystals from sides of pan now and then. Remove from heat.

Pour *hot* syrup *slowly* over stiff-beaten whites, beating constantly at high speed with electric mixer (about 5 minutes). Add vanilla. Continue beating till mixture forms soft peaks and begins to lose its gloss.

Drop by teaspoons on waxed paper; swirl each candy to a peak. If divinity becomes too stiff for twirling, add a few drops of hot water. Makes 1½ dozen candies.

Cherry Divinity: Add vanilla to Divinity; tint with few drops red food coloring and add ½ cup chopped candied cherries.

Maple Divinity

Butter sides of heavy 2-quart saucepan. In it, cook 2 cups maple-flavored cane syrup rapidly over high heat to hard-ball stage (250°) without stirring. Remove from heat.

At once beat 2 egg whites with ¼ teaspoon salt to stiff peaks. Following directions for Divinity, add *hot* syrup to egg whites and beat. Quickly add ½ cup broken pecans; drop by teaspoons on waxed paper; swirl each candy to peak. Makes 2 dozen candies.

Candies, rich and luscious

You won't wait till Santa season to make these candies—they're so good! Remarkable Fudge squares get trim of walnut halves; in center are puffs of Divinity—white and cherry-pink; along side are Creamy Praline Patties.

Almond Butter Crunch

1 cup butter
1⅓ cups sugar
1 tablespoon light corn syrup
3 tablespoons water
1 cup *coarsely* chopped blanched almonds, toasted
4 4½-ounce bars milk chocolate, melted
1 cup *finely* chopped blanched almonds, toasted

Melt butter in heavy 2-quart saucepan. Add sugar, corn syrup, and water. Cook, stirring often, to hard-crack stage (300°)—watch closely after temperature reaches 280°. Quickly stir in coarsely chopped nuts; spread in well-greased 13x9x2-inch pan. Cool thoroughly. Turn out on waxed paper; spread top with *half* the chocolate; sprinkle with *half* of finely chopped nuts. Cover with waxed paper; invert and top with remaining chocolate and nuts. If necessary, chill to firm chocolate. Break in pieces.

Peanut Brittle

2 cups sugar
1 cup light corn syrup
2 cups unroasted (raw) Spanish peanuts*
¼ teaspoon salt
1 teaspoon butter or margarine
¼ teaspoon soda

Slowly cook sugar, corn syrup, and *1 cup water* in heavy skillet, stirring till sugar dissolves. Cook to soft-ball stage (test a few drops in *cold* water). Add peanuts and salt. Cook to hard-crack stage, stirring constantly (remove from heat while testing). Add butter and soda; stir to blend. (Mixture will bubble.) Pour onto buttered platters.

Cool partially by lifting edges with spatula. Keep spatula moving under mixture so it won't stick. When firm but still warm, turn over; pull edges to make brittle thinner in center. Break in pieces when cold.

*Or use unroasted Virginia peanuts, but you'll need to blanch these ahead. Cover with boiling water, let stand 3 minutes; run under cold water. Remove coating.

Creamy Praline Patties

2 cups sugar
¾ teaspoon soda
1 cup light cream
1½ tablespoons butter (measure exactly)
2 cups pecan halves

In *deep* 3-quart saucepan, combine sugar and soda; mix well with wooden spoon. Stir in cream carefully. Bring to boil over medium heat; stir occasionally. Reduce heat; cook and stir to soft-ball stage (234°). Double-check for soft-ball stage: Use both a candy thermometer and the cold-water test.

Remove from heat. Add butter immediately. Add pecans. Beat mixture till thick, 2 to 3 minutes. Drop from metal spoon on waxed paper. (If necessary, add a little hot water.) Makes 24 to 30 1½-inch patties.

Southern Pralines

1½ cups brown sugar
1½ cups granulated sugar
3 tablespoons dark corn syrup
1 cup milk
1 teaspoon vanilla
1½ cups pecan halves

Combine brown sugar, granulated sugar, syrup, and milk. Cook to soft-ball stage (234°). Cool 10 minutes. Add vanilla and beat by hand about 2 minutes. Add pecans and beat until mixture loses its gloss. Drop by heaping tablespoons on a single thickness of buttered aluminum foil or 3 layers of buttered waxed paper. (If necessary, add a teaspoon or so of hot water to keep candy at right stage for forming into patties.) Makes nine 3½ inch pralines.

Crunch-crust Pie has filling of mint ice cream, a "confection" crust

Chocolate-fleck Cake—just delicious! Frosting is cocoa-whipped cream

Pineapple Parfaits—refreshing flavor, ready in no time!

1-2-3 desserts

Packaged foods give you a head start!

Magic with a box of cake mix

Fruit fix-ups—a breeze to make

Glamorous pies, elegant but easy

Party puddings from a package

Chilly desserts—marvelous!

Frankly fancy desserts with no fuss!

Magic with a cake mix

Cocoa Meringue Torte

Elegant and luscious, yet so easy!—

1 package yellow-cake mix
4 egg whites
⅛ teaspoon cream of tartar
Dash salt
¾ cup sugar
¾ cup chopped California walnuts
1½ cups heavy cream
½ cup sugar
⅛ cup cocoa

Prepare cake mix according to package directions and pour into 2 paper-lined 9x1½-inch round pans. Beat egg whites, cream of tartar, and salt till soft peaks form. Add ¾ cup sugar gradually, beating until glossy and sugar is dissolved. Fold in nuts. Spread mixture carefully over batter in both pans. Bake in moderate oven (375°) 25 to 30 minutes. Cool cakes in pans 10 minutes; then remove from pans to finish cooling.

Combine heavy cream, ½ cup sugar, and cocoa. Chill 1 hour, then whip. Frost between layers, then top and sides.

Apple Upside-down Cake

2 tart red apples

• • •

¼ cup butter or margarine
½ cup honey

• • •

½ cup broken California walnuts
⅛ cup chopped maraschino cherries

• • •

1 package spice-cake mix

Core unpeeled apples and slice in rings ¼ inch thick. Melt butter in an oven-going 10-inch skillet. Add honey and the apple rings; cook 3 minutes, turning once. Sprinkle with nuts and maraschino cherries.

Prepare cake-mix batter as directed on package. Pour 2 cups batter over apples. (Bake remaining batter as cupcakes.)

Bake cake in moderate oven (350°) 30 to 35 minutes or till done. (Bake the cupcakes 20 to 25 minutes.)

Cool upside-down cake 5 minutes in pan. Turn upside down on serving plate; serve warm. Top servings with whipped cream or ice cream, if desired.

Apple Upside-down Cake.
Catch a whiff of
the spicy goodness!

Honeyed apple rings, walnuts, and cherries line the pan. (The maraschino cherries give the apples a rosy tint.) Spice cake made from a mix bakes atop. Serve this treat oven warm, fruity side up. Added ruffle: daisy chain.

Rhubarb Upside-down Cake

3 tablespoons melted butter
½ cup sugar
Few drops red food coloring (optional)
2 cups (1 pound) finely diced rhubarb
1 package white-cake mix

Combine butter, sugar, and food coloring. Add rhubarb; toss lightly. Spread in 8¼x 1¾-inch round ovenware baking dish.

Prepare cake mix according to package directions. Pour half of batter* over fruit. Bake in moderate oven (375°) about 35 minutes. Loosen edges and invert on plate. Let stand 3 to 5 minutes; then lift off baking dish. Serve warm with whipped cream.

*Bake remaining batter as cupcakes. Or use loaf-size cake mix—it just fits.

Cranberry Upside-down Cake

2 1-pound cans (4 cups) whole
    cranberry sauce
3 tablespoons butter or margarine
1 package yellow-cake mix

Break up the cranberry sauce in a buttered 13x9x2-inch baking dish, spreading sauce over bottom. Dot with butter. Prepare batter from cake mix according to package directions; pour evenly over sauce. Bake in moderate oven (350°) 30 minutes or until done. Cut in squares, turning each upside down as you place it on plate. Serve warm with Yankee Sauce (page 64).

Note: If you like, make the cranberry sauce by cooking 3 cups fresh cranberries, 1½ cups sugar, and ⅓ cup water till the skins pop, about 5 minutes. Cool.

Chocolate-fleck Cake

With coffee, this cake makes a complete dessert. See it pictured on page 114—

1 package yellow- or white-cake mix
⅓ cup chocolate shot
1½ cups heavy cream
⅔ cup instant cocoa
¼ cup finely chopped pecans

Mix batter from cake mix according to package directions; fold in chocolate shot. Bake in 2 paper-lined 8x1½-inch round pans as directed on package. For frosting, combine cream and instant cocoa; chill, then whip. Frost cooled cake, sprinkling nuts between layers. Chill till serving time.

Almond Flip-top Cake

A crisp-topped cake, good for family or company. More speed—use packaged pie filling—

2 teaspoons butter or margarine
1 tablespoon sugar
⅓ cup chopped or ready-diced almonds
1 package white- or yellow-cake mix*
1 recipe Orange Filling, page 61

Melt butter in an 8x8x2-inch pan; spread over bottom and sprinkle with sugar, then with almonds. Prepare cake mix according to package directions. Carefully pour half of batter* over nuts. Bake in moderate oven (375°) 25 to 30 minutes. Invert on rack and cool. Split into 2 layers, spread cooled Orange Filling between. Makes 9 squares.

*Bake remaining batter as cupcakes. Or use loaf-size cake mix—it just fits.

Poppy-seed Torte

1 2-ounce can (about ⅓ cup)
    poppy seed
1 cup water
1 package white-cake mix
1 package vanilla pudding
½ teaspoon vanilla
1 cup heavy cream, whipped
Confectioners' sugar

Combine poppy seed and water; let stand at least 2 hours; drain. Prepare cake mix according to package directions. Add poppy seed. Bake in 2 paper-lined 9x1½-inch round pans at 350° about 20 to 25 minutes.

Make pudding following package directions, *but using only 1¾ cups milk.* Add vanilla; cover and cool. Fold in whipped cream.

Split cooled cakes, making 4 layers; spread filling between. Chill 2 to 3 hours. To serve, sift confectioners' sugar over top.

Peanut-topped Devil's Food

Prepare 1 package devil's-food-cake mix* and bake in greased 13x9x2-inch baking dish according to package directions.

Cream together ¼ cup soft butter or margarine, ¼ cup peanut butter, and ⅔ cup brown sugar. Stir in 1 cup coarsely chopped salted peanuts. Spread mixture over warm cake in pan. Broil 5 to 6 inches from heat 5 minutes or till frosting is bubbly and slightly brown. Serve warm.

*Or use spice- or peanut-cake mix.

Ginger Peach Squares

Another time, serve the maple-peach sauce over warm squares of spice cake—

1 package gingerbread mix

. . .

1 No. 2 can (2½ cups) sliced peaches, drained
½ cup maple-flavored syrup
1 quart vanilla ice cream

Mix and bake gingerbread according to package directions. Combine drained peaches and maple-flavored syrup; heat.

Cut warm gingerbread in squares; top each serving with a scoop of vanilla ice cream and spoon the warm peach sauce over.

Makes 8 or 9 servings.

Spicy Angel Cake

1 teaspoon cinnamon
¼ teaspoon cloves
¼ teaspoon nutmeg
1 package angel-cake mix

. . .

¼ cup instant cocoa

Add spices to flour mixture of angel-cake mix; sift to blend. Prepare batter according to package directions. Pour ⅓ of the batter into ungreased 10-inch tube pan; sprinkle with half of the cocoa. Add another ⅓ of the batter and sprinkle with remaining cocoa; top with the remaining batter. Bake at temperature and time given on package; or, for speed, bake in hot oven (425°) about 25 minutes. Invert; cool thoroughly.

Chocolate-Nut Fluff Layers

Give chocolate angel cake an elegant look and a wonderful taste—frost it with chocolate-flecked whipped cream!—

1 package chocolate angel-cake mix

. . .

1 6-ounce package (1 cup) semisweet chocolate pieces

. . .

1 cup blanched almonds, halved and toasted
2 cups heavy cream, whipped

Bake cake according to package directions. Cool; cut crosswise in 3 even layers.

Melt chocolate in top of double boiler over hot water. Cool to room temperature. Fold chocolate and almonds into whipped cream, allowing chocolate to harden in flecks. Spread between cake layers, then frost top and sides. Makes 12 servings.

Coffee-Toffee Torte

1 package angel-cake mix

. . .

1 package chocolate pudding
1 to 1½ tablespoons instant coffee

. . .

1 cup heavy cream, whipped
2 ¾-ounce chocolate-coated English toffee bars, chilled and crushed

Prepare angel-cake mix and bake in 10-inch tube pan according to package directions. Invert and cool thoroughly.

In saucepan, mix pudding and instant coffee. Prepare pudding following package directions, *but using only 1⅓ cups milk.* Cool. Beat until mixture is smooth; fold in *half* of the whipped cream.

Split cake in 3 layers. Spread *half* of the pudding-cream mixture between the layers. For the frosting, fold remaining whipped cream into remaining pudding mixture; use to frost top and sides of cake. Sprinkle frosted cake with crushed toffee bars. Chill till serving time.

Makes 12 servings.

Glamorous Coffee-Toffee Torte

← Here's a high, handsome dessert that's easy for a party—folks will be clamoring for the recipe! Packaged pudding and toffee bars give you a fast start on the frosting.

Chocolate Confetti Cake

Another time, sprinkle the chocolate shot between layers of batter before baking cake—

1 package angel-cake mix
¼ cup chocolate shot

. . .

1 recipe Butter Frosting, page 58
2 1-ounce squares unsweetened chocolate, melted

Mix cake batter according to package directions; fold in chocolate shot. Bake according to directions on package. Cool thoroughly. Frost with Butter Frosting. Drizzle melted chocolate around top edge.

Chocolate Angel Layers

Prepare 1 package chocolate angel-cake mix according to package directions, mixing 1 tablespoon of instant coffee with the flour mixture. Bake in ungreased 10-inch tube pan according to package directions.

Cut cooled cake crosswise in 3 even layers. Spread Milk-chocolate Frosting between layers and on sides and top. Chill for 45 minutes or until the frosting is set.

Milk-chocolate Frosting: In top of double boiler, place one 6-ounce package semisweet chocolate pieces or six 1-ounce squares semisweet chocolate, ¼ pound (16) marshmallows, and ½ cup milk. Heat over simmering water till blended, stirring occasionally. Chill. Stir till smooth. Whip 1 cup heavy cream; fold in. Makes 3 cups.

Java Angel Cake

1 package angel-cake mix
1 tablespoon instant coffee
1 teaspoon vanilla

. . .

1 recipe Mocha Topping

Prepare batter from angel-cake mix according to package directions, dissolving 1 tablespoon instant coffee in the water. Add vanilla. Bake following package directions. Invert and cool thoroughly.

For *Mocha Topping,* combine 1½ cups heavy cream, 3 tablespoons sugar, 2 to 3 teaspoons instant coffee, and ¾ teaspoon vanilla. Whip till mixture is fluffy; spread on cooled cake. Top with broken California walnuts. Chill till serving time.

Fruit fix-ups

Indian Summer Sauce

Refreshing! It's a can-opener special—

- 1 1-pound can (2 cups) purple plums, drained
- 1 1-pound can (2 cups) sliced peaches, drained
- 1 1-pound can (2 cups) whole apricots
- 1 9-ounce can (1 cup) pineapple tidbits
- ½ cup seedless green grapes
- 1 tablespoon lemon juice

Combine fruits and lemon juice; chill. If desired, dash in aromatic bitters to taste. Pass crisp cookies. Makes 8 to 10 servings.

A-B-C Dessert Salad

Three layers are put together at one time—

- 1 No. 2 can (2½ cups) pineapple tidbits
- 1 package lime-flavored gelatin
- 2 cups tiny marshmallows
- 1 cup heavy cream, whipped

Drain pineapple, reserving syrup. Add water to syrup to make 2 cups; heat to boiling; add gelatin and stir to dissolve. Add pineapple; pour into 10x6x1½-inch baking dish. Cover immediately with a layer of marshmallows. Spread top with whipped cream; chill till firm. Cut in 8 to 10 squares.

You can't beat Cantaloupe Sundae for a lightning dessert! Glamorous and good!

← You'll like the chilly, rich goodness of an old-fashioned cantaloupe sundae. Have melon icicle-cold, of course. Cut in half; remove seeds. Pile center high with scoops of vanilla ice cream. That's all!

Or give melon a fruit partner of grapes or strawberries, blueberries or raspberries. Garnish with plume of mint.

Try this summer special! Slice → cantaloupe or honeydew melon in circles; fill rings with raspberry sherbet. Surround with grapes and mint sprigs.

Another simple ending for mealtime: a rainbow of melon balls in gold, pink, and emerald — doubly refreshing served in parfait glasses with bubbly ginger ale poured over.

Ginger Fruit Cocktail

No ordinary fruit cup here! Chilly ginger ale adds tingling fizz—

1 fully ripe, flecked-with-brown banana
Lemon juice
1 1-pound can (2 cups) fruit cocktail, well chilled and drained
1 cup fresh strawberries, halved and chilled
1 cup honeydew, cantaloupe, or watermelon balls, chilled

. . .

1 small bottle (about 1 cup) ginger ale, chilled
Aromatic bitters (optional)

Peel banana; slice on bias. Dip banana slices in lemon juice to keep color bright. Combine with remaining fruits, mixing gently. Cover; keep chilled till serving time. Just before serving, pour ginger ale over fruit. Dash with aromatic bitters. Ladle into chilled sherbets. Makes 6 servings.

Apple-Date Crumble

1 packet or ½ package date-muffin mix
¼ cup brown sugar
1 teaspoon cinnamon
1 teaspoon nutmeg

. . .

4 cups sliced pared tart apples
¼ cup water
1 tablespoon lemon juice

Combine muffin mix, brown sugar, and spices. Spread *half* the apples in bottom of buttered 8-inch round baking dish; top with *half* the dry muffin mixture. Repeat layers. Combine water and lemon juice; drizzle over all. Bake in moderate oven (375°) 35 to 40 minutes. Serve warm with cream or ice cream. Makes 6 to 8 servings.

Fig-cooky Cream

14 fig-bar cookies, cut in fourths
1 No. 2½ can (3½ cups) fruit cocktail, drained
2 tablespoons lemon juice
1 teaspoon vanilla

. . .

1 cup heavy cream, whipped

Combine first 4 ingredients. Fold in whipped cream. Pile into sherbets; chill. Trim with maraschino cherries. Makes 6 servings.

Quick Frosty Ambrosia

Partially thaw one 14-ounce can frozen pineapple chunks. Toss with 1 banana, sliced, 1 cup halved fresh strawberries, and ½ cup moist shredded coconut. Serve while pineapple is still frosty. Makes 4 servings.

Orange Cherry Cobbler

1 No. 2 can (2½ cups) cherry-pie-filling mix
2 teaspoons lemon juice
¼ teaspoon cinnamon
¼ cup water
½ package (1 packet) orange-muffin mix
½ cup broken pecans

Combine first 4 ingredients in 10x6x1½-inch baking dish; heat 15 minutes in hot oven (400°). Meanwhile prepare batter from muffin mix according to package directions; stir in nuts. Spoon in mounds or spread over *hot* cherry filling. Bake in hot oven (400°) 15 to 20 minutes. Serve warm. Pass cream.

Banana Brittle Dessert

Peel 2 fully ripe bananas; slice thinly. Fold banana slices, ¾ cup crushed peanut brittle, and 1 teaspoon vanilla into 1 cup heavy cream, whipped. Spoon into sherbets. Chill 1 hour. Makes 4 servings.

Cinnamon Applesauce Revel

2 packages lemon-flavored gelatin
½ cup red cinnamon candies
2½ cups boiling water
2 cups unsweetened applesauce
1 tablespoon lemon juice
Dash salt
½ cup broken California walnuts
½ cup heavy cream, whipped

Dissolve gelatin and candies in boiling water. Stir in next 3 ingredients; chill till partially set. Stir in walnuts. Pour into 10x6x1½-inch dish. Spoon whipped cream atop; swirl through gelatin. Chill till firm. Cut in 8 squares. Pass whipped cream.

Peach Shortcake Dessert Cups

Fill spongecake dessert cups (from a package) with sweetened whipped cream. Top with chilled canned peach halves, hollow side up. Add dollop of whipped cream.

Pies, simple but special

Crunch-crust Pie

1 6-ounce package (1 cup) semisweet
  chocolate pieces
3 tablespoons butter or margarine
2 cups crisp rice cereal
1 quart green mint ice cream, slightly
  softened
1 1-ounce square unsweetened chocolate,
  shaved

In top of double boiler, melt chocolate and
butter over hot water, stirring to blend. Add
rice cereal; mix well. Press into unbuttered
9-inch pie plate; chill till firm.

Let crust stand at room temperature 5
minutes; fill with alternating layers of ice
cream and shaved chocolate. Serve at once.

Note: Or freeze filled pie; let stand at
room temperature 10 to 15 minutes; serve.

Chocolate Marble Pie

1 package chocolate chiffon-pie filling
1 to 2 teaspoons instant coffee (optional)
1 9-inch Coconut Crust, page 71
½ cup heavy cream, whipped

Prepare chiffon-pie filling according to
package directions, but *add instant coffee to the
hot milk*. Pour into Coconut Crust. Spread
whipped cream over top; swirl cream
through filling to give marbled effect. Chill
until set, about 2 hours.

Fancy Cherry Pie

1 No. 2 can (2½ cups) frozen tart
  red pitted cherries
⅓ cup sugar
1½ tablespoons cornstarch
Baked 8-inch Pastry Shell and Cutouts

Drain cherries; reserve syrup. Add water to
syrup, if needed, to measure 1 cup. Combine ¾ *cup of the syrup* and sugar; heat to
boiling. Add cherries; cook 2 minutes. Mix
cornstarch with remaining ¼ cup cold
syrup; stir into hot mixture. Cook and stir
till thick and clear. Cool till just warm.
Pour into baked Pastry Shell. Let stand
several hours. Top with baked Cutouts.

Pastry Shell and Cutouts

Prepare 2 sticks pastry mix according to
package directions. Roll out *half* of pastry to
⅛ inch; line 8-inch pie plate. Trim crust
even with edge of pie plate. Prick bottom
and sides well with fork. Roll remaining
pastry. With *tiny* cutter, cut out pastry
hearts; overlap hearts around moistened
rim of unbaked pastry shell.

Using cooky cutters or cardboard pat-
terns, make cutouts for top of pie; place on
baking sheet. Bake in very hot oven (450°)
8 to 10 minutes for pie shell and about 5 minutes for cutouts or till golden brown. Cool.

*From the Pennsylvania Dutch comes this pair of
country-kitchen pies—easy to make and good!*

Short cuts from package
and can put these pies in
the easy-to-do class.

Fancy Cherry Pie is just
that! It gets party-going
look from collar of tiny
pastry hearts marching
around rim and pastry cutouts atop the filling.

In Peach Crumb Pie,
golden canned peach halves
are partly hidden beneath
a tasty cinnamon topping.

Speedy Apple Pie—
use packaged helpers

This pie lives up to its name! The crust and spicy nut-crumb topper are a breeze with pastry-mix sticks. Canned pie apples (they come already sliced) are the no-work filling. Serve with cheese triangles. Or top with scoops of vanilla ice cream.

Peach Crumb Pie

1 stick pastry mix
½ cup enriched flour
¼ cup granulated sugar
¼ cup brown sugar
½ teaspoon cinnamon
¼ cup butter or margarine
½ cup broken California walnuts
1 No. 2½ can (3½ cups) peach halves
1 tablespoon lemon juice

Prepare pastry according to package directions; line 8-inch pie plate; crimp edge.

Combine flour, sugars, and cinnamon. With pastry blender, cut in butter till like coarse crumbs. Add nuts to *half* of crumb mixture and spread in bottom of unbaked pastry shell. Drain peaches; arrange, cut side down, over crumbs. Sprinkle with lemon juice. Top with remaining crumbs. Bake at 425° about 45 minutes (cover edge of crust with foil for last 10 minutes of baking).

Speedy Apple Pie

2 sticks pastry mix
1 No. 2 can (2½ cups) sliced pie
   apples, drained
⅓ cup brown sugar
⅓ cup granulated sugar
⅓ cup broken California walnuts
½ teaspoon cinnamon
Dash salt

· · ·

3 tablespoons maple-flavored syrup

Prepare *one* stick of the pastry mix according to package directions. Line 8-inch pie plate with pastry; flute edge. Arrange apples in the unbaked shell.

With fork, combine remaining pastry-mix stick with sugars, nuts, cinnamon, and salt till crumbly; sprinkle over apples. Drizzle with syrup. Bake in hot oven (425°) 10 minutes; completely cover top with aluminum foil; bake 15 minutes more. Serve warm.

Make your own tart pans! You fashion the frilly pastry shells with aluminum foil. No pans to wash—just toss away the foil!

For 5 tarts, use 1 stick pastry mix. Roll to ⅛ inch. Cut in 5-inch circles. Lightly press pastry round atop same-size circle of heavy-duty aluminum foil. Prick pastry with fork.

Now you're ready to shape the pans *and* tarts. Holding pastry and foil together, flute edges to form in tart shells—it will take about 5 crimps. Place on cooky sheet.

Bake tart shells in very hot oven (450°) 10 minutes or till pastry is golden brown. Cool baked shells on wire rack. Remove aluminum foil. Next comes the filling—here it's cherry.

Cherry Tarts

Just 20 minutes from inspiration to table—including the baked pastry!—

5 or 6 baked tart shells

• • •

1 3-ounce package cream cheese, softened
1 No. 2 can (2½ cups) cherry-pie filling

Make tart shells as directed at left. Spread softened cream cheese on bottoms of baked tart shells. Spoon cherry-pie filling into shells. Chill if you like. Top with dollops of whipped cream cheese. Makes 5 or 6 servings.

Ice Cream in Choco Tarts

Scrumptious! Pastry shells get a coating of chocolate and toasted nuts, filling of peppermint-stick ice cream—

8 baked tart shells

• • •

1 6-ounce package (1 cup) semisweet chocolate pieces
⅓ cup chopped blanched almonds, toasted

• • •

1 quart peppermint-stick ice cream
Semisweet chocolate curls

Prepare tart shells as directed at left. Melt chocolate over hot water. Spread melted chocolate over bottom and sides of each tart; sprinkle with almonds. Cool.

Just before serving, fill each tart with scoop of ice cream. Trim with chocolate curls. Makes 8 servings.

Vanilla-fluff Tarts

Busy day? Try this dessert—delicious!—

6 to 8 baked tart shells
1 package vanilla pudding
½ teaspoon vanilla

• • •

½ cup heavy cream, whipped

Make tart shells as directed at left. Prepare pudding according to package directions, but *decrease milk to 1¾ cups*. Add vanilla. Chill; beat smooth; fold in whipped cream. Spoon into baked tart shells. Garnish each tart with shaved chocolate curls.

Makes 5 servings.

Dress-ups for packaged pudding

Creamy Apricot Dessert—whip up in a jiffy! For jaunty trim, poke in 3 vanilla wafers around edge of each pudding. Serve topped with whipped cream, California walnuts.

Ambrosia Pudding

1 package instant vanilla pudding
⅔ cup orange juice
1 9-ounce can (1 cup) crushed pineapple
1 cup heavy cream, whipped
Vanilla wafers
½ cup flaked coconut, toasted

Prepare pudding following the package directions, *using ⅔ cup orange juice for the liquid.* Add pineapple. Fold in whipped cream. Pile in 6 sherbets. Tuck wafers around sides. Chill. Top with coconut.

Quick Pudding Parfaits

Prepare one 3- or 3¼-ounce package vanilla pudding according to package directions, *but using only 1¾ cups milk;* chill. Beat smooth; fold in 1 cup heavy cream, whipped, and 1 teaspoon vanilla. In parfait glasses, alternate layers of chilled sliced strawberries (2 cups) and pudding. Makes 6 servings.

Cranberry Danish Cream

1 package currant-raspberry-flavored
  Danish dessert
1 pint cranberry-juice cocktail
1 package vanilla rennet-custard
½ cup heavy cream, whipped (optional)
Slivered blanched almonds, toasted
  (optional)

Prepare Danish dessert according to directions, *but using cranberry-juice cocktail for the liquid.* Cool about 30 minutes.

Meanwhile prepare rennet-custard according to directions. Pour into sherbets. Let stand 15 to 20 minutes. Spoon Danish dessert *carefully* over custard; chill till set, about 3 hours. Top with fluffs of whipped cream and almonds. Serves 6 to 8.

Creamy Apricot Dessert

Next time try unsweetened pineapple juice—

1 3- or 3¼-ounce package vanilla
  pudding
1 12-ounce can (1½ cups) apricot nectar
1 cup heavy cream, whipped
¼ cup broken California walnuts

Prepare pudding following package directions, but *use 1½ cups apricot nectar instead of milk.* Cool thoroughly. Beat smooth. Fold in whipped cream and nuts; chill. Spoon into sherbets. Makes 4 servings.

Mandarin Orange Dessert

Takes just a few minutes with instant pudding and canned mandarin oranges—

1 package instant vanilla pudding
3 cups milk
2 11-ounce cans (2½ cups) mandarin
  orange sections, drained

Combine instant pudding and milk according to package directions. Pour into serving bowl and let stand till set, about 10 minutes or till slightly thicker than custard sauce. Serve over mandarin orange sections, using a few for trim. Makes 5 or 6 servings.

Chilly desserts—a snap!

Easy Pineapple Parfaits

Open a couple of cans—turn out a "million-dollar" dessert! See it on page 115—

- 1 1-pound can (2 cups) fruit cocktail, chilled, well drained
- 1 6-ounce can frozen pineapple-juice concentrate
- • • •
- 1 quart vanilla ice cream

Combine fruit cocktail and pineapple concentrate. Alternate layers of ice cream and fruit mixture in chilled parfait glasses. Garnish with pineapple chunks and maraschino cherries. Makes 6 servings.

Spicy Ice-cream Peach Cups

Try spicy ice cream on apple crisp, too—

- 1 quart vanilla ice cream
- 1 teaspoon cinnamon
- 6 spongecake dessert cups
- 3 large peaches, peeled, sliced, and sweetened

Stir ice cream just to soften; blend in cinnamon. Freeze till firm. Fill dessert cups (from a package) with the ice cream; spoon peach slices over all. Makes 6 servings.

Frosty Brittle Crunch—simple! And so tasty, you'll make it often.

Cream-cheese Freeze

A real smoothie! And just four ingredients—

- 2 3-ounce packages cream cheese, softened
- ⅔ cup sugar
- 2½ teaspoons vanilla
- 2 cups light cream

Cream together the cheese, sugar, and vanilla. Slowly add the cream, mixing thoroughly. Freeze in refrigerator tray till firm; break in chunks and beat with electric mixer till smooth.* Return to tray; freeze until firm. Makes 6 servings.

*Or freeze till partially frozen; beat smooth with rotary beater.

Strawberry Parfaits

Drain one 10-ounce package frozen strawberries, thawed; reserve juice. Dissolve 1 package strawberry-flavored gelatin in 1 cup hot water. Add ¼ cup cold water, 1 tablespoon lemon juice, dash salt, and reserved juice. Chill till partially set.

Whip till fluffy; fold in 1 cup heavy cream, whipped, and drained strawberries. Spoon into parfait glasses, alternating layers of gelatin mixture with one 10-ounce package frozen strawberries, *partially thawed* (still some crystals remaining). Chill parfaits 1 to 2 hours. Makes 6 servings.

Strawberry Freeze

Combine 2 cups dairy sour cream, one 10-ounce package frozen strawberries (partially thawed), and 1 cup sugar. Partially freeze in 1-quart refrigerator tray. Beat smooth, about 1 minute. Return to tray and freeze firm. Makes 6 servings.

It's frozen whipped cream flecked with candy!
Frosty Brittle Crunch: Crush ½ pound peanut brittle; fold into 2 cups heavy cream, whipped.
Pour mixture into a 1-quart refrigerator tray. Freeze till firm; do not stir. Makes 6 servings.

Fudge Ribbon Parfaits

½ pound (about 32) marshmallows
2 1-ounce squares unsweetened chocolate
1 6-ounce can (⅔ cup) evaporated milk
1 teaspoon vanilla
. . .
1 quart vanilla ice cream
1 pint chocolate ice cream

In double boiler heat marshmallows, chocolate, and *2 tablespoons* of the milk, stirring frequently, until blended. Remove from heat; gradually stir in remaining milk and vanilla. Cool. In chilled parfait glasses, alternate fudge sauce, vanilla ice cream, and chocolate ice cream. Top with fluffs of whipped cream. Makes 8 servings.

One-step Sherbet

Use one 10-ounce package frozen raspberries *or* one 14-ounce can frozen pineapple. Break up frozen fruit, place in blender. Turn blender on. With rubber spatula, work fruit down slowly until smooth and of sherbet consistency (about 1 minute for raspberries, 3 minutes for pineapple). Serve immediately.

For more solid sherbet, empty into refrigerator tray; freeze till ready to serve. Makes about 3 servings.

Double-mint Fluff

3 egg whites
1 10-ounce jar (about 1 cup) mint jelly
1½ tablespoons lemon juice
Few drops green food coloring
1 cup heavy cream, whipped

Beat egg whites till foamy; gradually add ½ cup of the jelly (reserve remainder), beating till stiff. Add lemon juice. Tint with coloring. Fold in whipped cream. Freeze firm in refrigerator tray. Melt reserved jelly, stirring occasionally. Serve over ice cream. Makes about 8 servings.

Frozen Peacharoon Torte

Combine 2 cups mashed peaches, 1 to 1¼ cups sugar, and 1 tablespoon lemon juice. Fold in 1 cup heavy cream, whipped.

Place ½ cup coarse macaroon crumbs in bottom of 1-quart refrigerator tray; pour in peach mixture. Top with additional ½ cup macaroon crumbs. Freeze firm, about 4 to 6 hours. Makes 6 to 8 servings.

Hurry-up Eclairs go together fast—and make a fine finale!

Make the shells from cream-puff mix; the filling is packaged pudding with whipped cream folded in. Frost the tops with a confectioners' icing and sprinkle with candy confetti decorettes. Offer a bowl of salted mixed nuts for nibbling.

Frankly fancy desserts

Hurry-up Eclairs

½ 8½-ounce package (1 stick)
   cream-puff mix
1 package vanilla pudding
1 cup heavy cream, whipped
½ teaspoon vanilla
Confectioners' sugar
1 slightly beaten egg white
Multicolored candy decorettes

Prepare cream-puff mix and bake according to the package directions for eclairs. Cool thoroughly and split.

Prepare vanilla pudding according to package directions, but *using only 1¾ cups milk;* chill. Beat pudding smooth; fold in whipped cream and vanilla. Fill eclairs.

Add enough confectioners' sugar to slightly beaten egg white to make frosting of spreading consistency. Frost tops of eclairs and sprinkle with candy decorettes for a confetti effect. Chill till serving time. Makes 8 eclairs.

Cocktail Pie

Vanilla wafers (about 32)
2 cups dairy sour cream
½ cup sugar
1 teaspoon vanilla
1 No. 2½ can (3½ cups) fruit
   cocktail, well drained

Line bottom and sides of 9-inch pie plate with whole vanilla wafers. Combine sour cream, sugar, and vanilla; fold in drained fruit. Pour into cooky-lined pie plate. Bake in moderate oven (350°) about 25 minutes or till set. Cool, then chill thoroughly.

Springtime Berry Bowl

Partially thaw one 14-ounce can frozen pineapple chunks; drain, reserving syrup.

In crystal serving bowl, arrange 1 pint fresh sliced strawberries, then pineapple. Top with 1 pint fresh red raspberries. Pour pineapple syrup over. Makes 6 servings.

To-each-his-own Alaskas

1 pint vanilla ice cream
½ cup crushed peppermint candy or chopped California walnuts

. . .

1 recipe Meringue
4 cake dessert cups (1 package)

Scoop ice cream in 4 balls. Roll in candy or walnuts. Freeze firm.

Prepare Meringue as for pie, using 3 egg whites—see step-by-step recipe, page 73.

Put dessert cups on ungreased baking sheet; place ice-cream ball in each. *Quickly* swirl meringue over top and sides, sealing to cake. Bake in extremely hot oven (500°) 2 minutes or till meringue is lightly browned. Serve immediately.

Rainbow Sundae Buffet

Prepare 9-inch Meringue Shell following recipe, page 73. Bake and cool as directed.

Scoop ice cream of several flavors and colors into shallow pan and freeze firm.

At party time, fill meringue shell with the rainbow of ice creams and pass an assortment of In-a-minute Sundae Sauces.

In-a-minute Sundae Sauces: Simply stir your favorite fruit preserves for easy spooning over ice cream. Could be peach, cherry, raspberry—your choice!

Coffee Clouds

A melt-in-your-mouth dessert! When minutes count, buy meringue shells at bake shop—

3 egg whites
1 teaspoon vanilla
¼ teaspoon cream of tartar
Dash salt
1 cup sugar
1 teaspoon instant coffee
1 6-ounce package butterscotch pieces
3 tablespoons water
1 tablespoon instant coffee
Dash salt
1 beaten egg
1 cup heavy cream, whipped

Shells: Combine first four ingredients; beat till frothy. Mix sugar and 1 teaspoon instant coffee; gradually beat into egg-white mixture; beat till stiff peaks form. Shape and bake 8 shells as directed in Individual Meringue Shells, page 73.

Filling: In saucepan, combine butterscotch pieces, water, 1 tablespoon instant coffee, and dash salt. Cook and stir over low heat till candy melts; then cook 1 or 2 minutes longer. Stir small amount of hot mixture into beaten egg; return to hot mixture and cook about 1 minute, stirring constantly. Chill. Fold butterscotch mixture into whipped cream. Pile filling into meringue shells. Chill several hours. Makes 8 servings!

A beauty!
Rainbow
Sundae Buffet
with speedy
sauces

Get meringue shell in the oven—the work's all done! The filling is ice cream—here it's chocolate, pistachio, and strawberry.

Sauces to glorify your Rainbow Buffet are fruit preserves — choose your favorite flavor. Just stir up, then spoon over!

Dessert spectaculars

Baked Alaska—a truly memorable dessert

Cheesecakes, baked and chilled

A treasury of terrific tortes

High-hat souffles, light and airy

Napoleons, cream puffs, eclairs

Pancakes—dolled-up for dessert!

A dazzler of a dessert, easier than you think

← Mile-high Mocha Alaska is one for your "special occasion" file. Top nut-laden brownie layer with a dome of coffee ice cream *and* chocolate ice cream; cover with meringue. When time is precious, count on mixes to see you through.

Bake an elegant Alaska

Melba Alaska

1 pint vanilla ice cream
1 pint raspberry sherbet
1 9-inch round layer sponge or
  yellow cake
1 recipe Meringue
1 1-pound can sliced peaches, drained

Line 8-inch round cake pan with waxed paper or foil. Stir vanilla ice cream to soften slightly. Pack in bottom of pan. On top, pack a layer of raspberry sherbet. Cover with waxed paper or foil; flatten top by smoothing with hands. Freeze *firm*.

Place cake on cooky sheet or wooden cutting board. Prepare Meringue as for pie—see picture-recipe, page 73—but use 4 egg whites, ½ teaspoon vanilla, ¼ teaspoon cream of tartar and ½ cup sugar.

Remove paper or foil from ice cream; invert on cake layer. Remove pan, peel off liner.

Completely cover dessert with meringue, spreading it thicker over ice cream and thinner around cake. Sift confectioners' sugar over top of meringue. Bake at once or return to freezer until just before serving time. Bake in extremely hot oven (500°) about 3 minutes or till meringue is browned. Trim top with peach slices; serve at once with remaining peaches. Makes 8 servings.

Ribbon Alaska Pie

Peppermint-candy meringue tops vanilla ice cream layered with fudge sauce—

2 tablespoons butter
2 1-ounce squares unsweetened chocolate
1 cup sugar
1 6-ounce can (⅔ cup) evaporated milk
1 teaspoon vanilla

. . .

2 pints vanilla ice cream, softened
1 9-inch baked pastry shell

. . .

1 recipe Meringue
¼ cup crushed peppermint-stick candy

Make Fudge Sauce: Mix butter, chocolate, sugar, and evaporated milk in saucepan; cook and stir over low heat till thick and blended. Remove from heat. Add vanilla. Cool thoroughly.

Spread *1 pint* ice cream in pastry shell; cover with *half* the cooled Fudge Sauce; freeze. Repeat layers; freeze *firm*.

Prepare Meringue as for pie, using 3 egg whites—see step-by-step recipe, page 73. Reserve 2 teaspoons candy; fold remainder into meringue; spread over pie, sealing to edges. Sprinkle with remaining candy. Bake in very hot oven (475°) about 3 minutes or till lightly browned. Serve at once or freeze.

Easy Baked Alaska awes guests, turns dessert time into an occasion!

1 On cutting board or cooky sheet, trim layer of sponge cake or layer cake 1 inch bigger on all sides than a 1-quart brick of ice cream. Make meringue.

2 *Meringue:* Gradually add ⅔ cup sugar to 5 stiff-beaten egg whites; beat till peaks form. Now place 1 quart brick ice cream on the cake.

3 Spread meringue over ice cream, cake, sealing well to cake. Bake at 450° about 5 minutes. Slide onto plate—paper strip underneath helps.

Neat trick: Completely assemble

Alaska ahead; freeze till needed

Stack cake layer and ice cream on cooky sheet or wooden cutting board. Spread with meringue as directed. Return to freezer. Just before serving, whisk Alaska from freezer to oven.

White Mountain Alaska

It's beautiful and luscious! A specialty of Hartwell Farm in Massachusetts—

1 baked 9-inch pastry shell
1 quart peppermint ice cream
4 egg whites
1 teaspoon cream of tartar
½ cup light corn syrup
. . .
1 recipe Chocolate Sauce

Fill pastry shell with scoops of ice cream and push down to make as solid as possible; freeze firm. Beat egg whites till frothy; add cream of tartar and beat till stiff peaks form. Gradually add syrup, beating till very stiff (about 10 minutes). Pile meringue high atop ice cream, mounding to a peak in the center. Make deep swirls with tip of spoon or spatula from the base of pie to the peak (like mountain crevices).

Place on a wooden cutting board and bake in extremely hot oven (500°) until meringue is golden brown, about 3 to 5 minutes. Serve with Chocolate Sauce. Makes 6 servings.

Chocolate Sauce: In top of double boiler, combine four 1-ounce squares unsweetened chocolate, 1 cup sugar, ⅔ cup strong, freshly brewed coffee, and ¼ teaspoon salt. Cook over boiling water about 20 minutes, stirring occasionally as sauce thickens. Makes about 1 cup sauce.

Mile-high Mocha Alaska

2 pints chocolate ice cream
1 to 2 pints coffee ice cream
1 recipe Brownie Layer
5 egg whites (about ⅔ cup)
⅔ cup sugar

For a mold, line a deep 1½-quart bowl with aluminum foil, allowing 1 inch extra to extend over edge of bowl. Stir chocolate ice cream to soften *slightly;* spread a layer, about 1 inch thick, over bottom and sides of foil liner (use back of spoon; work quickly).

Keep mold in freezer while you stir coffee ice cream to soften *slightly;* pack into center of mold. Cover with foil. Press with hands to smooth top. Freeze *firm.*

To assemble: Place cooled Brownie Layer on a cooky sheet or wooden cutting board. Let bowl of ice cream stand at room temperature, while you make meringue: Beat egg whites till soft peaks form; gradually add sugar, beating to stiff peaks.

Remove foil from top of ice cream; invert ice cream onto Brownie Layer, lift off bowl, then peel off foil. Quickly cover ice cream and brownie base with meringue, swirling it in peaks. (Be sure to spread plenty of meringue around the edge where ice cream and cake meet. Work fast so ice cream stays firm.) At once place on lowest rack in extremely hot oven (500°) and bake about 3 minutes or till meringue is browned. Let stand a few minutes for easier cutting. Cut in wedge-shaped slices. Makes 12 servings.

Brownie Layer: Prepare 1 recipe cake-type Brownies (page 108); bake in greased 8-inch *round* pan at 350° about 30 to 35 minutes or till done. Cool; remove from pan.

Note: For a speedy Alaska, use brownie mix. Prepare according to package directions for cake-type brownies, baking like Brownie Layer. Cool and remove from pan.

N-M Fresh Flowerpot

From Neiman-Marcus—individual baked Alaskas in real red-clay flowerpots!—

Line bottoms of small new red-clay flowerpots with rounds of sponge cake. Top with several kinds of ice cream, then high meringue. Brown a few minutes in very hot oven. Poke two soda straws into each dessert as channels for flower stems. Insert flower in each straw—in the Zodiac Room at Neiman-Marcus, they use garnet roses.

Choice cheesecakes

Best-ever Cheesecake

Crust:

1 cup sifted enriched flour
¼ cup sugar
1 teaspoon grated lemon peel
½ cup butter or margarine
1 slightly beaten egg yolk
¼ teaspoon vanilla

Combine first 3 ingredients. Cut in butter till mixture is crumbly. Add egg yolk and vanilla; blend well. Pat ⅓ of dough on bottom of 9-inch spring-form pan (sides removed). Bake at 400° about 8 minutes or till golden; cool. Attach sides to bottom, butter; and pat remaining dough on sides to a height of 1¾ inches.

Cheese Filling:

5 8-ounce packages cream cheese
¼ teaspoon vanilla
¾ teaspoon grated lemon peel
1¾ cups sugar
3 tablespoons enriched flour
¼ teaspoon salt
4 or 5 eggs (1 cup)
2 egg yolks
¼ cup whipping cream

Let cheese soften at room temperature, 1 to 1½ hours. Beat creamy. Add vanilla and peel. Mix next 3 ingredients; slowly blend in. Add eggs and yolks one at a time; beat after each just to blend. Gently stir in cream.

Turn into crust-lined pan. Bake at 450° for 12 minutes; reduce heat to 300°, bake 55 minutes. Allow to cool. Loosen sides with spatula after ½ hour. Remove sides at end of 1 hour. Cool 2 hours longer. Glaze with Pineapple or Strawberry Glaze. Serves 12.

Pineapple Glaze
(or use Strawberry Glaze)

In saucepan combine 3 tablespoons sugar, 1 tablespoon cornstarch; stir in 1 cup unsweetened pineapple juice and ¼ teaspoon grated lemon peel. Heat and stir till boiling; cook and stir till thick and clear. Cool to room temperature; spread atop cooled cheesecake; chill 2 hours. Trim with mounds of whipped cream and pineapple.

Strawberry Glaze
(or use Pineapple Glaze)

2 to 3 cups fresh strawberries
1 cup water
1½ tablespoons cornstarch
½ to ¾ cup sugar

Crush *1 cup* of the strawberries; add the water, and cook 2 minutes; sieve. Mix cornstarch with sugar (amount of sugar depends on sweetness of berries); stir into hot berry mixture. Bring to boiling, stirring constantly. Cook and stir till thick and clear. (Add a few drops red food coloring, if needed.) Cool to room temperature. Place remaining strawberries atop cooled cheesecake; to match picture, circle with halved pineapple rings. Pour glaze over the fruit and chill about 2 hours.

Creamy Cheesecake Pie

Crust:

1¼ cups plain- or cinnamon-graham-
 cracker crumbs
¼ cup butter or margarine, melted

Filling:

1 8-ounce package cream cheese
½ cup sugar
1 tablespoon lemon juice
½ teaspoon vanilla
Dash salt
2 eggs

Topping:

1 cup dairy sour cream
2 tablespoons sugar
½ teaspoon vanilla

Combine crumbs and butter; press into buttered 8-inch pie plate, building up sides. Beat softened cream cheese till fluffy; gradually blend in ½ cup sugar, lemon juice, vanilla, and salt. Add eggs, one at a time, beating well after each. Pour filling into crumb crust. Bake in slow oven (325°) 25 to 30 minutes or till set.

For topping, combine last three ingredients; spoon over top of pie. Bake 10 minutes more. Cool. Chill several hours. Serve with red-ripe strawberries.

Best-ever Cheesecake—
and it really is just that!

It's so big and luscious, worth every penny! Filling is smooth and rich with cream cheese, crust almost like a lemon cooky.

Crowning glory: Strawberry Glaze with fresh strawberries, pineapple.

Improvise a spring-form pan with aluminum foil

1 You'll need heavy-duty aluminum foil, a 9x1½-inch round cake pan, heavy cardboard, a ruler, pencil, and scissors. Cut two strips of foil 2x16 inches, and crisscross them in the pan, as shown.

Cut a strip of cardboard 3x30 inches and a cardboard circle that will fit inside the pan. Cover strip and circle with foil. Drop circle into pan.

2 Curve foil-covered cardboard strip to fit inside pan; overlap ends and fasten at top and bottom with paper clips. Now pour in cheesecake mixture.

At serving time, pick up foil strips and lift cheesecake from cake pan to platter. Pull off paper clips and take off foil-covered cardboard strip. Slip the foil strips from under cake. Trim; serve.

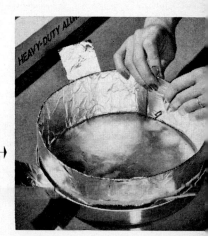

Chilled Pineapple Cheesecake

2⅓ cups fine vanilla-wafer crumbs
½ cup butter or margarine, melted
1 No. 2 can (2½ cups) crushed
    pineapple
2 envelopes (2 tablespoons) plus 1
    teaspoon unflavored gelatin
4 slightly beaten egg yolks
1 cup sugar
2 teaspoons grated lemon peel
¼ teaspoon salt
2 12-ounce cartons (3 cups) small-curd
    cream-style cottage cheese
1 tablespoon vanilla
2 cups heavy cream, whipped
4 stiff-beaten egg whites

Mix crumbs, butter. Press onto bottom and sides of a buttered 9-inch spring-form pan.

Drain pineapple, reserving syrup. Soften gelatin in ½ cup pineapple syrup. In double boiler, combine egg yolks, sugar, lemon peel, salt, and 2 tablespoons pineapple syrup. Cook and stir over *hot, not boiling* water 5 to 8 minutes or till like smooth stirred custard (mixture will seem to get thin as it cooks).

Remove from heat; add softened gelatin; stir till dissolved. Add crushed pineapple, cottage cheese, and vanilla. Fold in whipped cream, then egg whites. Pour into crumb-lined pan. Chill about 5 hours, or till firm. In removing cake from pan, first loosen sides with spatula. Makes 16 servings.

Lemon Refrigerator Cheesecake

1 cup sugar
2 envelopes unflavored gelatin
¼ teaspoon salt
2 eggs, separated
1 6-ounce can (⅔ cup) evaporated milk
1 teaspoon grated lemon peel
2 12-ounce cartons (3 cups) cream-style
    cottage cheese, sieved
1 tablespoon lemon juice
1½ teaspoons vanilla
1 cup heavy cream, whipped

In double boiler, combine ¾ *cup* sugar, gelatin, and salt. Stir in *beaten* egg yolks and evaporated milk. Cook and stir over simmering water till gelatin dissolves and mixture thickens slightly, about 10 minutes. Remove from heat; add lemon peel; cool. Stir in cottage cheese, lemon juice, and vanilla. Chill, stirring occasionally, till partially set. Beat egg whites to soft peaks. Slowly add ¼ *cup* sugar, beating to stiff peaks. Fold into gelatin mixture. Fold in whipped cream.

Pour into Corn-flake Crust; top with reserved crumbs. Chill firm, about 3 hours.

Corn-flake Crust: Mix 1½ cups finely crushed corn flakes, ½ cup finely chopped nuts, ⅓ cup sugar, 1 teaspoon cinnamon, ¼ teaspoon nutmeg, and ⅓ cup butter, melted. Reserve ¾ cup. Press remainder on bottom of 8- or 9-inch spring-form pan. Chill.

A grand finale—
Chilled Pineapple
Cheesecake, coffee

You couldn't ask for a more breath-taking dessert than this! Flavor's delicious — crushed pineapple with the fresh nip of grated lemon peel. This cottage cheese and gelatin beauty "bakes" in your refrigerator.

For trim: Circle platter with half slices of pineapple and maraschino cherries. Slit pineapple rings and twist in S-shapes atop cheesecake; tuck in more cherries. Each guest gets some of the garnish! A must: hot coffee.

Turn out a terrific torte!

Party Cherry Torte

3 egg whites
1 teaspoon vanilla
Dash salt
1 cup sugar
¾ cup chopped walnuts
½ cup saltine-cracker crumbs
1 teaspoon baking powder

• • •

1 No. 2 can (2½ cups) frozen pitted
   tart red cherries
¼ cup sugar
2 tablespoons cornstarch
1 cup heavy cream, whipped

Beat egg whites with vanilla and salt till foamy. Gradually add 1 cup sugar, beating to stiff peaks. Mix nuts, cracker crumbs, and baking powder; fold into egg whites. Spread in well-greased 9-inch pie plate, building up sides. Bake at 300° about 40 minutes or till dry on outside. Cool.

Drain cherries, reserving syrup. Combine ¾ *cup of the syrup* and ¼ cup sugar; heat to boiling. Add cherries; cook 10 minutes. Mix cornstarch with remaining cold cherry syrup; add to hot mixture. Cook, stirring constantly, till thick and clear. Cool.

Line shell with *half* the whipped cream. Fill with cherry mixture; top with remaining whipped cream. Makes about 6 servings.

Coconut-crunch Torte

1 cup graham-cracker crumbs
½ cup chopped flaked coconut
½ cup chopped California walnuts
4 egg whites
¼ teaspoon salt
1 teaspoon vanilla
1 cup sugar
1 pint butter-brickle ice cream

Combine crumbs, coconut, and nuts. Beat egg whites with salt and vanilla to soft peaks; gradually add sugar, beating till very stiff peaks form and all sugar has dissolved. Fold crumb mixture into egg whites.

Spread in well-greased 9-inch pie plate. Bake at 350° about 30 minutes. Cool. Cut in 6 to 8 wedges; top with scoops of ice cream.

Angel Pineapple Torte

A glamorous dessert to delight guests—

12 egg whites (1½ cups)
2 teaspoons vanilla
1½ teaspoons vinegar
3 cups sugar

• • •

1 cup heavy cream
1 cup well-drained canned crushed
   pineapple
½ cup maraschino cherries, chopped
   and well drained
2 cups heavy cream

To egg whites, add vanilla and vinegar. Beat until mixture forms soft peaks. Gradually add sugar, beating till very stiff and all sugar is dissolved. Spread in 3 paper-lined 9x1½-inch round cake pans. Bake in slow oven (300°) 1¼ to 1½ hours, or till dry on top and lightly browned. Cool thoroughly in pans. Turn out; remove paper.

Whip 1 cup heavy cream till stiff; add pineapple and cherries. Spread between layers. Chill 12 hours or overnight.

To serve, whip 2 cups heavy cream; frost top and sides of torte. Trim with California walnuts and cherry flowers (make 5 lengthwise cuts in cherry, not quite through; spread flat). Makes 12 to 16 servings.

Brownie Pie

3 egg whites
Dash salt
¾ cup sugar
¾ cup fine chocolate-wafer crumbs
½ cup chopped California walnuts
½ teaspoon vanilla
Sweetened whipped cream

Beat egg whites and salt till soft peaks form; gradually add sugar, beating till stiff peaks form. Fold in crumbs, nuts, and vanilla; spread evenly in lightly buttered 9-inch pie plate.

Bake at 325° about 35 minutes. Cool thoroughly. Spread top with sweetened whipped cream; chill well, 3 to 4 hours. Trim with curls of shaved unsweetened chocolate.

Chocolate Torte Royale

1 6-ounce package (1 cup) semisweet
    chocolate pieces
Cinnamon Meringue Shell
2 beaten egg yolks
¼ cup water
1 cup heavy cream
¼ cup sugar
¼ teaspoon cinnamon

Melt the chocolate over *hot, not boiling* water. Then spread 2 tablespoons of the chocolate over bottom of cooled Cinnamon Meringue Shell. To remaining chocolate, add egg yolks and water; blend *very thoroughly.* Chill till mixture is thick.

Combine cream, sugar, and cinnamon; whip till stiff. Spread *half* over chocolate in shell; fold remainder into chocolate mixture and spread on top. Chill several hours or overnight. Garnish with whipped cream and sliced pecans. Makes 8 to 10 servings.

Cinnamon Meringue Shell: Cover a cooky sheet with a piece of heavy paper; draw an 8-inch circle in center. Beat 2 egg whites with ¼ teaspoon salt, and ½ teaspoon vinegar till soft peaks form. Blend ½ cup sugar and ¼ teaspoon cinnamon; gradually add to egg whites, beating till very stiff peaks form and all sugar has dissolved.

Spread within circle—make bottom ½ inch thick and mound around edge, making it 1¾ inches high. Form ridges on outside with back of teaspoon. Bake at 275° for 1 hour. Turn off heat; let dry in oven (door closed) about 2 hours. Peel off paper.

Lemon Angel Torte

Preheat oven to 450°. Place 4 egg whites, ¾ cup sugar, ¼ teaspoon salt, and ¼ teaspoon cream of tartar in small bowl; beat at high speed with electric mixer about 15 minutes to *very stiff* peaks. Spread in *well-buttered* 9-inch pie plate. Place in preheated oven; *turn off heat.* Let stand in closed oven 5 hours or overnight (don't peek).

Whip 1 cup heavy cream; spread half in torte shell. Top with Lemon Filling, then remaining whipped cream. Chill 5 hours. Makes 8 servings.

Lemon Filling: In top of double boiler, beat 4 egg yolks till thick and lemon-colored. Gradually beat in ½ cup sugar, dash salt, 1 tablespoon grated lemon peel, and 3 tablespoons lemon juice. Cook and stir over hot water till thick, about 5 minutes. Cool.

Peach Mystery Meringue

Preheat oven to 450°. Beat 5 egg whites with ¼ teaspoon salt till soft peaks form. Gradually beat in 1 cup sugar; continue beating to stiff peaks (about 15 minutes).

Spread in well-greased 8x8x2-inch pan. Place in preheated oven and close door; *turn off heat.* Let stand overnight or at least 5 hours before removing from oven.

To serve: Cut meringue in 6 to 8 squares. Placed drained, canned peach half, cut side up, atop each. Fill centers with whipped cream. Top with sliced maraschino cherries or strawberries and California walnuts.

Chocolate Torte Royale —heavenly! And it's made ahead, too!

This is the kind of dessert you can serve the bridge club and be confident the compliments will be tossed your way!

And this dessert is easier than it looks! It's "built" of a crunchy cinnamon-meringue crust daintily lined with pure chocolate, filled with spiced whipped cream, then spiced chocolate whipped cream. All this the day before!

Top with whipped cream and pecans. Rich, rich—one torte makes refreshment for two foursomes.

Candy-confetti Torte

Cake:

1½ cups sifted enriched flour
¾ cup sugar
½ cup (8) egg yolks
¼ cup cold water
1 tablespoon lemon juice
1 teaspoon vanilla
1 cup (8) egg whites
1 teaspoon cream of tartar
1 teaspoon salt
¾ cup sugar

Sift flour and ¾ cup sugar into bowl. Make well in center; add egg yolks, water, juice, and vanilla. Beat till smooth. Beat egg whites with cream of tartar and salt just till very soft peaks form; add remaining sugar gradually, 2 tablespoons at a time; continue to beat till stiff meringue forms. Fold first mixture gently into the meringue.

Pour batter into ungreased 10-inch tube pan. Carefully cut through batter, going around tube 5 or 6 times with knife to break air bubbles. Bake at 350° 50 to 55 minutes, or till top springs back when lightly touched. Invert pan 1 hour, or till cool. Remove cake. Split crosswise in 4 equal layers. Assemble torte with whipped cream and Almond-brittle Topping, as directed.

Almond-brittle Topping:

1½ cups sugar
1 teaspoon instant coffee
¼ cup light corn syrup
¼ cup water
1 tablespoon *sifted* soda
2 cups heavy cream
1 to 2 tablespoons sugar
2 teaspoons vanilla
½ cup blanched almond halves, toasted

While cake bakes, fix candy-brittle part of topping: In saucepan, mix first 4 ingredients. Cook to hard-crack stage (285° to 290°). Remove from heat; add soda at once. Stir vigorously, but only till mixture blends and pulls away from sides of pan. Quickly pour foamy mixture into buttered 9x9x2-inch pan. *Do not spread or stir.* Cool. Tap bottom of pan to remove candy; with rolling pin, crush candy into coarse crumbs.

When cake is thoroughly cool, whip cream and fold in sugar and vanilla. Spread half of cream between layers and remainder over top and sides. Cover with candy crumbs; trim with almond halves, as shown at right.

How to assemble the Torte

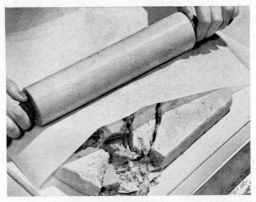

1 Invert pan of cooled candy, and tap sharply on table to remove. With rolling pin, coarsely crush brittle between sheets of waxed paper.

2 Remove loose crumbs from cake layers. Starting at bottom, spread each layer generously with whipped cream, right to edge. Frost top and sides. Chill if candy trim isn't ready.

3 Cover whipped cream with the candy crumbs. Poke in toasted almond halves porcupine style all over the cake. It's ready to serve!

High-hat souffles

Chocolate Cloud Souffle

Feathery light, flavor-rich—

⅓ cup light cream
1 3-ounce package cream cheese
½ cup semisweet chocolate pieces
3 egg yolks
Dash salt
3 egg whites
3 tablespoons sifted confectioners' sugar

Blend cream and cream cheese over very *low* heat. Add chocolate pieces; heat and stir till melted. Cool. Beat egg yolks and salt till thick and lemon-colored. Gradually blend into chocolate mixture.

Beat egg whites till soft peaks form. Gradually add sugar, beating to stiff peaks; fold in chocolate mixture.

Pour into *ungreased* 1-quart souffle dish or casserole. Bake in slow oven (300°) 45 minutes or till knife inserted comes out clean. Makes 5 or 6 servings.

Orange Souffle

Melt ¼ cup butter or margarine; blend in 6 tablespoons enriched flour and a dash salt. Gradually stir in 1 cup milk; cook over low heat, stirring constantly, till thick.

Measure ¼ cup frozen orange-juice concentrate from a 6-ounce can (reserve remainder for Orange Sauce); combine with ½ cup water and 1½ teaspoons grated lemon peel. Stir into the hot mixture.

Beat 6 egg yolks till thick and lemon-colored; gradually add hot mixture; mix well. Beat 6 egg whites to soft peaks; gradually add ¼ cup sugar, beating to stiff peaks. Fold yolk mixture into egg whites.

Pour into *ungreased* 1½-quart casserole with paper collar (see directions, next page). Set dish in shallow pan, filling pan to 1 inch with hot water. Bake in slow oven (325°) about 1½ hours or till knife inserted comes out clean. Peel off paper. Serve at once, breaking apart gently with two forks. Pass Orange Sauce. Makes 8 servings.

These tips assure you a souffle that's puffed to airy heights

Beat egg yolks till *thick* and lemon-colored. Then *slowly* stir in hot sauce. Pour mixture over stiffly beaten egg whites; fold with rubber spatula—be gentle but thorough.

Pour mixture into *ungreased* casserole—souffle climbs right up the sides. For a souffle that's extra high, fasten on a waxed-paper collar. Now bake in a slow oven (300° to 325°).

Ginger Souffle

2 tablespoons butter or margarine
3 tablespoons enriched flour
¼ teaspoon salt
¼ teaspoon ground ginger
¾ cup milk
3 egg yolks
1 teaspoon vanilla
2 to 4 tablespoons diced candied ginger
3 egg whites
¼ teaspoon cream of tartar
¼ cup sugar

Melt butter; blend in flour, salt, and ground ginger. Gradually stir in milk. Cook and stir over low heat till thick. Beat egg yolks till thick and lemon-colored; gradually add hot mixture to yolks; mix well. Stir in vanilla and candied ginger.

Beat egg whites with cream of tartar till soft peaks form. Gradually add sugar, beating till stiff peaks form. Fold yolk mixture into egg whites. Pour into *ungreased* 1-quart baking dish fitted with paper collar (see directions, right). Set in shallow pan, filling pan to 1 inch with hot water.

Bake at 325° about 1½ hours or till knife inserted comes out clean, or top springs back and feels dry when touched lightly. Peel off paper. Serve at once. Pass warm Citrus-Ginger Sauce. Makes 5 or 6 servings.

Orange Sauce (*for Orange Souffle*)

½ cup sugar
1½ tablespoons cornstarch
Dash salt
½ cup frozen orange-juice concentrate
1 cup water
1 tablespoon butter or margarine

Combine sugar, cornstarch, and dash salt. Stir in concentrate and water. Cook and stir till thick. Stir in butter. Serve warm.

Citrus-Ginger Sauce
(*for Ginger Souffle*)

In saucepan, combine ½ cup sugar, 1 tablespoon cornstarch, and dash salt. Stir in 1 cup water; bring to boiling; cook, stirring constantly, till thick. Cool slightly.

Stir in ½ teaspoon *each* grated orange and lemon peel, 3 tablespoons orange juice, 1 tablespoon lemon juice, and 2 tablespoons finely diced candied ginger. Serve warm.

Paper collar for souffle: Measure enough waxed paper to go around casserole, with 1-inch overlap. Fold in thirds lengthwise. Lightly butter one side; sprinkle with sugar. Collar (buttered side in) should extend 2 inches above casserole. Pull tight so collar is smaller at top; fasten with cellophane tape.

Showy Orange Souffle makes a special event of any meal!

Bake this wonderful, can't-wait dessert while guests enjoy dinner. Whisk souffle to the table and break apart in servings with two forks. Pass Orange Sauce.

For high-style model with spoke design: After 10 to 15 minutes baking time, mark top with tip of sharp knife in pie-shaped wedges ½ inch deep. Wipe the knife clean after each mark.

Cream puffs and eclairs

Cream Puffs

½ cup butter or margarine
1 cup boiling water

• • •

1 cup sifted enriched flour
¼ teaspoon salt
4 eggs

Melt butter in boiling water. Add flour and salt all at once; stir vigorously. Cook, stirring constantly, till mixture forms a ball that doesn't separate. Remove from heat and cool slightly. Add eggs, one at a time, beating vigorously after each until smooth.

Drop dough by heaping tablespoons 3 inches apart on greased cooky sheet.

Bake in very hot oven (450°) 15 minutes, then in slow oven (325°) 25 minutes. Remove cream puffs from oven; split. Turn oven *off* and put cream puffs back in oven to dry out, about 20 minutes. Cool on rack.

Just before serving, fill centers with a double recipe of French Custard Filling (page 61). Replace tops; drizzle with Chocolate Sauce. Sprinkle chopped nuts atop. Makes about 10 big puffs.

Chocolate Sauce (*for Cream Puffs*)

1 cup sugar
¾ cup water
½ cup light corn syrup
3 1-ounce squares unsweetened chocolate, melted
1 teaspoon vanilla

In saucepan combine sugar, water, and corn syrup; bring to a boil. Gradually add to chocolate, blending well. Boil gently 10 to 15 minutes, stirring occasionally. Add vanilla. Cover entire surface with clear plastic wrap; cool. Makes 1⅔ cups.

Chocolate Eclairs

Mix batter as directed for Cream Puffs. Put mixture through a pastry tube or paper cone, making 4-inch strips, ¾ inch wide, on greased cooky sheet.

Bake as for Cream Puffs. Frost eclairs with Chocolate Icing. Fill with double recipe of French Custard Filling (page 61) just before serving. Makes about 14 eclairs.

Cream Puffs look complicated, but they aren't—just follow these easy steps

1 Add the butter or margarine to boiling water in a saucepan. Stir with wooden spoon till butter melts. Add sifted flour and salt all at once and stir vigorously.

2 Cook and stir till dough pulls away from sides of pan and forms a ball around spoon. Remove from heat; vigorously beat in eggs, *one at a time*.

3 Drop dough by tablespoonfuls on greased cooky sheet. Bake. Split puffs; turn off heat; let dry in oven 20 minutes. Cool.

Crisp Cream Puffs with luscious filling, fudge topper

Here Cream Puffs are filled with smooth French Custard; another time try ice cream, Cocoa Cream, or pudding from a package.

Spoon on rich Chocolate Sauce and sprinkle with nuts. Pass extra sauce. Time a-flying? Make Hurry-up Eclairs, page 129.

Chocolate Icing (for Eclairs)

2 1-ounce squares unsweetened chocolate
1½ tablespoons butter or margarine

. . .

⅔ cup sifted confectioners' sugar
2 tablespoons milk

Melt chocolate and butter in top of double boiler. Remove from heat. Stir in confectioners' sugar and milk, blending till mixture is smooth and of spreading consistency. Spread on tops of Chocolate Eclairs.

Cream Puff Miniatures

Dainty morsels—perfect for a tea table—

Prepare batter as for Cream Puffs. Drop from the tip of a teaspoon about 1½ inches apart on greased cooky sheet.

Bake puffs in hot oven (425°) 10 minutes, then reduce heat to 325°; bake 10 minutes longer. For crisper puffs, turn oven *off;* cut tops from puffs and leave in oven 10 minutes to dry out. Cool on rack.

Frost tops with Chocolate Icing. Fill with Cocoa Cream. Makes 5 to 6 dozen tiny puffs.

Cocoa Cream

1½ cups heavy cream
½ cup sugar
⅓ cup cocoa

Combine ingredients. Chill 1 hour. Then beat till stiff. Spoon into cream puffs.

Peach-Orange Fluff in Cream Puffs

2 beaten eggs
¼ cup sugar
½ cup orange juice
¼ cup lemon juice
½ cup heavy cream, whipped

. . .

1½ to 2 cups drained sweetened sliced peaches
6 Cream Puffs, tops removed

Combine eggs and sugar. Blend in juices. Cook over *hot, not boiling,* water till thick, stirring constantly. Chill. Fold in whipped cream. Place peaches in puffs; cover with half of orange custard.

Put tops on puffs; pour remaining custard over. Garnish with additional peach slices, if you like. Makes 6 servings.

Napoleons

Puff Pastry

The ultimate in a French pastry-chef's art!—

1 cup chilled butter or margarine
1¾ cups sifted enriched flour
½ cup ice water

Reserve 2 tablespoons butter; chill. Work remaining chilled butter with back of wooden spoon or in electric mixer just till it's pliable as putty. Pat or roll between sheets of waxed paper in 8x6-inch rectangle, ¼ inch thick. Chill thoroughly, at least 1 hour in refrigerator or 20 minutes in freezer. (Keep utensils cold—chill before each use.)

Measure flour into mixing bowl; cut in reserved butter with pastry-blender or blending fork till mixture resembles coarse meal. Gradually add ice water, tossing with fork to make stiff dough. Shape in ball. Turn onto lightly floured surface; knead till smooth and elastic, about 5 minutes. Cover dough; let rest 10 minutes.

On *lightly* floured surface, roll dough in 15x9-inch rectangle, ¼ inch thick. Peel top sheet of waxed paper from chilled rectangle of butter; invert on half the dough; peel off other sheet of waxed paper. Fold over other half of dough to cover butter.

Seal edges of dough by pressing down with side or heel of hand. Wrap in waxed paper; chill thoroughly, at least 1 hour in refrigerator or 20 minutes in freezer.

Unwrap. On lightly floured surface, roll dough in 15x9-inch rectangle, ¼ inch thick. (Roll dough from center, *just to* the edges. Don't flatten edges by rolling over them—dough should be even thickness.) Brush any excess flour from pastry; fold in thirds, then turn dough around and fold it in thirds again. Dough is now in 9 layers.

Seal edges with side or heel of hand. Wrap in waxed paper; chill thoroughly, at least 1 hour in refrigerator or 20 minutes in freezer. Repeat rolling, folding, and thorough chilling 2 or 3 times more. Puff Pastry's now ready to shape into Napoleons.

Unbaked pastry will keep several weeks in freezer or several days in refrigerator. To store *baked* puff pastry, wrap in foil or clear plastic wrap for freezing; place in box for protection, and put in freezer.

Napoleons

Roll Puff Pastry into 14x8-inch rectangle, ⅜ inch thick. With floured sharp knife, cut off all edges. Prick dough thoroughly with fork—no uneven puffing while it bakes. Cut in sixteen 3½x2-inch rectangles.

Place on cooky sheets covered with 3 or 4 thicknesses of paper towels. Chill thoroughly. Brush with mixture of 1 slightly beaten egg white and 1 tablespoon ice water.

Bake in very hot oven (450°) 6 minutes, then in slow oven (300°) 25 to 30 minutes, till lightly browned and crisp. Remove from pan; cool on rack. (If baked in advance, place on baking sheet covered with 4 thicknesses of paper towels; heat in slow oven (300°) about 10 minutes.)

Separate each pastry in 3 layers. Fill between layers with Napoleon Filling; spread top with Vanilla Glaze. Using pastry tube, decorate top with 2 lengthwise, wavy strips of Chocolate Icing. Makes 16 pastries.

Napoleon Filling

1 cup sugar
¼ cup enriched flour
¼ cup cornstarch
½ teaspoon salt
3 cups milk
4 beaten egg yolks
2 teaspoons vanilla

Combine sugar, flour, cornstarch, and salt. Gradually stir in milk. Cook, stirring constantly, till mixture boils and thickens.

Stir a little of hot mixture into egg yolks; return to hot mixture. Stirring constantly, bring just to boiling. Cool; add vanilla. Chill. Beat with electric or rotary beater till smooth. Makes about 3 cups.

Vanilla Glaze (*for Napoleons*)

2 cups sifted confectioners' sugar
Dash salt
¼ teaspoon vanilla
3 to 4 tablespoons boiling water

Combine sugar, salt, and vanilla. Add boiling water, mixing well. Makes ¾ cup.

Chocolate Icing (*for Napoleons*)

Melt one 1-ounce square unsweetened chocolate with 1 teaspoon butter or margarine over hot water. Cool slightly. Stir in 3 tablespoons sifted confectioners' sugar and dash salt; mix till smooth. Makes ⅓ cup.

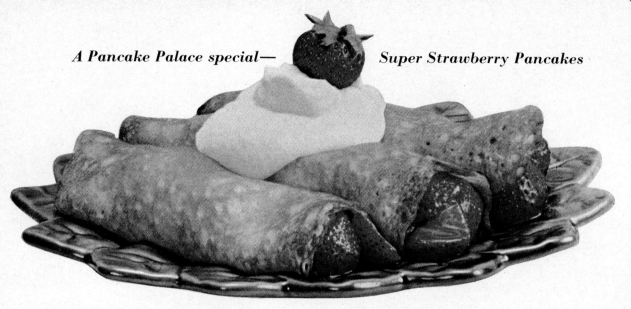

A Pancake Palace special— *Super Strawberry Pancakes*

Pancakes–dolled up!

Super Strawberry Pancakes

Pride of the Pancake Palace at San Francisco's International Airport—

Thaw two 10-ounce packages frozen strawberries; drain. Fill each Swedish Pancake with spoonful of strawberries and roll up. Arrange three pancakes for a serving. Sift powdered sugar over. Add a puff of whipped cream and a berry.

Swedish Pancakes: Beat 2 eggs just to blend; add 1 cup light cream. Sift in $\frac{1}{2}$ cup sifted enriched flour, $1\frac{1}{2}$ teaspoons sugar, and $\frac{1}{4}$ teaspoon salt; beat smooth with rotary beater. Let stand at least 2 hours, so batter thickens. Heat electric griddle or skillet to 375° or till drop of water will dance on surface. Butter lightly.

Beat batter again. Use 2 tablespoons batter for each cake. Brown on both sides. (If difficult to turn pancakes, loosen edge with spatula; lift pancake with fingers, peeling it off griddle.) Roll pancakes; place on ovenproof platter; cover. Keep warm in slow oven (300°). Make Super Strawberry Pancakes. Or serve with Lingonberry Butter. Makes 1 dozen 5-inch pancakes.

Lingonberry Butter: Whip $\frac{1}{4}$ pound slightly softened butter with electric mixer or wooden spoon till fluffy. Fold in $\frac{1}{2}$ cup drained canned lingonberries (or $\frac{1}{2}$ cup drained whole cranberry sauce).

Royal Sunshine Roll-ups

Pancakes: Heat $\frac{2}{3}$ cup milk with $1\frac{1}{2}$ tablespoons butter till butter melts. Cool to lukewarm. Beat 1 egg till light; blend in milk mixture and $\frac{1}{3}$ cup pancake mix.

Lightly grease small skillet; heat. Pour in 2 tablespoons batter; lift pan from heat and tip from side to side so batter covers pan. Return to heat; cook till underside is lightly browned. Remove. Fry remaining pancakes; stack till ready to fill.

Cheese Filling: Soften two 3-ounce packages cream cheese. Blend in 2 tablespoons sugar, $2\frac{1}{4}$ teaspoons grated orange peel, $1\frac{1}{2}$ tablespoons orange juice, and 2 tablespoons chopped pecans. (Add $\frac{1}{4}$ cup chopped dates, if desired.) Whip mixture till fluffy.

Spoon about 2 tablespoons filling across center of each pancake; roll up. Place folded side down in skillet. (You may fill the pancakes ahead and refrigerate till needed.)

Orange Sauce: Mix $\frac{1}{2}$ cup sugar, $1\frac{1}{2}$ tablespoons cornstarch, and dash salt; blend in $\frac{1}{4}$ cup orange juice. Heat $1\frac{1}{4}$ cups orange juice to a boil; stir in sugar mixture, and cook and stir till thick and clear. Remove from heat. Add $\frac{1}{4}$ cup broken pecans and 2 tablespoons butter. Stir till butter melts.

Just before serving, pour Orange Sauce over filled pancakes and heat till sauce bubbles. Serve warm. Makes 8 servings.

Do-ahead desserts

Luscious refrigerator desserts

Frosty desserts—your favorite
ice creams and sherbets

Dress-ups with a carton of ice cream

Desserts for weight-watchers—
you make them ahead!

Delightful desserts—no last-minute fuss!

← These beauties you fix and forget! Pink Pinwheel Bavarian
is velvety and berry-rich; Tutti-frutti Tortoni—
professional-looking, yet made in a wink; low on calories,
that's Apricot Chiffon Pie; Choco-Cherry Dessert is
stacked with good flavor; Lemon-drop Ice Cream—wonderful!

Refrigerator desserts

Mocha Chip Squares

- 1 envelope (1 tablespoon)
  unflavored gelatin
- ¼ cup sugar
- 2 tablespoons instant coffee
- Dash salt
- 2 egg yolks
- 1¼ cups milk
- ½ teaspoon vanilla
- 2 egg whites
- ¼ cup sugar
- 1 cup heavy cream, whipped
- 1 6-ounce package (1 cup) semisweet
  chocolate pieces, chopped
- ½ cup broken California walnuts

In top of double boiler, thoroughly mix gelatin, ¼ cup sugar, coffee, and salt. Beat together egg yolks and milk; stir into gelatin mixture. Cook and stir over *hot, not boiling* water till slightly thick. Add vanilla; chill till partially set.

Beat egg whites till soft peaks form; gradually add ¼ cup sugar, beating till stiff peaks form; fold into gelatin.

Reserve ½ cup of *whipped* cream and 2 tablespoons chocolate for garnish. Fold in remaining cream, chocolate, and nuts. Pour into 10x6x1½-inch dish; chill till firm. Cut in squares; garnish. Makes 6 to 8 servings.

Choco-Cherry Dessert

Wafer Crust: Mix 2 cups fine vanilla-wafer crumbs with ⅓ cup melted butter; reserve 2 tablespoons for top. Press remainder in bottom of 1-quart refrigerator tray.

Butter Fluff Layer: Cream ½ cup butter with 1½ cups sifted confectioners' sugar. Add 2 eggs, one at a time, beating well after each. Spread mixture over crumbs.

Chocolate-Cherry Layer: Combine ¼ cup sugar, 2 tablespoons cocoa, and 1 cup heavy cream; whip. Fold in 1 cup chopped walnuts, 1 fully ripe banana, mashed, and ¼ cup sliced maraschino cherries. Pile atop mixture in tray. Sprinkle reserved crumbs over. Chill 24 hours or freeze. Cut in wedges. Makes 9 to 12 servings.

Fluffy Lemon Dessert

- 1 envelope (1 tablespoon)
  unflavored gelatin
- ½ cup cold water
- 3 slightly beaten egg yolks
- ½ cup sugar
- ½ teaspoon salt
- ½ teaspoon grated lemon peel
- ½ cup lemon juice

• • •

- 1 cup marshmallow creme
- 3 egg whites
- ¼ cup sugar

Soften gelatin in cold water. In top of double boiler, combine egg yolks, ½ cup sugar, salt, lemon peel, juice; cook and stir over *hot, not boiling* water till thick. Remove from heat; add gelatin; stir till dissolved. Add marshmallow creme; cool. Beat egg whites till soft peaks form; gradually add ¼ cup sugar, beating till stiff peaks form. Fold into gelatin mixture. Pour into 8x8x2-inch pan; chill till firm. Top with sweetened whipped cream and chopped nuts; cut in 9 squares.

Pink Pinwheel Bavarian

- 2 cups sweetened sliced fresh strawberries or 2 10-ounce packages frozen
- 2 envelopes (2 tablespoons)
  unflavored gelatin
- ½ cup cold water
- 2 tablespoons lemon juice
- ½ teaspoon salt
- 2 cups heavy cream, whipped
- About 5 1-inch slices jelly roll

If using frozen berries, thaw and let warm to room temperature. Soften gelatin in cold water; dissolve over hot water. Stir in strawberries, lemon juice, and salt. Chill until partially set. Fold in whipped cream. Tint pink with few drops red food coloring. Place jelly-roll slices around edge of 8-inch spring-form pan. (Buy the jelly roll or make it—see page 48.) Fill with strawberry mixture; chill until firm, about 4 hours. Garnish with strawberry halves—see picture, page 146. Makes 8 to 10 servings.

Apricot Bavarian

1 cup sugar
2 envelopes unflavored gelatin
Dash salt
2 12-ounce cans (3 cups) apricot nectar
⅓ cup lemon juice
1 unbeaten egg white
½ cup heavy cream, whipped

Thoroughly mix sugar, gelatin, and salt. Heat 1 can of apricot nectar just to boiling; add to gelatin, stir to dissolve. Add remaining nectar and lemon juice. Pour ¾ cup of mixture into 1½-quart mold; chill till firm.

Cool remaining mixture to room temperature; add unbeaten egg white. Chill till partially set, then beat until light and fluffy. Fold in whipped cream. Pour over first gelatin layer. Chill till firm. Unmold; trim with sprigs of mint and chilled fruits. Makes 6 to 8 servings.

Strawberry Bavarian Cups

1 10-ounce package frozen sliced
  strawberries
1 envelope (1 tablespoon)
  unflavored gelatin
1 tablespoon light corn syrup
¼ cup sugar
¼ teaspoon salt
2 beaten egg yolks
1¼ cups milk
½ teaspoon vanilla
2 egg whites
¼ cup sugar
1 cup heavy cream, whipped
½ cup slivered blanched
  almonds, toasted

Thaw strawberries; drain, reserving syrup. To 2 tablespoons of the syrup, add *1 teaspoon* gelatin; dissolve over hot water. Add to remaining syrup; mix well. Combine berries and corn syrup; add gelatin mixture. Divide among 9 individual molds; chill firm.

Meanwhile, in top of double boiler, mix *2 teaspoons* gelatin, ¼ cup sugar, and salt. Combine egg yolks and milk; slowly add to gelatin mixture. Cook and stir over *hot, not boiling* water just till mixture coats spoon. Add vanilla; chill till partially set.

Beat egg whites till soft peaks form; gradually add ¼ cup sugar, beating till stiff peaks form. Fold into gelatin mixture. Fold in whipped cream and almonds. Pour over gelatin in molds; chill till firm.

Chocolate Charlotte Russe

1 envelope (1 tablespoon)
  unflavored gelatin
2 tablespoons cold water
3 1-ounce squares unsweetened chocolate
½ cup water
4 eggs, separated
½ cup sugar
1 teaspoon vanilla
½ teaspoon cream of tartar
¼ cup sugar
1 cup heavy cream, whipped
½ cup chopped California walnuts
3 dozen single ladyfingers or 18 double

Soften gelatin in 2 tablespoons cold water. Melt chocolate in ½ cup water over low heat, stirring constantly. Remove from heat; add softened gelatin; stir to dissolve.

Beat egg yolks till thick, lemon-colored; gradually beat in ½ cup sugar; add vanilla and *dash salt*. Gradually stir in chocolate mixture. Cool; then stir till smooth.

Beat egg whites and cream of tartar to soft peaks; gradually add ¼ cup sugar, beating to stiff peaks. Fold into chocolate mixture. Fold in whipped cream and nuts.

Set aside about 10 ladyfingers for center layer. Line bottom of 8-inch spring-form pan with ladyfingers, cutting to fit; line sides by standing ladyfingers on end all around. Fill with half the chocolate mixture, then add reserved ladyfingers, making layer. Top with chocolate mixture. Chill 8 hours, or overnight. Makes 8 to 10 servings.

Raspberry Bavarian Mold

1 10-ounce package frozen red raspberries, thawed
1 package red-raspberry-flavored gelatin
1 cup hot water
1 tablespoon lemon juice
1 6-ounce can (⅔ cup) evaporated
  milk, chilled *icy cold*

Drain raspberries, reserving syrup. Dissolve gelatin in hot water; add reserved syrup, lemon juice, and *dash salt*. Chill till partially set. Add milk. Beat at high speed on mixer till fluffy and soft peaks form, about 4 minutes.* Fold in raspberries. Tint pink with red food coloring. Pour into 1-quart mold. Chill firm. Trim with dessert topping, if desired. Makes 6 servings.

*For extra fluffy dessert, beat mixture about 7 minutes. Pour into 1½-quart mold.

Freeze a frosty dessert

Vanilla Custard Ice Cream
(*freezer*)

¾ cup sugar
2 tablespoons enriched flour
¼ teaspoon salt
2 cups milk
2 beaten eggs

. . .

2 cups heavy cream
1½ tablespoons vanilla

Combine sugar, flour, and salt; gradually stir in milk. Cook and stir over low heat till thick. Add small amount of hot mixture to eggs and mix well; return to hot mixture; cook and stir 1 minute. Chill.

Add cream and vanilla. Freeze in 2-quart (or larger) ice-cream freezer. Let ripen. Makes 1¼ quarts.

To freeze ice cream: Pour ice cream mixture into freezer can (cool mixture first, if cooked). Fill can only ⅔ full to allow for expansion. Fit can into freezer.

If using electric ice cream freezer, follow manufacturer's directions.

Adjust dasher and cover. Pack crushed ice and ice-cream salt around can, using proportions of 6 parts ice to 1 part salt. Turn dasher slowly till ice partially melts and forms brine—add more ice and salt to maintain ice level. Then turn handle rapidly and constantly till crank turns hard. Remove ice to below the lid of can; take off lid. Remove dasher.

To ripen ice cream: Plug opening in lid. Cover can with several thicknesses of waxed paper or foil for tight fit; replace lid.

Pack more ice and salt (use 4 parts ice to 1 part salt) around can to fill freezer. Cover freezer with heavy cloth or newspapers. Let ice cream ripen about 4 hours.

Or ripen ice cream in freezer or refrigerator freezing unit.

Wonderful Coffee Ice Cream
(*freezer*)

In recipe for Vanilla Custard Ice Cream, reduce vanilla to 1½ *teaspoons* and add 1½ to 2 tablespoons instant coffee with vanilla. Serve with chocolate sauce.

Vanilla Ice Cream (*freezer*)

4 eggs
2½ cups sugar
6 cups milk
4 cups light cream
2 tablespoons vanilla
½ teaspoon salt

Beat eggs until light. Add sugar gradually, beating until mixture thickens. Add remaining ingredients; mix thoroughly. Freeze in ice-cream freezer. Makes 1 gallon.

Vanilla Ice Cream (*refrigerator*)

1 rennet tablet
1 tablespoon cold water

. . .

1 cup light cream
½ cup sugar
1¼ teaspoons vanilla
1 cup heavy cream, whipped

Crush rennet tablet in cold water; dissolve. Combine light cream and sugar; heat slowly till warm (110°), not hot. Stir in rennet tablet. Add vanilla; stir quickly for few seconds. Pour into refrigerator tray.

Let stand at room temperature till set— about 10 minutes. Freeze firm. Break in chunks with wooden spoon; turn into chilled bowl; beat smooth with electric or rotary beater. Fold in the whipped cream. Return quickly to *cold* tray; freeze until firm. Makes 4 to 6 servings.

Chocolate-Almond Velvet

⅔ cup canned chocolate syrup
⅔ cup sweetened condensed milk
2 cups heavy cream
½ teaspoon vanilla

. . .

⅓ cup slivered blanched almonds, toasted

Combine the chocolate syrup, condensed milk, cream, and vanilla; chill. Whip till fluffy and soft peaks form. Fold in nuts. Pile into refrigerator tray; freeze firm. Serve sprinkled with toasted almonds, if desired. Makes 8 to 10 servings.

*A rich, smooth
dessert—and
besides
that, it's easy!*

Words can't tell you how delicious Chocolate-Almond Velvet is— find out for yourself! Go with for this ice cream: Cherry Winks with crunchy cereal jackets, cherry centers.

Chocolate-fleck Ice Cream

Dotted with bits of chocolate—

2 egg yolks
2 tablespoons sugar
½ teaspoon vanilla
1 cup heavy cream, whipped

• • •

2 egg whites
1 tablespoon sugar
3 1-ounce squares semisweet chocolate,
   coarsely grated

Beat the egg yolks until thick and lemon-colored. Add 2 tablespoons sugar and continue beating till light and fluffy. Blend in vanilla. Fold into whipped cream.

Beat egg whites until fluffy; add 1 tablespoon sugar and beat until soft peaks form. Fold into cream mixture; fold in chocolate. Pour into refrigerator tray; freeze till firm. Makes 6 servings.

Pink Peppermint Ice Cream

1 envelope (1 tablespoon)
   unflavored gelatin
½ cup cold milk
1½ cups milk, scalded
1 cup crushed hard
   peppermint-stick candy
¼ teaspoon salt

• • •

2 cups heavy cream, whipped
Few drops red food coloring (optional)

Soften gelatin in cold milk; dissolve in hot milk. Add candy and salt; stir till candy dissolves. Pour into refrigerator tray. Freeze till firm; break in chunks and beat with electric beater till smooth.*

Fold in whipped cream. Add food coloring to tint delicate pink. Return to tray; freeze firm. Makes 6 to 8 servings.

*Or freeze till partially frozen, beat smooth with rotary beater.

Strawberry Ice Cream

1 envelope unflavored gelatin
¼ cup cold water
2 well-beaten egg yolks
¾ cup sugar
¼ teaspoon salt
1½ teaspoons vanilla
2 cups crushed fresh strawberries
2 cups heavy cream
2 egg whites
¼ cup sugar

Soften gelatin in cold water; dissolve over hot water. Combine next 6 ingredients; add gelatin; mix well. Pour into 2-quart refrigerator tray; freeze firm.

Beat egg whites till soft peaks form; gradually add ¼ cup sugar, beating till stiff peaks form and sugar is dissolved.

Break frozen mixture in chunks; beat till fluffy with electric mixer (or partially freeze; beat with rotary beater). Fold in egg whites. Return quickly to *cold* tray; freeze firm. Makes 8 to 10 servings.

Lemon-drop Ice Cream

1 cup sugar
2 teaspoons grated lemon peel
3 tablespoons lemon juice
1 14½-ounce can (1⅔ cups) evaporated milk
4 drops yellow food coloring
½ cup crushed lemon drops

Thoroughly combine sugar, lemon peel, and juice; blend well. Stir in milk and food coloring. Pour into refrigerator tray.

Freeze till firm. Break in chunks and beat with electric beater till smooth (or partially freeze; beat with rotary beater). Fold in crushed lemon drops; return to tray. Freeze firm. Makes 4 to 6 servings.

Peach-tree Ice Cream

Drain 2 cups finely chopped peaches, reserving juice. Add water to juice to make ¾ cup. Combine peaches, juice mixture, and one 15-ounce can (1⅓ cups) sweetened condensed milk; pour into refrigerator trays.

Freeze till firm. Break in chunks; beat with electric beater till fluffy. Fold in 1 cup heavy cream, whipped, and ½ cup slivered, blanched almonds, toasted. Return to trays. Freeze firm. Spoon into sherbets; trim with slivered almonds. Makes 8 to 10 servings.

Rhubarb Ice Cream

2 cups chopped rhubarb
1 cup granulated sugar
1 cup water
Few drops red food coloring
1 to 2 teaspoons lemon juice
1 egg white
1 tablespoon sifted confectioners' sugar
1 cup heavy cream, whipped

Combine rhubarb, granulated sugar, water; cover and simmer till rhubarb is tender. Tint with food coloring. Chill. Add lemon juice. Pour into refrigerator trays. Freeze firm. Break in chunks; beat with electric beater till smooth (or partially freeze; beat with rotary beater). Beat egg white till fluffy; add confectioners' sugar and beat till soft peaks form. Fold into rhubarb mixture. Fold in whipped cream. Return to trays. Freeze firm. Makes 8 to 10 servings.

Coffee Tortoni

1 cup heavy cream
¼ cup sugar
1 tablespoon instant coffee
1 teaspoon vanilla
Few drops almond extract
1 egg white
2 tablespoons sugar
¼ cup finely chopped toasted almonds
¼ cup toasted flaked coconut, crumbled

Whip cream; fold in ¼ cup sugar, instant coffee, and flavorings. Beat egg white to soft peaks; gradually add 2 tablespoons sugar and beat to stiff peaks. Combine almonds and coconut. Fold egg white and *half* of nut mixture into whipped cream. Spoon into 8 paper bake cups set in muffin pan. Sprinkle remaining nut mixture atop; freeze firm. Trim with maraschino cherry halves.

Pink Raspberry Snow

Thaw two 10-ounce packages frozen raspberries; sieve. Combine one 3-ounce package raspberry-flavored gelatin and ½ cup sugar; dissolve in 1½ cups hot water. Cool. Add ¼ cup lemon juice, ¼ cup orange juice, and the sieved berries. Pour into 2-quart refrigerator tray; freeze firm.

Break in chunks; beat smooth. Return to tray; freeze 3 to 4 hours. (Mixture won't freeze firm.) Makes 8 to 10 servings.

Chocolate Marlow

¼ pound (about 16) marshmallows
2 1-ounce squares semisweet chocolate
   or ⅓ cup semisweet chocolate pieces
⅓ cup water
Dash salt
1 teaspoon vanilla
1 6-ounce can (⅔ cup) evaporated
   milk, chilled *icy cold*
⅓ cup graham-cracker crumbs

In double boiler heat marshmallows, chocolate, water, and salt, stirring frequently, until smooth. Remove from heat and add vanilla. Chill till slightly thick.

Whip evaporated milk until stiff; fold in marshmallow mixture. Pour into 1-quart refrigerator tray, sprinkle crumbs over top. Freeze firm. Cut in 6 servings.

Frozen Caramallow

¼ pound (14) caramels
1 cup tiny marshmallows
½ cup milk

   •   •   •

1 cup heavy cream, whipped
½ cup chopped pecans

In double boiler melt caramels and marshmallows in milk, stirring now and then. Chill. Fold in whipped cream and nuts. Pour into refrigerator tray and place in freezing compartment till super-chilled, about 2½ hours. Makes 4 to 5 servings.

Cranberry Sherbet

¾ cup sugar
½ envelope (1½ teaspoons)
   unflavored gelatin
Dash salt
1 pint bottle (2 cups) cranberry-juice
   cocktail

   •   •   •

2 tablespoons lemon juice

In saucepan, mix sugar, gelatin, and salt. Stir in 1 *cup* of the cranberry-juice cocktail. Heat and stir over medium heat till sugar and gelatin dissolve. Remove from heat; add remaining cranberry juice and the lemon juice. Freeze in refrigerator tray till firm; break in chunks and beat with an electric beater till smooth.* Return to tray; freeze several hours. Makes 8 servings.

*Or freeze till partially frozen; beat smooth with a rotary beater.

Pineapple Sherbet

½ envelope (1½ teaspoons)
   unflavored gelatin
2 tablespoons cold water
2 cups buttermilk
¾ cup sugar
1 9-ounce can crushed pineapple
1 teaspoon vanilla
1 egg white
¼ cup sugar

Soften gelatin in cold water; dissolve over hot water. Combine buttermilk, ¾ cup sugar, pineapple, vanilla, and gelatin; mix well. Pour into refrigerator tray; freeze till firm.

Break in chunks and beat smooth. Beat egg white till soft peaks form; gradually add ¼ cup sugar, beating to stiff peaks. Fold into pineapple mixture. Return quickly to *cold* tray. Freeze firm. Makes 4 to 6 servings.

Lemon-Orange Sherbet

½ cup orange juice
⅓ cup lemon juice
¾ cup sugar
1 cup milk
1 6-ounce can (⅔ cup) evaporated
   milk, chilled *icy cold*

Combine fruit juices; add sugar. Gradually stir in milk; pour into refrigerator tray.

Freeze till firm; break in chunks and beat with an electric beater till smooth. Whip evaporated milk till stiff; fold into frozen mixture. Return to tray; freeze firm. Makes 6 servings.

For a sunny sauce, combine ½ cup orange marmalade and 1 tablespoon lemon juice.

Lemon-Lime Velvet

3 egg yolks
¼ cup sugar
¾ teaspoon grated lemon peel
2 tablespoons lemon juice
2 tablespoons lime juice
½ cup heavy cream, whipped
3 egg whites
¼ cup sugar

Beat yolks. Gradually add ¼ cup sugar, beating till thick and lemon colored. Stir in peel, juices, and dash salt. Fold in cream. Beat whites till soft peaks form. Gradually add ¼ cup sugar, beating to stiff peaks; fold in. Pour into refrigerator tray; freeze firm. Makes 1 quart.

Fix-ups with ice cream

Coconut Ice-cream Balls

Chill a cooky sheet in freezer. Place scoops of ice cream on chilled cooky sheet; freeze. Roll in Minted or Coffee Coconut. Package in plastic bag; store in freezer.

To serve, place ice-cream balls in sherbets; top with Fudge Sauce.

Minted Coconut: In glass jar, mix 1 teaspoon water, 6 drops green food coloring, and 4 drops peppermint extract. Add one 3½-ounce can (1¼ cups) flaked coconut. Cover; shake till well mixed.

Coffee Coconut: In jar, mix 1½ teaspoons *each* instant coffee and water. Add one 3½-ounce can flaked coconut. Shake.

Crispy-crunch Freeze

2 tablespoons butter or margarine
¼ cup brown sugar
1 cup corn flakes
⅓ cup salted peanuts
• • •
1 quart vanilla ice cream

In skillet, melt butter; add sugar, and heat slowly, stirring till blended. Add corn flakes; toss to coat well. Remove from heat; add peanuts. Cool; break up any large chunks. Reserve ⅔ cup mixture for topping. Stir ice cream just to soften; fold in remaining cereal mixture. Freeze firm. Sprinkle with topping. Makes 6 to 8 servings.

Strawberry Ice-cream Mountain
—easy does it, and so elegant!

Cream ¼ cup butter; mix in ¼ cup sugar, 1½ cups fine graham-cracker crumbs. Line 5-cup mixing bowl.

Soften 3 pints strawberry ice cream; press into crumb lining. Freeze firm, about 6 hours. To unmold, run spatula around sides, bottom. Invert on plate.

Garnish with whipped cream, strawberries. Makes about 9 servings.

Chocolate-chip Cups

2 1-ounce squares semisweet chocolate
 or ⅓ cup semisweet chocolate pieces
1 teaspoon butter or margarine
1 pint vanilla ice cream
¼ cup finely chopped almonds, toasted

Melt chocolate and butter over hot water. Stir ice cream to soften; fold in nuts. Drizzle melted chocolate over ice cream, folding constantly to "chip" chocolate. Pour into six or seven 2-ounce paper cups or small dishes. Freeze till nearly firm. Remove from freezer; top each serving with maraschino-cherry half and circle it with whole almonds, pointed end down. Freeze firm.

Tutti-frutti Tortoni

Stir 1 pint vanilla ice cream to soften. Add ¼ cup chopped candied fruits and peels, ¼ cup seedless raisins, and 1½ teaspoons rum flavoring. Spoon into four or five paper bake cups set in muffin pan. Freeze and trim, following recipe above.

Fruit-Nut Freeze

1 quart vanilla ice cream
2 fully ripe bananas, mashed
2 tablespoons lemon juice
1 cup pitted dates, cut up
½ cup chopped candied cherries
½ cup slivered blanched
 almonds, toasted

Stir ice cream just to soften. Combine bananas and lemon juice; stir into ice cream. Quickly fold in dates, cherries, and nuts. Freeze firm. Makes 8 to 10 servings.

Ice-cream Mince Pie

1 quart vanilla ice cream
1 cup well-drained mincemeat
¼ to ½ teaspoon rum flavoring
1 recipe Graham-cracker Crust

Stir ice cream to soften; stir in mincemeat and flavoring. Spoon into Graham-cracker Crust. Freeze firm.

Graham-cracker Crust: Combine 1½ cups fine graham-cracker crumbs (18 crackers), ¼ cup sugar, and ½ cup melted butter or margarine; mix well. Press firmly in unbuttered 9-inch pie plate. Chill until set, about 45 minutes, before filling.

Coconut Ribbon Loaf

Cake and ice cream all in one dessert!—

Rub brown crumbs off one 10x4x2-inch loaf angel cake. Cut cake lengthwise in three layers. Stir 1 pint pink peppermint-stick ice cream and 1 pint lime sherbet to soften. Spread bottom layer with peppermint-stick ice cream. Add second cake layer; spread with lime sherbet. Add last cake layer. Place in freezing compartment or freezer till ice cream is firm.

To serve, whip 1½ cups heavy cream; stir in 1 teaspoon sugar and ½ teaspoon vanilla. Spread over top and sides of loaf. Sprinkle with one 3½-ounce can flaked coconut, toasted. Makes 8 to 10 servings. (See Coconut Ribbon Loaf, page 4.)

Pumpkin Ice-cream Pie

1 cup canned or mashed cooked pumpkin
½ cup brown sugar
½ teaspoon salt
½ teaspoon cinnamon
½ teaspoon ginger
¼ teaspoon nutmeg
1 quart vanilla ice cream
1 recipe Graham-cracker Crust

Combine pumpkin, brown sugar, salt, and spices. Stir ice cream to soften; then fold into pumpkin mixture. Spoon into the Graham-cracker Crust (see recipe at left). Freeze firm. Garnish with pecans.

Strawberry Ice-cream Pie

1 3½-ounce can (1¼ cups)
 flaked coconut
1 quart vanilla ice cream
1½ cups sugared sliced fresh
 strawberries *or* 1 10-ounce package
 frozen, partially thawed
6 Frozen Cream Toppers

Toast coconut in moderate oven (350°) about 10 minutes, stirring often to brown evenly. Cool. Lightly press onto bottom and sides of well-buttered 9-inch pie plate. Stir ice cream only to soften *slightly;* spoon into shell; smooth top. Freeze firm.

To serve, spoon strawberries over ice cream. Trim with *Frozen Cream Toppers:* Whip ½ cup heavy cream. Stir in 2 tablespoons sifted confectioners' sugar. Place 6 heaping spoonfuls on chilled baking sheet. Freeze firm. Makes 6 servings.

Low-calorie desserts

Make-ahead desserts right for dieters! So good, you'd never guess they're low-cal!

Berry Pink Cloud

    1 2-ounce package dessert-topping mix
    Few drops red food coloring
    2½ cups sliced, unsweetened
      strawberries
    1 No. 2 can (2½ cups) dietetic-pack
      pineapple chunks, drained

Prepare the dessert-topping mix according to package directions. Tint pale pink with few drops red food coloring. Fold in strawberries and pineapple; chill. Stir before serving (add a little milk if the mixture is too thick).

    Trim with strawberries. Makes 8 servings. *Calories per serving: 125.*

Cranberry Fluff

    In large bowl, dissolve 1 envelope low-calorie raspberry-flavored gelatin according to directions on envelope; chill till partially set. With rotary or electric beater, whip till soft peaks form.

    Dissolve ¼ cup nonfat dry milk in ¼ cup cold water; gradually add to gelatin, beating till stiff peaks form. Gradually beat in ½ cup canned jellied cranberry sauce, till stiff peaks form again. Pile into sherbet glasses and chill.

    Or, for sherbet: Spoon mixture into refrigerator tray and freeze firm. Cut a few cubes of sauce for trim, if desired. Makes 8 servings. *Calories per serving: 45.*

←

Berry Pink Cloud—luscious!

Good enough to be fattening, yet a big helping has few calories! Strawberries, pineapple chunks are folded through dessert topping. (Or pick a grapefruit half—just 75 calories.)

Sunburst Souffle

Slim-jims cheer this delightful dessert—

½ teaspoon soft butter or
    margarine
1 tablespoon sugar

. . .

4 egg yolks
¼ cup sugar
1½ teaspoons grated lemon peel

. . .

4 egg whites
¼ teaspoon salt
2 tablespoons lemon juice

Lightly butter a 6-cup melon mold or 1½-quart casserole; sprinkle with 1 tablespoon sugar. Beat egg yolks till thick and lemon-colored; gradually beat in ¼ cup sugar; add peel. Beat whites with salt and lemon juice till stiff peaks form. Fold yolks into whites. Pour into mold and set in shallow pan; fill pan to 1 inch with hot water.

Bake in moderate oven (350°) about 35 minutes, or till knife inserted in center comes out clean. Loosen edges; invert on plate. Garnish dessert with lemon slices, if desired. Serve hot or chilled. Makes 6 servings. *Calories per serving: 95.*

Autumn Custard

Like pumpkin pie, but fewer calories—

2 cups canned or mashed
    cooked pumpkin
½ teaspoon salt
1 teaspoon cinnamon
½ teaspoon ginger
¼ teaspoon nutmeg
¼ teaspoon cloves

. . .

3 slightly beaten eggs
2 cups reliquefied nonfat dry milk*
Noncaloric sweetener equivalent to
    8 tablespoons (½ cup) sugar*

Combine pumpkin, salt, and spices; add remaining ingredients. Pour into nine 5-ounce custard cups and set in shallow pan; fill pan to 1 inch with hot water. Bake in moderate oven (350°) about 40 minutes, or till mixture doesn't adhere to a knife. Serve warm or chilled. Top with whipped dry milk sweetened with noncaloric sweetener, if desired. *Calories per serving: 60.*

*Follow package or label directions.

Coffee Delight

2 tablespoons sugar
½ envelope (1½ teaspoons)
    unflavored gelatin
2 to 3 teaspoons instant coffee
1 cup reliquefied nonfat dry milk*
1 beaten egg yolk
1 egg white
½ teaspoon vanilla

In saucepan, mix sugar, gelatin, coffee, and dash salt. Stir ½ *cup of the milk* into egg yolk; stir into first mixture. Cook and stir over *low* heat till gelatin dissolves. Remove from heat; add remaining milk. Chill till partially set. Add egg white and vanilla; beat with rotary or electric beater till about double. Spoon into 6 dishes. Chill till firm. *Calories per serving: 45.*

*Follow package directions.

Frozen Orange Pudding

2 eggs
⅓ cup cold water
⅓ cup nonfat dry milk
Dash salt
¼ cup sugar
1 6-ounce can frozen orange-juice or
    tangerine-juice concentrate, thawed

In small bowl, combine eggs, water, nonfat dry milk, and salt. Beat with electric or rotary beater until light and fluffy; gradually add sugar and concentrate, beating till thick and lemon colored. Freeze. Makes 8 servings. *Calories per serving: 100.*

Apricot Chiffon Pie

Thoroughly mix 1 envelope (1 tablespoon) unflavored gelatin, ⅓ cup sugar, and dash salt. Heat one 12-ounce can (1½ cups) apricot nectar just to boiling; add to gelatin mixture, stirring till dissolved.

Add 1 teaspoon lemon juice and ⅛ teaspoon almond extract. Chill till partially set. Add 2 unbeaten egg whites and beat till soft peaks form. Pile into cooled Lacy Coconut Crust. Chill until firm. *Calories per serving (1/7 of pie): 180.*

Lacy Coconut Crust: Butter a 9-inch pie plate, using 1 teaspoon butter or margarine. Empty a 3½-ounce can (1¼ cups) flaked coconut into pie plate; press against bottom and sides. Bake at 325° about 10 minutes or till edges are golden. Cool.

Index